DISASTER ILLUSTRATED

Two Hundred Years of American Misfortune

Compiled, Illustrated, and Written by

Woody Gelman

and

Barbara Jackson

Harmony Books
New York

To Lillian Gelman and Martin Jackson for all of their help.

Publisher: Bruce Harris
Editor: Linda Sunshine
Book and Cover Design: Dana Levy
Copyeditor: Arnold Leo
Photographer: Martin Jackson
Research: Lillian Gelman
Production: Murray Schwartz, Robert Schwartz

Harmony Books, a division of Crown Publishers, Inc.,
One Park Avenue, New York, New York 10016

Published simultaneously in Canada by General Publishing Company Limited
Printed in the United States of America

Library of Congress Cataloging in Publication Data

Gelman, Woody.
    Disaster illustrated 200 years of American misfortune.

    1. Disasters—United States.   I. Jackson, Barbara
Gelman, 1945-   joint author.   II. Title.
E179.G33   973   76-17809
ISBN 0-517-52542-9
ISBN 0-517-52543-7 pbk.

72550

CONTENTS

INTRODUCTION

The First Two Hundred Years Are The Hardest

Two hundred years ago, our forefathers did, indeed, bring forth upon this continent a new nation, dedicated to — among other things — the proposition that life was tough enough, right here, without having to pay homage, taxes, or anything else to a distant monarch. For every one of our two hundred years, life has been proving just how tough it really can be — with fires, floods, fevers and other furious displays of nature and/or human error. In a sense, this book is the story of America's fight for survival against nature's most destructive elements and the blind spots in the human mind that cause men to unwittingly bring the world crashing down around their ears.

No disaster in this book — so far as we know — was deliberate in origin. With the questionable exception of the *Lusitania*, there are no acts of war, no mad bombers, no mass murderers. Only nature and/or "accidents" are the culprits here. And if one or two catastrophes are not strictly American (we do have some spectacular contributions from our Canadian cousins), they all involve great numbers of American people.

We couldn't, of course, hope to fit every disaster that's taken place over the past two hundred years into one volume, so we've narrowed down the field, in most cases, to those tragic events which definitely record 50 fatalities or more. However, when a disaster seemed particularly bizarre, mind-boggling or especially American, we've tried to include it even when the statistics were not staggering.

From all of our research we've made an interesting discovery. Americans love a good story. And catastrophes — no matter how tragic — make good stories. Calamity victims have been known to gasp stories from their deathbeds — without forgetting one gory detail. In a way, this book is not only about them, but by them. Their stories are what make these disasters a part of our folklore.

To that we can only add that, hopefully, the first two hundred years were the hardest.

Reprinted from *Frank Leslie's Illustrated Newspaper*, September 11, 1886.

In minutes it can move or make mountains, destroy cities, create canyons, lakes, and rivers, and snuff out lives. It is called an earthquake, and of all the calamities of nature, it is the most incomprehensible to the senses. The sea may well up into waves as big as houses, but the sea is liquid and we can imagine amazing walls of water even if we've never seen them. A breeze that turns into a gale or even a hurricane may seem to be a mad excess of nature, but it is possible and conceivable.

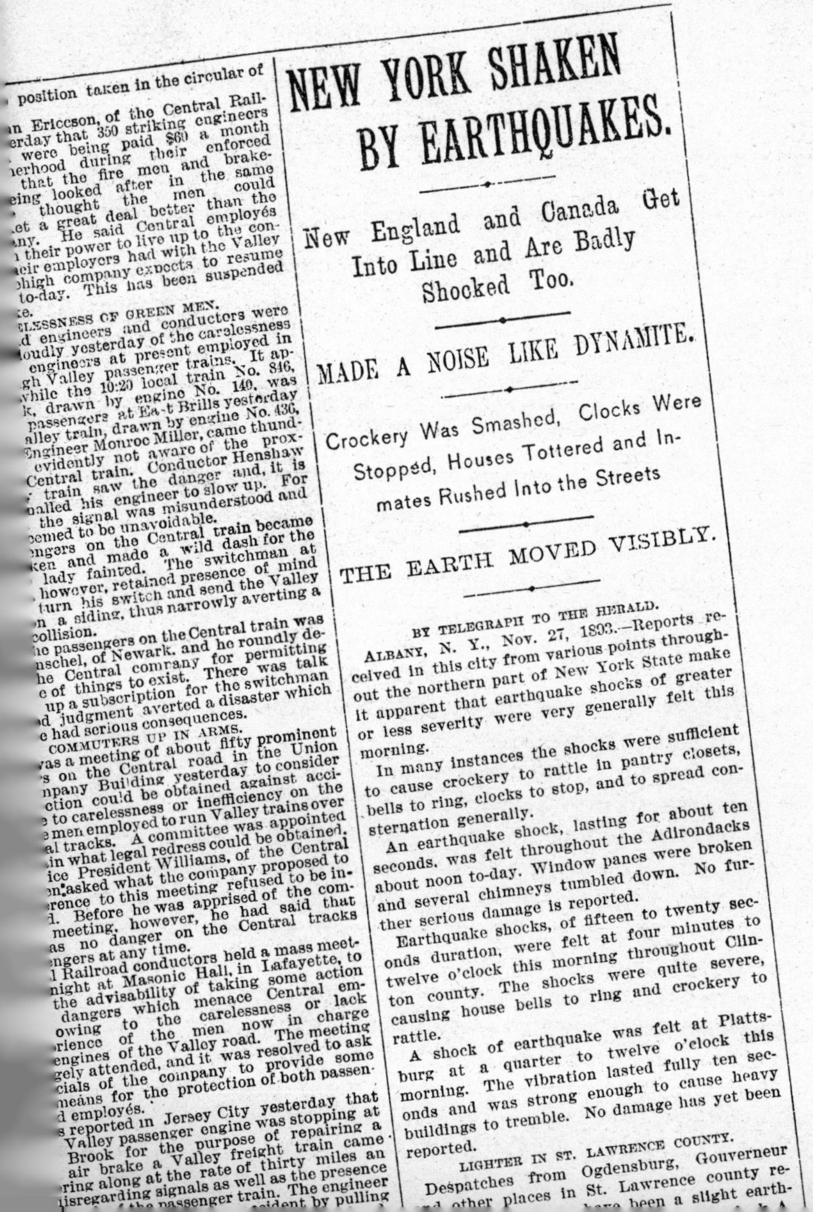

However, when the earth—which we feel is solid beneath our feet—begins to pitch and sway, rising and falling like liquid, it defies everything our senses know about this earth and is terrifying in the extreme. As a survivor of the 1906 San Francisco earthquake described it, "We were not like people upon the earth, but like fleas on the back of a quivering, quaking dog. Human beings, who'd braved every other catastrophe known to man, became blind with unreasoning panic."

Despite our senses, the earth, as one scientist put it, is not as solid (or as dead) as a giant bowling ball. The analogy of a quaking dog is, in fact, much more accurate. The earth is a living thing, with a miles-thick crust—or shell or even "skin"—that covers and floats on a large central core of hot liquid. Not much else is known about the earth's internal structure, except that like all vital things it is constantly in motion. Every minute of every day, there are tremors somewhere on this planet. Mostly, they're too weak to cause any real damage, if they are felt at all. But there are certain areas which, under certain conditions, do erupt into the heaving, buckling terrors we call earthquakes.

Those places are on or near what seismologists call "faults"—great cracks in the surface of the earth. The current theory is that the earth's surface, which is composed mostly of rock that is miles thick, was once fairly whole and without cracks. Dry land consisted of one immense continent; the rest was sea. Then something cataclysmic happened, perhaps a series of gigantic earthquakes; the earth's surface both above and below the sea was broken into a kind of huge jigsaw puzzle. The surfaces began to drift, eventually creating the continents and the seas. Each single surface, both above and below the sea, is known as a "continental plate." Where the continental plates meet are the deepest, largest cracks—and our major earthquake faults. Motion and pressure beneath the surface cause these immense slabs of rock to rub against each other in a variety of ways, even overlapping at times. This pushing together creates great pressure, and when it reaches a certain point, an earthquake is the result.

Our West Coast lies in the place where the Pacific plate

NEW YORK SHAKEN BY EARTHQUAKES.

New England and Canada Get Into Line and Are Badly Shocked Too.

MADE A NOISE LIKE DYNAMITE.

Crockery Was Smashed, Clocks Were Stopped, Houses Tottered and Inmates Rushed Into the Streets

THE EARTH MOVED VISIBLY.

BY TELEGRAPH TO THE HERALD.

ALBANY, N. Y., Nov. 27, 1893.—Reports received in this city from various points throughout the northern part of New York State make it apparent that earthquake shocks of greater or less severity were very generally felt this morning.

In many instances the shocks were sufficient to cause crockery to rattle in pantry closets, bells to ring, clocks to stop, and to spread consternation generally.

An earthquake shock, lasting for about ten seconds, was felt throughout the Adirondacks about noon to-day. Window panes were broken and several chimneys tumbled down. No further serious damage is reported.

Earthquake shocks, of fifteen to twenty seconds duration, were felt at four minutes to twelve o'clock this morning throughout Clinton county. The shocks were quite severe, causing house bells to ring and crockery to rattle.

A shock of earthquake was felt at Plattsburg at a quarter to twelve o'clock this morning. The vibration lasted fully ten seconds and was strong enough to cause heavy buildings to tremble. No damage has yet been reported.

LIGHTER IN ST. LAWRENCE COUNTY.

Despatches from Ogdensburg, Gouverneur and other places in St. Lawrence county report that there have been a slight earth-

[partial left column, overlapping newspaper clipping:]

position taken in the circular of
... Ericsson, of the Central Railroad ... that 350 striking engineers ... were being paid $60 a month ... ierhood during their enforced ... that the fire men and brake... ... eing looked after in the same ... thought the men could ... et a great deal better than the ... any. He said Central employés ... their power to live up to the con... ... ieir employers had with the Valley ... high company expects to resume ... to-day. This has been suspended ...

...LESSNESS OF GREEN MEN.
... engineers and conductors were ... loudly yesterday of the carelessness ... engineers at present employed in ... gh Valley passenger trains. It ap... ... while the 10:20 local train No. 846, ... k, drawn by engine No. 140, was ... passengers at East Brills yesterday ... alley train, drawn by engine No. 436, ... Engineer Monroe Miller, came thund... ... evidently not aware of the prox... ... Central train. Conductor Henshaw ... train saw the danger and, it is ... nalled his engineer to slow up. For ... the signal was misunderstood and ... cemed to be unavoidable. The ... engers on the Central train became ... ken and made a wild dash for the ... lady fainted. The switchman at ... however, retained presence of mind ... turn his switch and send the Valley ... n a siding, thus narrowly averting a ... collision.

... he passengers on the Central train was ... nschel, of Newark, and he roundly de... ... he Central company for permitting ... e of things to exist. There was talk ... up a subscription for the switchman ... d judgment averted a disaster which ... e had serious consequences.

COMMUTERS UP IN ARMS.
... vas a meeting of about fifty prominent ... s on the Central road in the Union ... npany Building yesterday to consider ... ction could be obtained against acci... ... e to carelessness or inefficiency on the ... men employed to run Valley trains over ... al tracks. A committee was appointed ... in what legal redress could be obtained. ... ice President Williams, of the Central ... nasked what the company proposed to be in... ... rence to this meeting refused of the com... ... d. Before he was apprised of the com... ... meeting, however, he had said that ... as no danger on the Central tracks ... engers at any time.

... l Railroad conductors held a mass meet... ... night at Masonic Hall, in Lafayette, to ... the advisability of taking some action ... the dangers which menace Central em... ... owing to the carelessness or lack ... rience of the men now in charge ... engines of the Valley road. The meeting ... gely attended, and it was resolved to ask ... cials of the company to provide some ... means for the protection of both passen... ... d employés.

... s reported in Jersey City yesterday that ... Valley passenger engine was stopping at ... Brook for the purpose of repairing a ... air brake for a Valley freight train came ... ring along at the rate of thirty miles an ... disregarding signals as well as the presence ... the passenger train. The engineer ... ... dent by pulling

IMPORTANT AMERICAN EARTHQUAKES

DATE	LOCATION	FATALITIES	REMARKS
1811 12/16	New Madrid, Mo., was center of quake that was felt over two-thirds of the U.S.	Unestimable. Thinly populated area, with settlements far apart. Death reports came in slowly and could not be checked.	Ohio and Mississippi valleys greatly affected. The landscape of several states was altered.
1886 8/31	Charleston, S.C.	60	Charleston's one and only earthquake in more than 300 years.
1906 4/18	San Francisco, Calif.	700 known dead	The earthquake by which all U.S. earthquakes are measured—our worst and most legendary.
1918 10/11	Puerto Rico	116	Entire island was affected, but most deaths took place in Mayagüez and Aguadilla. In Mayagüez, building fronts fell into a plaza where people had taken refuge. In Aguadilla, a seismic wave was the killer.
1933 3/10	Long Beach, Calif.	116	Destruction of old schoolhouses, which might have been filled with children at an earlier hour, started southern Californians thinking about building codes.
1946 4/1	Dutch Harbor, Alaska	200 (in Hawaii alone)	April Fools' Day quake in Alaska caused seismic waves that hit the Aleutian Islands, U.S. West Coast and Hawaii. How many were killed between the Aleutians and California is unknown, but it was many. Hawaii, 4,000 miles away, was worst hit.
1964 3/27	Port Arthur, Alaska, was center of quake, but Anchorage and nearby towns were badly damaged, some permanently.	131 (in Alaska alone)	Tidal wave caused by quake traveled down West Coast, killing 4 campers in Oregon. In Crescent City, Calif., 10 were reported drowned and 50 missing.
1971 2/9	Southern California	65	Not a strong quake, but many old buildings, including schools, were destroyed, as were highway overpasses. Had quake come during school day or rush hour, fatalities would have been greater. Two-thirds of victims were patients at 47-year-old Veterans' Administration Hospital, which collapsed, burying patients.

meets the Atlantic plate, and this has made California and Alaska the earthquake zone of America. Earthquakes have happened more frequently and killed more people in those two states than anywhere else in this country. It is predicted that they will strike again. Earthquakes strike in the same places over and over again. The great San Francisco earthquake of 1906 was the third time that city was hit. And San Francisco is due for another quake. The size of its current population could make this future shock the worst on American record. At least 10,000 would die, seismologists agree.

But that's only if it happens soon, for we have learned much about earthquakes, and to a degree they can be predicted. Recently, in China — a nation torn by the worst quakes in history — an area was evacuated on the advice of Chinese seismologists. Hours later a very destructive quake struck, making mincemeat of the area, but nobody was killed.

More important, earthquake scientists feel it may become possible to control quakes. It's only theory now, with no experimentation, but it would be done, partly, by actually causing tremors. Without more research, seismologists are a little afraid they could set off something that would make the terrors of yore seem like a rocking cradle. Meanwhile, earthquake engineers and architects are continually looking into new ways of constructing buildings so they will be less subject to destruction from shocks and tremors.

Unfortunately, the West Coast is not our only earthquake area. Where continental plate meets continental plate may be where the most obvious faults lie, but the earth's surface may develop a crack or weakness or fault anywhere. One of our biggest quakes happened in the Midwest. Our East Coast has been subject to some mighty destructive shocks. And actually, almost every area in every state is subject to some risk. Only two places seem totally free — southern Texas and southern Florida. But before you pack up and move to either of these places, please read our section on hurricanes.

New Madrid, Missouri, 1811

Date	Location	Fatalities	Remarks
12/16	New Madrid, Mo., was center of quake that was felt over two-thirds of the U.S.	Unestimable. Thinly populated area, with settlements far apart. Death reports came in slowly and could not be checked.	Ohio and Mississippi valleys greatly affected. The landscape of several states was altered.

The 1811 earthquake was one of the strongest in U.S. history—or perhaps in all history—seismologists believe today. It affected an area 200 million miles square, compared to the mere 375,000 square miles touched by the great San Francisco earthquake nearly a century later. More lives and property were lost in the San Francisco disaster, but only because there were more people and buildings to be destroyed in the Golden Gate city of 1906. In 1811, most of the country, particularly the central portions, was sparsely populated, mostly by adventuresome pioneers who thought they'd seen every hardship nature could produce.

On December 16, at 2:00 A.M., settlers at New Madrid, Missouri, were awakened by a fearful roaring that grew louder and louder. They rushed from their cabins when the ground beneath them began to pitch and roll. It heaved up in great waves and tore apart, leaving wide fissures. In seconds, the entire town had crumpled. The skies were lit by an "eerie red glow," and the frightened shrieks of both wild and domestic animals added to the confused cries of the people.

The center of the earthquake seemed to be at New Madrid, so far as could be determined without instruments. But the shocks were felt throughout two-thirds of the nation. As far away as Boston, Washington, D.C., and Charleston, South Carolina, buildings swayed precariously and church bells tolled by themselves. But the Mississippi River and Ohio River valleys suffered the greatest upheaval.

There is no accurate count of the lives taken by the earthquake of 1811. Settlements were far apart, and reports of deaths came in much later, when it was too late to check the veracity of the wild tales. In western Tennessee, people told of neighbors being swallowed up by great fissures in the earth. One of those yawning chasms became Reelfoot Lake, 20 miles of bird sanctuary and tourist attraction today. Folks along the

THE GREAT EARTHQUAKE AT NEW MADRID

"Then the houses crumbled, the trees waved together, the ground sunk; while ever and anon vivid flashes of lightning, gleaming through the troubled clouds of night, rendered the darkness doubly horrible"

Mississippi River watched in amazement as the big river began to flow backward, and then changed its course. High waves on the river sank boats bound for New Orleans and drowned a number of people. In Kentucky, the ornithologist John J. Audubon witnessed the same strange illumination that was seen in New Madrid. At the mouth of the Ohio River, people saw great lakes created, drained, and destroyed within an hour. Near New Madrid, a crevice 37 miles long and half a mile wide became Lake Francis.

The most severe jolts came on December 16, but shocks and tremors continued until March of 1812. By then, eastern Missouri had become a land of splintered trees and huge mounds that looked like waves on a frozen sea. The earth was disfigured with crevices, and strange, pale sand covered everything. These conditions delayed settlement of the area by 50 years.

1. THE PANIC-STRICKEN CITIZENS SEEKING REFUGE ON BATTERY PLACE.

SOUTH CAROLINA.—THE TERRIBLE EARTHQUAKE AT CHARLESTON—SCENE AFTER THE FIRST SHOCK.

Charleston Earthquake, 1886

Date	Location	Fatalities	Remarks
8/31	Charleston, S.C.	60	Charleston's one and only earthquake in more than 300 years.

"The most calamitous earthquake ever experienced in the United States laid half of Charleston, South Carolina, in ruins on the night of Tuesday, the thirty-first."

So read the report in *Frank Leslie's Illustrated* for the week ending September 11, 1886. In terms of human lives lost and damages estimated, it was, at that date, the worst American earthquake. It was the first quake to hit a heavily populated area, and most surprising, even today, is that it happened in Charleston.

Unlike lightning, earthquakes seem to strike the same place repeatedly. Charleston has been the exception. From the time of its settlement in 1670, it had suffered no more than the minor tremors felt in almost every area of the United States— nothing strong enough to set a brick out of place.

Thus, on the night of August 31, 1886, the city was completely unprepared for its disaster. It began at 9:50 P.M., when good townsfolk were tucked away safely (they hoped) in their beds. Those not yet asleep heard a loud rumbling, and seconds later the whole town was awake, some thrown from their beds in wildly swaying houses. Chimneys toppled, and then the air was filled with the sound of "thousands of panes of glass rattling to the pavement."

People rushed to the streets in panic, but bricks, timbers, and telegraph poles were crashing through the air, and the streets themselves were deep in mortar dust. Dressed mostly in their nightclothes, people pushed their way to open squares and parks where they hoped to be safe from toppling buildings.

It may indeed have been Charleston's beautiful open squares and parks that kept the death total from rising above 60. Safe from falling debris, "the terrified people spent the night in the open air," reported *Frank Leslie's Illustrated*, "fearing to enter such houses as were left standing. There were, however, many brave hearts and strong arms to care for the injured and rescue those imprisoned in fallen buildings. Even women, it is related, fought valiantly to release the unfortunates."

The injured spent the night camped out in the open air with the rest of the population, where they were ministered to and sometimes prayed over with a fervor that was in keeping with the earthquake itself. Some of the black population belonged to a fundamentalist religious sect, and spent the night crying in thunderous tones for God to forgive, help, and save them.

By morning, most of Charleston's population had been saved, and to this day, the city has never been struck by another serious earthquake. But to seismologists, a fault is a fault, and can act up at any moment. Charleston apparently lies right on top of one, or it wouldn't have had an earthquake at all. On the strength of that disastrous night in August, the city must be ranked on the list of high-risk earthquake zones. Hopefully, only the memory of that one quake will keep it on the list.

Above: Wounded and dying in Washington Park. *Left:* After first shock, people took to the streets — seen here fleeing from Charleston Hotel. *Below:* Marion Square became a city of tents after quake.

The San Francisco Earthquake, 1906

Date	Location	Fatalities	Remarks
4/18	San Francisco, Calif.	700 known dead	The earthquake by which all U.S. earthquakes are measured—our worst and most legendary.

Map of burned district from *Binghampton Press and Leader,* April 21, 1906.

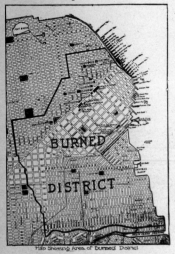

In 1906, San Francisco's native son and star writer, Jack London, was already a man with visions of revolution, an ardent socialist who was disenchanted with the society around him. What he wanted to do with society, he said, was to "topple it over, along with its rotten life and its unburied dead, its monstrous selfishness and sodden materialism."

But on the morning of April 18, when the city was toppled over by the worst earthquake in United States history, Jack London was a bereaved man. "I'll never write about this for anyone," he told his wife Charmian. "What use trying? One could only string big words together, and curse the futility of them."

Then a wire came from *Collier's Weekly,* in New York. The magazine wanted an eyewitness report for a special issue they were preparing that was devoted to the catastrophe. London, a pro despite grief or politics, went to work immediately. The following is an excerpt from his story, originally printed in *Collier's Weekly,* May 5, 1906:

THE STORY OF AN EYE-WITNESS

By JACK LONDON, Collier's Special Correspondent

Seismographic record of the quake registered at 5:15 A.M., April 18, at Yountville, fifty miles from San Francisco.

5.15 a.m.
April 18, '06.
Veterans Home, Cal
Napa Ci.

The earthquake shook down in San Francisco hundreds of thousands of dollars' worth of walls and chimneys. But the conflagration that followed burned up hundreds of millions of dollars' worth of property. There is no estimating within hundreds of millions the actual damage wrought. Not in history has a modern imperial city been so completely destroyed. San Francisco is gone. Nothing remains of it but memories and a fringe of dwelling-houses on its outskirts.

On Wednesday morning at a quarter past five came the earthquake. A minute later the flames were leaping upward. In a dozen different quarters south of Market Street, in the working-class ghetto, and in the factories, fires started. There was no opposing the flames. There was no organization, no communication. All the shrewd contrivances and safeguards of man had been thrown out of gear by thirty seconds' twitching of the earth-crust.

By Wednesday afternoon, inside of twelve hours, half the heart of the city was gone. At that time I watched the vast conflagration from out on the bay. It was dead calm. Not a flicker of wind stirred. Yet from every side wind was pouring in upon the city. The heated air rising made an enormous suck. Thus did the fire of itself build its own colossal chimney through the atmosphere.

Wednesday night saw the destruction of the very heart of the city. Dynamite was lavishly used, and many of San Francisco's proudest structures were crumbled by man himself into ruins, but there was no withstanding the onrush of the flames.

An enumeration of the buildings destroyed would be a directory of San Francisco. An enumeration of the buildings undestroyed would be a line and several addresses. An enumeration of the deeds of heroism would stock a library and bankrupt the Carnegie medal fund. An enumeration of the dead — will never be made. All vestiges of them were destroyed by the flames.

Remarkable as it may seem, Wednesday night, while the whole city crashed and roared into ruin, was a quiet night. There were no crowds. There was no shouting and yelling. There was no hysteria, no disorder. I passed Wednesday night in the path of the advancing flames, and in all those terrible hours I saw not one woman who wept, not one man who was excited, not one person who was in the slightest degree panic-stricken.

Before the flames, throughout the night, fled tens of thousands of homeless ones. Yet everybody was gracious. The most perfect courtesy obtained. Never, in all San Francisco's history, were her people so kind and courteous as on this night of terror.

Surrender was complete. There was no water. The sewers had long since been pumped dry. There was no dynamite. Another fire had broken out further uptown, and now from three sides conflagrations were sweeping down. The fourth side had been burned earlier in the day.

The following will illustrate the sweep of the flames and the inability of men to calculate their spread. At eight o'clock Wednesday evening I passed through Union Square. It was packed with refugees. Thousands of them had gone to bed on the grass. Government tents had been set up, supper was being cooked, and the refugees were lining up for free meals.

At half-past one in the morning three sides of Union Square were in flames. The fourth side, where stood the great St. Francis Hotel, was still holding out. An hour later, ignited from top and sides, the St. Francis was flaming heavenward. Union Square, heaped high with mountains of trunks, was deserted. Troops, refugees, and all had retreated.

 **BINGHAMTON PRESS**
AND LEADER

EXTRA EXTRA

VOL. 29. NO. 9   * STATE EDITION   FRIDAY EVENING, APRIL 20, 1906.   TWELVE PAGES   PRICE ONE CENT

LITTLE LEFT OF 'FRISCO, THOUSANDS HOMELESS

PARKS ARE FULL OF THE SUFFERERS

MAP OF THE DESOLATE CITY AND ITS ENVIRONS

GOLDEN GATE

Collier's
SAN FRANCISCO

San Francisco street scene after quake, photographed by the well-known Arnold Genthe.

On Thursday morning, at a quarter past five, just twenty-four hours after the earthquake, I sat on the steps of a small residence on Nob Hill. To the east and south, at right angles, were advancing two mighty walls of flame.

I went inside with the owner of the house on the steps of which I sat. He was cool and cheerful and hospitable. "Yesterday morning," he said, "I was worth six hundred thousand dollars. This morning this house is all I have left. The flames will be here in fifteen minutes."

There was no sun when the second day dawned on the strickened city. I was creeping past the shattered dome of the City Hall. There was no better exhibit of the destructive force of the earthquake. Most of the stone had been shaken from the great dome, leaving standing the naked framework of steel. Here and there through the smoke, creeping warily under the shadows of tottering walls, emerged occasional men and women. It was like the meeting of the handful of survivors after the day of the end of the world.

On Mission Street lay a dozen steers, in a neat row stretching across the street, just as they had been struck down by the flying ruins of the earthquake. The fire had passed through afterward and roasted them.

All day Thursday and all Thursday night, all day Friday and Friday night, the flames still raged.

Friday night saw the flames finally conquered, though not until Russian Hill and Telegraph Hill had been swept and three-quarters of a mile of wharves and docks had been licked up.

San Francisco, at the present time, is like the crater of a volcano, around which are camped tens of thousands of refugees. The refugees were carried free by the railroads to any point they wished to go, and it is estimated that over one hundred thousand people have left the peninsula on which San Francisco stood. The Government has the situation in hand, and, thanks to the immediate relief given by the whole United States, there is not the slightest possibility of a famine. The bankers and business men have already set about making preparations to rebuild San Francisco.

Top: Quake effect on the pavement and car tracks in front of the post office. *Far left:* Refugees with household goods gathered on Market Street. *Left:* Ruins of the brand-new City Hall which had been the pride and joy of San Francisco. Reprinted from *Collier's,* May 5, 1906.

The burning of San Francisco, April 19, 1906. *Insets:* Section of Ea Street before fire (*above*) and 15 minutes after the fire started (*below*

Picture postcards depicting scenes of the quake were made from photos taken at the time. These cards were very popular.

Southern California, 1933

Date	Location	Fatalities	Remarks
3/10	Long Beach, Calif.	116	Destruction of old schoolhouses, which might have been filled with children at an earlier hour, started southern Californians thinking about building codes.

In March 10, 1933, the California Institute of Technology, at Pasadena, was in a state of excitement. They were entertaining an important guest, Dr. Albert Einstein himself, who'd come to visit their own Dr. Beno Gutenberg, an authority on earth disturbances.

Earth disturbances, in fact, was the topic of conversation as the two men strolled the campus together, so engrossed in their talk they scarcely noticed anything else. Suddenly Dr. Gutenberg noticed numbers of people running frantically out of the university's buildings. He and Einstein stopped and stared, and for the first time, they felt that the earth beneath their feet was trembling. Southern California was in the throes of an earthquake. Over 200 miles of earth, from Santa Barbara to San Diego, had begun to undulate. Einstein and Gutenberg managed to stay calm, but panic spread in the streets of tottering cities and towns. The writhing San Andreas Fault — the cause of most of California's earth disturbances—was doing it again.

The first, most powerful shocks hit the Los Angeles–Long Beach area at 5:55 P.M., and many natives were caught in the rush-hour traffic going home. Those at home, perhaps hoping to relax for the first time that day, were no doubt horrified to see great, gaping cracks appear in what they thought were the solid walls of their houses. Old hands knew what was happening at once, of course, and rushed outside rather than risk being crushed under their own walls. But some were killed in the streets by falling debris.

On the highways, commuters' cars were tossed about like small craft on the high seas. From Long Beach to Los Angeles, fires illuminated the sky. An airplane pilot flying over the area reported seeing thousands of panicked people on the shores of Long Beach.

The first shocks had been the worst, but tremors continued all night. Everyone was in the streets by now, except the injured. In Los Angeles, over 4,000 injured persons were in hospitals. When a tremor caused a wall at one hospital to collapse, and caused cracks in the walls at others, patients panicked and rushed for the doors. Only nimble-witted efforts by the hospital staffs kept people from trampling each other to death.

By morning the worst was over. Long Beach and the surrounding area had been hardest hit. The city was in ruins and 65 of its residents were dead. Los Angeles and nearby towns contributed the rest of the fatalities. But perhaps the biggest shock for the area was a little announcement from the Carnegie Institute in Pasadena. They had measured the shocks and tremors on their instruments, and the earthquake had not been all that severe. It was certainly weaker than the shocks that rocked San Francisco in 1906. It was more like the quake that had occurred in Santa Barbara in 1925, which killed 11 people and caused 10 million dollars' worth of damage. At that time, seismologist Harry O. Wood had pointed out that the total energy of the quake was small. What had caused most of the damages and fatalities were buildings that were unsuitable for an earthquake zone. Mr. Wood warned that southern California was in for some stronger shocks and stated that engineers and architects should start to promote buildings that were designed to withstand quake shocks.

Not much was done until after the earthquake of 1933, when the population finally understood the danger. Building codes were set up, but were optional. Owners of old buildings were not required to make their structures more quake-resistant, and new builders threw quake-resistant architecture to the winds in order to be more economical. However, after the earthquake of 1971 in southern California, when an old hospital collapsed and killed many patients, it was possible to convince southern Californians to enforce the building codes more strictly.

Above: Jefferson Junior High School, Long Beach. *Left:* Downtown business section of Compton. *Right:* Downtown Los Angeles. Reprinted from *Mid-Week Pictorial,* March 25, 1933.

Alaska's Bad Friday, 1964

Date	Location	Fatalities	Remarks
3/27	Port Arthur, Alaska, was center of quake but Anchorage and nearby towns were badly damaged, some permanently.	131 (in Alaska alone)	Tidal wave caused by quake traveled down West Coast, killing 4 campers in Oregon. In Crescent City, Calif., 10 were reported drowned and 50 missing.

It was early evening, and downtown Anchorage was filled with people leaving work. It was Good Friday and everyone was looking forward to the Easter weekend. But they hadn't gotten very far when, without warning, the streets began to ripple and pitch beneath them. People tried to scramble to safety, but there was nowhere to go. Thirty blocks of downtown Anchorage were crumbling. Crevasses 12 feet deep and 50 feet wide opened in the streets, and cars, people, and buildings slipped away. There was nothing to do but watch helplessly, and to try to brace against the relentless shocks. The same scene and worse was being enacted in the ring of towns surrounding Anchorage.

At Seward, Kodiak, Whittier, and Valdez—coastal towns—seismic waves did more damage than the quake. At Valdez, a hole opened up in the dock area and a man and 2 children were swallowed up in it. Moments later, a pier with 12 stevedores on it disappeared. The scenes at Valdez were so horrifying that its residents moved out afterward, never to return.

When it was over, the Alaskans learned that 131 people had died. The shock, centered at Port Arthur, some 75 miles distant from Anchorage, was one of the strongest ever recorded in the United States. It far exceeded the shocks that destroyed San Francisco. Only the thin distribution of the population and the lack of high skyscrapers had kept the fatality rate down.

Aerial view of Anchorage after quake. Those are not just breaks in the snow, but deep crevasses in the earth.

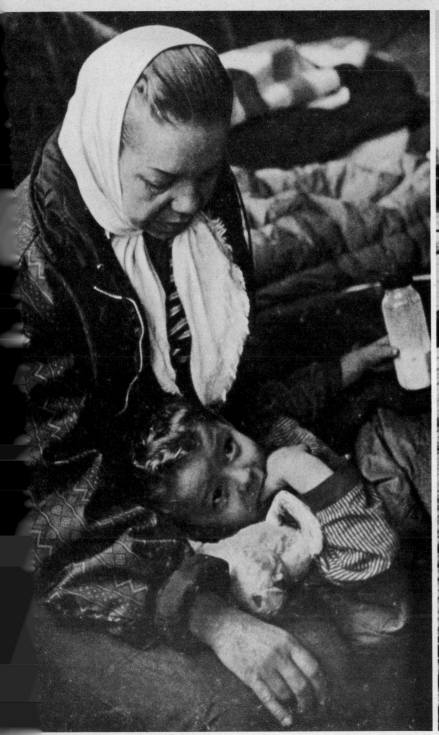

Left: Homeless victims from Seward, Alaska. *Right:* March 27, 1964.

Army personnel helped recover victims lost in the cold sea. As many people were killed by quake-caused tidal wave as by the shattering quake itself.

IMPORTANT AMERICAN FLOODS

DATE	LOCATION	FATALITIES	REMARKS
1771	Richmond, Va.	150	James River overflowed.
1870 Oct.	Lynchburg, Richmond, Harper's Ferry, Va.	50+	Potomac and James Rivers overflowed, flooding nearby towns, including Washington, D.C. More than 50 known dead at Harper's Ferry alone; other records are inaccurate.
1874 5/16	Mill Creek, Mass.	143	Dam on Mill Creek (tributary of Connecticut River) burst, inundating Williamsburg and surrounding towns.
1889 5/31	Johnstown, Pa.	2,200	The worst American dam disaster, and the worst American flood not caused by a hurricane.
1903 6/15	Heppner, Oreg.	200	A strange flood, difficult to explain, preceded by a very brief rain and an unusual amount of hail.
1913 3/27	Ohio, Indiana	732	The worst flood to hit the area since it was settled. Dayton, Ohio, and surrounding area were hit hardest, but the whole Ohio River Valley was affected.
1913 12/1–12/5	Brazos River, Tex.	177	River flooded, making 1913 the third worst flood year of the twentieth century.
1921 6/4	Pueblo, Col.	120	Arkansas River broke levees at Pueblo. People went down to river to see "great wall of water," were cut off from high ground, and died.
1927 March/April	Mississippi River Valley, from Illinois to Gulf of Mexico	313	Damages were so bad, it was first single flood to make Federal Government take a hand in rescue and relief operations, and may have helped elect Herbert Hoover as President.
1928 3/13	Santa Paula, Calif.	450	St. Francis Dam collapsed at night. Nobody knows exact time Santa Paula was wiped out.
1969 1/18–1/26	Southern California	91	Several rivers flooded in area.
1969 8/25	Virginia	236	Western part of state flooded.
1972 2/26	Buffalo Creek, W. Va.	125	A natural dam, created by coal slag and mining waste, burst.
1972 6/9	Rapid City, S. Dak.	236	Canyon Lake Dam burst.

THE FLOOD AT ST. PAUL, MINNESOTA—VIEW OF THE SUBMERGED PORTION OF THE CITY.

In 1541, Hernando de Soto discovered a mighty river that was known to the Indians as "Father of Waters." It was the Mississippi, and since it was springtime, the river was in full flood. This held up De Soto's expedition for one month, giving his chronicler, Garcilaso de la Vega, time to describe the event. It was the first recorded flood in the history of the United States.

The big river overflows its banks at some point almost every year; thus the Mississippi is our most frequent and damaging flooder. It caused the Federal Government to take a hand in flood control, and ultimately to begin a flood-relief program. But the Mississippi is by no means our only flood problem, or even our biggest killer. Every state has at least one serious flood area. In every season in every year, some section of the country is under water. Not all floods are the result of a river's overflowing its banks.

Some of our worst floods have been caused by other disasters, such as sea wapes pushed up by hurricanes, or tidal waves produced by earthquakes. These are covered in appropriate sections in this book. We're concerned here with pure floods, and that still leaves more than one way to drown a community.

For example, the dam that bursts — sometimes in the night and often unexpectedly, bringing sudden and terrifying death. The Johnstown Flood, our worst disaster

SCENE DURING THE INUNDATION AT CAIRO, ILLINOIS.

FLOODS

by water in number of fatalities, was the result of a collapsed dam. In those days, dams were no marvels of engineering. More often than not, they were great heaps of dirt and stone.

We still make mistakes today. Sometimes we don't maintain dams properly, or repair them often enough. Sometimes we ignorantly build them on rock that is weak — even, in one case, on an earthquake fault that was subject to shifts in the earth if not outright quakes. All too often we build them on rivers that run down into populated areas. We keep a sharper eye on them than we used to, and our systems of instant communication make early warnings and evacuation possible. But people don't always heed warnings, even today.

Just as deadly as a dam collapse, and far stranger, is the phenomenon we call a "flash" flood. Usually the result of a brief, unexpected storm or "cloud burst," it's capable of turning quiet creeks and dry culverts into raging torrents. Towns sheltered in cozy wind-free hollows have disappeared in an instant. Sometimes it doesn't take much of a cloud burst to do it. If the ground is already saturated from earlier rains—or hard, dry, and nonporous so it can't absorb water—a good shower can bring on a flash flood. Unfortunately, the squalls that precede such instant deluges are often unpredictable. But when ground conditions are as described above, a sudden shower will cause the Weather Bureau to issue flash-flood warnings. Anyone near a stream or gulley who doesn't take heed is foolish indeed.

Fortunately, a flooding river sometimes overflows its banks or bursts its levees slowly enough to allow evacuation of endangered populations. But not always. Sometimes a flood wave, or waves, can make a river, or convergence of rivers, crest so much more quickly and higher than expected that the results are as sudden and deadly as those produced by the burst dam or flash flood. More often, the river flood kills by inches, destroying all a community has worked for in the past, and sometimes all possibility of future subsistence. In terms of regularity and damage, river floods are the worst enemy, though much has been done to control them. Dams and reservoirs have been built to control flooding, as well as levees that are very effective. We, the taxpayers, have spent billions on flood control, but there are limits to how far nature can be controlled. There are places where a river will and must flood, no matter what. Thus floods occur as frequently today as ever, although the results are not so fatal as they once were.

These areas of periodic flooding are called "flood plains"—flat land lying below or on a level with a large body of water (a lake, reservoir, river, or large creek). For years, the Government has discouraged people from living on the plains. Today, flood insurance is provided by the Government to flood-plains communities, but anyone who collects money from this insurance is pressured to move away. The Government would like to make public parks of all its flood plains.

Flood plains, however, contain some of the best farm land. They are also sought as sites for factories, for they provide water power and a river dump for waste. As sites for residences, they are attractive—and expensive. And one look at this book will tell you that life is a dangerous proposition anywhere.

Homeless and adrift during a western flood of 1852.

Virginia Flood, 1870

Date	Location	Fatalities	Remarks
Oct.	Lynchburg, Richmond, Harper's Ferry, Va.	50+	Potomac and James Rivers overflowed, flooding nearby towns, including Washington, D.C. More than 50 known dead at Harper's Ferry alone; other records are inaccurate.

Reprinted from *Harper's Weekly*, October 22, 1870.

INUNDATION OF RICHMOND.—[From a Photograph by C. R. Rees and Co., Richmond.]

Mill Creek Disaster, 1874

Date	Location	Fatalities	Remarks
5/16	Mill Creek, Mass.	143	Dam on Mill Creek (tributary of Connecticut River) burst, inundating Williamsburg and surrounding towns.

Illustration by Milton Bradley reprinted from *Frank Leslie's Illustrated Newspaper,* May 30, 1874.

Johnstown flood memorial print issued by Kurz & Allison, Art Publishers, Chicago, May 31, 1889.

RSTING OF THE RESERVOIR.　　　2. SAVED BY HER FAITHFUL HORSE.　　　HUNDREDS ROASTED ALIVE AT THE RAIL-ROAD BRIDGE.　　　4. RECOVERING THE VICTIMS.　　　5.—IDENTIFYING

THE GREAT CONEMAUGH VALLEY DISASTER.—FLOOD & FIRE AT JOHNSTOWN, PA.

FRIDAY, MAY 31ST 1889

Johnstown Flood, 1889

Date	Location	Fatalities	Remarks
5/31	Johnstown, Pa.	2,200	The worst American dam disaster, and the worst American flood not caused by a hurricane.

He came riding down the mountain like something out of a nightmare. "The dam is going! The South Fork Dam is going!"

The panic in civil engineer John G. Parke's voice alarmed the folks in South Fork, which lay just two miles below the dam. Every spring, it seemed someone came galloping down the mountain, yelling that the Conemaugh Lake Reservoir was about to dump its water into the valley below.

It never happened. The first few times, everyone as far down as Johnstown, a city of 30,000 people 16 miles away, had run for the nearby hills. But not anymore.

This time, however, there was something in John Parke's voice that sent the population of South Fork heading for the hills.

John Parke reached the village of South Fork just before noon, and immediately sent two men to the telegraph office to warn the towns and cities down in the valley. Years later, some would claim that Conemaugh and Johnstown and the other towns and villages never got any warning because the telegraph wires were down as a result of the torrential rains that had plagued the area for a full week. But according to *Harper's Weekly* of June 15, 1889, the message was received by the widow Mrs. Ogle, manager of Johnstown's Western Union office for 25 years. It's inconceivable that she would not have spread the alarm, especially since she, her daughter Minnie, and her entire staff relayed warning after warning to the towns beyond Johnstown that might also lie in the path of the impending flood. Why would Johnstown ignore Mrs. Ogle's warning? As *Harper's* put it: "Thousands of people discredited the alarm because it was like the false warnings they had heard before."

From their hillside perches, the people of South Fork could see a crew of men trying desperately to keep the dam from collapsing. From time to time, little avalanches of stone and dirt came rumbling down, reminding them of just how long the dam's critics had been calling it a "heap of dirt."

The Pennsylvania Railroad had built the dam long ago, as part of its water supply. They abandoned it, and it was allowed to deteriorate. Some people thought it would be best to drain the reservoir and do away with the dam, but in 1879, seventeen years after it had been abandoned, the dam was leased by "some millionaire fellahs from Pittsburgh," as part of their private hunting and fishing club. They did try to repair the dam by making it higher and wider, but there was no masonry involved, no stone or concrete, and all they'd done was to make an even bigger "heap of dirt." What's more, they were accused of not repairing the waste gates at the bottom, where water could escape instead of building up. Fish could escape through those waste gates as well as water, and the club didn't want that.

Johnstown and its neighbor, Conemaugh, were created and largely owned by the Cambria Iron Works, "one of the largest and most flourishing establishments of its kind in Pennsylvania." Together, both towns were known as Johnstown City, a classic example of a company town. Most of its citizens were Cambria Works laborers and their families. They lived in wooden row houses, built and owned by the company, down on the flats of the city, in a kind of triangle surrounded on two sides by the Conemaugh River and Stony Creek. The flats had churches and schools and even a public library, all paid for by the Cambria Iron Works. The officers of the company, the professionals, and the merchants lived up in the hills above the flats.

The thriving city after the flood, a muddy flat. Scarcely a fourth of its buildings were left standing.

Up in the mountains, the South Fork villagers had begun to wonder if it wasn't another false alarm. The dam was leaking, but nothing else seemed to be happening. Suddenly, a section of the huge dam seemed to move off, and a 75-foot wall of water roared into the valley. South Fork and the little towns beyond disappeared in the twinkling of an eye, and the great wall of water surged toward Johnstown at 40 miles an hour.

In Johnstown, Mrs. Ogle and staff remained alert and had begun to send regular reports to the main office at Pittsburgh. The rest of the town seemed in a gay, almost holiday mood. Down by the river banks, men on horseback joked with the people in their second-story windows. And in one of the town churches, a young couple was being married.

Then, at 3:00 P.M., Pittsburgh received a report from Mrs. Ogle that said, "This is my last message." They did not hear from Mrs. Ogle or her staff again, for the huge wall of water had squeezed through a very narrow pass at Woodvale, just above Johnstown. It reared up to 90 feet and with a mighty roar fell like a judgment on the town.

Those who could do so ran for high embankments or the hills. Many were caught unawares in their homes, some were stunned and unable to move, and still others were too burdened with children and loved ones to move fast enough.

From precarious footholds on high ground, people watched in horror as the whirling waters destroyed their town and tossed their neighbors about in the debris. They tried to help, holding out straps, ropes, or hands to drag anyone they could to safety. But the job soon became hopeless.

At the far end of Johnstown was a viaduct—a big, concrete railroad bridge supported by arches. The bridge withstood the force of the water, but the arches filled up with the debris that had once been the town, and created a natural dam. It saved the towns below Johnstown, but created a 25-foot whirlpool, nearly a mile wide, in Johnstown itself. It was impossible to reach anyone in the swirling waters, which seemed to carry everything toward the railroad bridge. Then, as the pile of ruins grew against the bridge, new hope was born. Those still left alive in the water could climb up on the heap, and survive until the waters went down.

At 6:00 P.M., the gigantic mass of rubble—covered with petroleum from overturned freight cars—caught fire. The screams of those who perished in the flames would haunt the survivors for a lifetime.

In South Fork, the only fatality was a man who had not joined his thousand fellow villagers in the hills. From South Fork to Johnstown, more than 2,200 died. People tried to find each other in the confusion, but some never did. A man who'd lost a family of four went into a hardware store, bought a gun, and shot himself. The bride and groom whose wedding ceremony was interrupted by the flood waters were said to be found locked in each other's arms, dead. But amid the rubble that in 12 short hours floated down to Pittsburgh, 75 miles away, a 5-month-old baby was found floating on a wooden floor. She was alive and without a scratch on her.

Ohio River Valley, 1913

Date	Location	Fatalities	Remarks
3/27	Ohio, Indiana	732	The worst flood to hit the area since it was settled. Dayton, Ohio, and surrounding area were hit hardest, but the whole Ohio River Valley was affected.

It rained from March to December. At some time during at least one of those months, large areas in New York, Pennsylvania, Virginia, British Columbia, Nebraska, California, and Texas could be found only under water. In Illinois, Kentucky, Tennessee, Louisiana, and Arkansas, picturesque creeks and streams became raging torrents and deluged towns and countryside. Every place along the banks of the Mississippi, north and south, spent all spring bailing out. In American history, 1913 ranks as the third worst flood year of the twentieth century. For Ohio and Indiana, 1913 ranks first and worst for all time.

THE NEW YORK HERALD.
NEW YORK, SATURDAY, MARCH 29, 1913.—TWENTY-TWO PAGES.—   ***** PRICE THREE CENTS.

NIGHT PILLAGERS IN DAYTON SHOT TO DEATH; WATER RECEDES AND CARLOADS OF FOOD ARRIVE

RESCUERS TAKING PHYSICIAN TO AID MAROONED INJURED AT HAMILTON, OHIO

Only 200 May Be Dead in Dayton, but Property

The trouble began on March 23, with a gigantic rainstorm that swept the entire Ohio River basin. The ground had been saturated with rain from February and the rivers were high. People living along the Ohio River and its main tributaries, both in Ohio and Indiana, were alarmed. Dayton, the capital of Ohio, was protected by levees, but experienced residents knew that, with or without levees, the Ohio, and its nearby tributary, the Miami River, were historically bad troublemakers. Together, they'd overflowed their banks almost as many times as the Mississippi, into which they flowed.

Escaping by wire and wagon.

In Indiana, the same scene was enacted. The beautiful Wabash of song and story turned angry and menacing, swollen beyond capacity. The Ohio River swamped the Indiana plains and claimed 232 lives.

When the flood waters finally receded in Ohio and Indiana the final count of known victims was appalling. Only two American floods of the twentieth century had claimed more victims —and both had been caused by hurricanes and inundations from the sea (Galveston Hurricane, 1900; Lake Okeechobee Hurricane, 1928). In terms of river-flooding, this was the worst. The people of Ohio were determined to prevent another flood disaster from happening again. They formed a Flood Prevention Committee, and, seven weeks after the flood, they hired Arthur E. Morgan, an engineer, to show them how to do it.

Morgan had a plan. Deepen the channel of the Miami River, making it able to contain more water, and build detention reservoirs on its tributaries which would hold excess water.

Today, this is a normal flood-control procedure, with the Federal Government frequently paying the bill for both channel-clearing and dam-building. But in 1913, the Government did not allocate funds for state flood protection and the people of Dayton decided to pay for it themselves. They raised money despite opposition of people who were afraid of change, and overcame a four-year court battle. By 1923, they had their dams, and since then they've never suffered a really bad flood. It was a first in flood-prevention and a model to other cities threatened by flood.

At 1:00 A.M., the Miami River crested at Dayton, exceeding all of its previous high-water levels. At almost the same moment, the Scioto River also crested, and its waters rushed to meet those of the Miami at the main stem of the Ohio River. Simultaneously, a huge 25-foot flood wave was rushing down the Muskingum in the same direction. In this conspiracy of rivers against Ohio, the waters won. Within twenty-four hours, the rushing tides of the three rivers met and turned Dayton and the surrounding area into an enormous lake.

The scramble for survival was terrific. Every available floating object was maneuvered through the streets to pick up as many passengers as possible. People walked along dead telephone and electric wires, like tightrope artists, to escape from their submerged homes; others waited it out on protruding rooftops. Bales of wire and rope were strung between high poles, trees, and other standing objects, in hope that survivors could grasp them and pull themselves to safety through swift currents and high waters. Over 500 people did not make it.

Mississippi River Valley, 1927

Date	Location	Fatalities	Remarks
March/ April	Mississippi River Valley, from Illinois to Gulf of Mexico	313	Damages were so bad, it was first single flood to make the Federal Government take a hand in rescue and relief operations, and may have helped elect Herbert Hoover as President.

The Mississippi River in flood is never a dull affair. But in 1927, this granddaddy of North American rivers outdid itself in every way. It broke all of its previous water-level records and spread out over 18 million acres of land—from Cairo, Illinois, to New Orleans—causing at least 6 states to declare a state of emergency. New Orleans managed to save itself from total inundation by dynamiting some of its levees and allowing the river to flood its bayou islands instead. In the rest of the country, the big river wreaked 300 million dollars' worth of havoc, killed 313 people, and left 637,000 homeless and stranded in water that was literally over their heads.

The size and importance of the Mississippi, and its almost annual inundations, had long ago forced the Federal Government to take a hand in trying to control its flooding, but little was done for its victims. After the flood of 1927, it would have to do more. Secretary of Commerce Herbert Hoover was put in charge of rescue operations.

His first act was to organize the National Guard, Army Corps of Engineers, Weather Bureau, Navy, Red Cross, and available local help into a consolidated working unit. He commandeered 40 river steamers, got himself 1,000 outboard-motored rough boats, and floated all the stranded to high ground. There, he set up sturdy tent cities, replete with sewers, electricity, huge kitchens and dining halls, even hospitals. Nor did the Hoover group fade with the receding waters. They stayed long enough to try to rehabilitate people back on their land, giving them basic supplies with which to start over again.

The Federal Government did not pay for any of this. Since, in Mr. Hoover's words, "at this time we all believed in self-help," he raised the money through a Red Cross drive, which netted 15 million dollars, and he managed to get another million from the Rockefeller Foundation. He did induce the Government to take one step forward. Through the Department of Commerce, a nonprofit organization was set up from which flood victims could get low-interest loans, every penny of which was paid back, Mr. Hoover was proud to say.

Melville, Louisiana, 1927. Most towns in the Mississippi River Valley, from Illinois to the Gulf of Mexico, looked this way during April.

Let's Give a Dime to the Flood Victims

By WILL ROGERS

All I know is just what I read in the papers. And what I am akicking about is that I haven't read enough in the papers about something that ought to have had more in the papers about it than it has had. That is this Flood.

Your Earthquake (Pardon me, fire) in Frisco, or the Tidal wave in Miami or the Tornados in the middle west didont start to wreck the amount of damage that this flood has. The Red Cross asked for five million. Why, that won't start to do any good. There is a million people that have lost by it. That would only be five dollars a head. Five dollars ain't much good to you, even if the water's just up to your ankles.

Five million dollars won't start to give all these people any kind of relief. There is 120 million people in America. We will says there are 10 million children that are too little physically to give, and then there is another 10 million that are physically large enough, but conscientiously too small to give. So that still leaves us 100 million. Now five million for the sufferers is only a nickle apiece for One Hundred million to give. Now, I think we ought to spread this to about a quarter each (25 cents). Or if everybody can't spare a quarter why 20 cents would give them 20 million.

Now, if we sorter feel they didont get hardly wet enough for a couple of thin dimes per head, why let's kinder spread our generosity a little anyway and give a dime each and that will give them ten million. That's about ten dollars a head for the ones that suffered loss. Now you will hear lots of people say, "What do they do with all this money? Here people are giving millions!"

Well now, take for instance ten dollars a head in case my suggestion is acted on and everyone of the 100 million will give 10 cents. That will give the sufferers $10 a head. Now I know that is a pretty lump sum to go and squander on a fellow that hasn't lost anything but his house and barn and stock and all his seed that he has planted already. It is liable to bring on an era of squandering. But you take it as a rule and most people are mighty good when they know there is real need.

'Course, the Florida thing kinder hurt collections for National calamities. The minute a community would gather up something and start to send it they would get word from the authorities down there that "they wasent hurt a bit; that they didont need a thing." Well, would coulдent blame them from trying to hide it as bad as they could and make it as small as possible. But in doing so they didont realise the harm they were doing to the collections of future calamities. It was like the old "Wolf! Wolf!" Then when the

is as bad hit as the next. Your stock is either washed away or marooned on a piece of land with no food. A fire, they can get to your town or place from other places to lend you help, but water, when the bridges are all under, one place can't get to the other to help till they make temporary boats and rafts. Then the worst thing is their crops had lots of them been planted, and those that hadent had already plowed for seeding. Where are they going to get the money to re-seed and plow again? How are they going to rebuild their fences? All stock that hasn't drowned will just have to run loose, for there will be no fences or barns to put them in.

The poorest class of people in this country is the renter farmer, or the ones that tends the little patch of ground on shares. He is debt from one crop to the other to the store keeper, or the little local bank. He never has a dollar that he can call his own. City people don't realise the poverty of poor country folks.

They can talk all they want about country people being out in the air and in the open, but I want to tell you as a diet and nothing to go with it, I dont think there is a Scientist living that can show any more "Callories" in a few whiffs of Country air over air anywhere on Hester Street or the Bowery.

And as for the number of children, say the poor in the city would be accused of race suicide if they was stacked up alongside of the poor white family down in the bottom on a cotton farm. The poor man in the city hasent got any dog to feed. Why this first five millions wouldent even feed the dogs that have been caught in this flood. Thats one thing the poor country fellow will always have, his pack of

We went cuckoo over the Armenians, Russians and Poles.

dogs, and no man can be condemped for owning a dog. In fact you admire him, 'cause as long he's got a dog he's got a friend, and the poorer he gets the better friend he has. Then when you talk about poor people that have been hit by this flood, look at the thousands and thousands of negroes that never did have much, but now its washed away. You don't want to forget that water is just as high up on them as it is if they were white. The Lord so constituted everybody that no matter what color you are you require about the same amount of nourishment.

What gets my Goat is hearing constantly, "Why don't those people move out of there? There are floods every year." How are they going to move? Who is going to move 'em? Where are they going to move to, and what are they going to do when they move there? Why dont you move? Maybe you could do better some place else. That's the trouble with us it's Why don't everybody do something but us. Wait till a calamity hits where you are, and then they can ask, Why don't you move?"

Fifty million wouldent be too much for this cause, and I bet you Mr. Hoover will tell you so. If you have raised your Quota once, start in and raise it again. Then you can brag, but don't do it unless you have. Remember these people can't get any relief for themselves until a crop is harvested. We went Cuckoo over the Armenians. We took off our shirts and sent them to the Russians. We give the Poles our Socks.

Reprinted from *The Lexington Herald*, Sunday, May 8, 1927.

St. Francis Dam, 1928

Date	Location	Fatalities	Remarks
3/13	Santa Paula, Calif.	450	St. Francis Dam collapsed at night. Nobody knows exact time Santa Paula was wiped out.

There are no tales of terror, no vivid descriptions of great walls of water, no thrilling stories of miraculous escapes from the St. Francis Dam disaster. On the night of March 12, 1928, people went to bed as usual in Santa Paula, California, in the San Francisquito Valley below the St. Francis Dam. On the morning of March 13, there was no Santa Paula, just an appalling pile of rubbish. Its entire population of 450 people were dead. There were no eyewitnesses, no survivors. A huge gap in the enormous 205-foot structure that had been the St. Francis Dam told what had happened.

The St. Francis Dam, 45 miles north of Los Angeles, had been built only two years before, and with great care. Created to hold a water supply for Los Angeles, the dam was solid concrete, very strong, and more important, under constant surveillance. On March 12, in fact, the chief engineer of the Los Angeles waterworks had inspected the dam. Some cracks had developed and there was leakage, but he was not worried. After all, the earth is always shifting, and the most solid structures may develop cracks.

Only during the subsequent investigation of the disaster was it discovered that the dam had been built on a fault. This fracture or crack in the earth's crust was subject to tremors that could damage any structure built over it. Geologists also discovered, too late, that the dam had been built upon a kind of rock that was very weak and decayed on contact with water.

On March 12, sometime during the night or early morning, the dam gave way. Anyone who saw what happened did not live to tell the tale.

A piece of the broken St. Francis Dam was all that was left standing in the little town of Santa Paula, March 24, 1928.

The Rapid City Flood, 1972

Date	Location	Fatalities	Remarks
6/9	Rapid City, S. Dak.	236	Canyon Lake Dam burst.

In the Black Hills of South Dakota—home of Mount Rushmore, some of the best camping country in the world, and Rapid City ("the Denver of the hills")—the weather report was dreary, but not alarming. Variable cloudiness was predicted for June 9, with chances of scattered showers and thunderstorms. But on the ninth, the scattered showers became a steady downpour the likes of which Rapid City had never seen before.

So unusual was the prolonged deluge that the residents of Rapid City didn't know enough to be worried, and were totally unprepared for what was to come. In 6 hours, 14 inches of rain fell, an extraordinary record anywhere. The National Weather Bureau reported that the atmospheric conditions over the area on June 9 might occur once in a hundred years.

By 7:15 P.M., the local weather station was issuing high-water warnings. Rapid Creek, the pretty stream which wound down from the hills and which gave the city its name, was disturbingly full. However, it wasn't only the creek that troubled Mayor Dan Barnett. His worry was Canyon Lake, which lay above the city's most desirable residential section. A large, man-made lake that straddled the creek, it was held in place by a dam that was due for its five-year overhaul later that summer. Since it had been a wet month, Barnett wasn't sure the dam would hold against this extraordinary rainfall. He got together the chief of police, the director of public works, and a crew to inspect the condition of the dam.

At 10:00 P.M., the group received a call from a man who lived by the creek, up above the lake. He'd just seen a "wall of water" coming down the creek, and it would hit the lake in about 20 minutes.

The Mayor called the local radio station to issue announcements to abandon the area at once. He rallied the National Guard to evacuate people. He ran up and down the creek himself, asking people to leave. They all looked at him as if he were crazy.

"They wouldn't listen!" he said in amazement afterward.

"We thought he was kidding!" a survivor reported later, equally amazed.

Between 10:44 P.M. and 11:00 P.M., the dam broke.

With a "terrible roar," the wild wall of water hit the city and turned its streets into turbulent rivers. Frantic people ran for their cars, only to have them quickly fill with water, cutting off all means of rapid escape. Houses sailed down the streets with people clinging to the rooftops. National Guardsmen did their best to help, and one was swept away in the fierce tide as he let go of his truck door in an effort to save a little girl. Others watched helplessly as a house with a roof full of people floated down the creek and struck a bridge, forcing everyone into the churning waters.

Those lucky enough to be in, or on, standing houses were as helpless as the National Guard to help less fortunate victims. In nearby treetops, they could see children trying to hang on for dear life, until someone could save them. Some of them were rescued, but not all. "Our daughter just floated away," one brokenhearted father reported afterward. "She tried holding on to a tree, but she just floated away."

All power failed before 2:00 A.M. There was no light, no communication. Nobody knew what was happening outside their own little realm of horror. It wasn't until 6:00 A.M. that any of them knew that the worst was over when someone managed to broadcast on a citizen's band. The first message received was not cheering: "Stay in your homes. Do not impede emergency-vehicle traffic. Do not drink the water. Boats are needed immediately. If you do find a body, do not move or touch it. Wait for emergency personnel. . . ."

Before the day was out, it was obvious that this was South Dakota's biggest disaster, and certainly the worst thing that had ever happened to Rapid City. Senator George McGovern interrupted his campaign for the Democratic nomination for President and flew to the stricken city, where he waited with fellow citizens to hear the sad results of the flood. By afternoon, 150 bodies had been recovered, and National Guardsmen and volunteers were still dredging the creek and digging through muck and debris for the missing.

There had been a lot of campers in the area, out in the nearby woods of the Black Hills. What had become of them? "They'll be picking them out of there all summer," sighed the chief of police.

By summer's end, the official fatality count was 236, with 124 still missing. Nobody ever knew whether the missing were dead, had gone on to homes elsewhere without notifying authorities, or had left before the flood and simply were not where they were expected to be. In Rapid City, they knew one thing for sure. When you live on a flood plain — like the one that exists below Canyon Lake — and someone tells you to get out, you get out.

Cars, like houses, were carried along in the swift flood tide — stopping only for an immovable obstacle.

IMPORTANT AMERICAN FIRES

DATE	LOCATION	FATALITIES	REMARKS
1835 12/16	New York City	No accurate record, probably few.	"Great New York Fire." 700 buildings destroyed, a large portion of New York in those days.
1845 3/10	Pittsburgh, Pa.	No accurate record.	1,000 buildings destroyed.
1849 7/4	St. Louis, Mo.	No accurate record.	15 blocks gone in this first destruction of St. Louis. Tornado would destroy her later.
1866 7/4	Portland, Maine	Several, no accurate record.	City destroyed.
1871 10/8	Chicago, Ill.	250+	Most famous fire in American history. Only found bodies were counted, but probably an equal number were killed and never found.
1871 10/8	Michigan, Minnesota, Wisconsin	1,182	Simultaneous forest fires ravaged small towns in three states. Peshtigo, Wis., was hardest hit, but was typical of what happened during worst fire in U.S. history.
1872 11/9	Boston, Mass.	Most escaped with "nothing but their lives."	600 buildings destroyed.
1876 12/5	Brooklyn, N.Y.	300+	"Flying" scenery hit gas lamp at Conway's Theater. Many theaters caught fire the same way, but this was worst of its time.
1894 9/1	Hinckley, Minn.	413	Fire destroyed town and 160,000+ acres of forest.
1900 6/30	Hoboken, N.J.	326	Hoboken docks burned, destroyed.
1902 9/19	Birmingham, Ala.	115	Panic and stampede in Shiloh Baptist Church was the killer. There was no fire at all.
1903 12/30	Chicago, Ill.	602	Chicago's second great fire took place at Iroquois Theater. Worst theater fire in U.S. history. The actors helped save many lives.
1904 2/7	Baltimore, Md.	No fatalities recorded.	75 city blocks burned.
1908 1/13	Boyertown, Pa.	170	Rhoades Opera House caught fire during Sunday school program.
1908 3/4	Collinwood, Ohio	176	Children trapped by fire in school. Two teachers also killed.
1908 4/12	Chelsea, Mass.	Few	City destroyed.
1911 3/25	New York City	145	Fire in Triangle shirt factory, a sweatshop in Greenwich Village, brought changes in legislation concerning working and safety conditions in factories.
1914 6/25	Salem, Mass.	Few	1,700 buildings destroyed.
1916 3/21	Paris, Tex.	Few	1,440 buildings destroyed.
1918 10/13	Minnesota, Wisconsin	1,000	Forest fires raked towns in both states. In Cloquet, Minn., 400 were killed.
1919 6/20	San Juan, Puerto Rico	150	Mayagüez Theater burned.
1923 5/17	Camden, S.C.	76	School burned.
1923 9/17	Berkeley, Calif.	Few, if any.	600 buildings destroyed.
1929 5/15	Cleveland, Ohio	125	Burning X-ray films caused suffocation in clinic.
1930 4/21	Columbus, Ohio	320	Ohio State Penitentiary inmates were trapped in locked cells of the west block.
1940 4/23	Natchez, Miss.	198	Dance hall burned.
1942 11/28	Boston, Mass.	492	Fake palm tree at Cocoanut Grove nightclub caught fire; flames quickly spread in packed club
1944 7/6	Hartford, Conn.	168	Ringling Bros. and Barnum & Bailey Circus tent caught fire and trapped ringside spectators.
1946 6/5	Chicago, Ill.	61	LaSalle Hotel burned.
1946 12/7	Atlanta, Ga.	119	Winecoff Hotel burned; worst hotel fire in U.S. history.
1949 4/5	Effingham, Ill.	77	Fire in St. Anthony's Hospital.
1957 2/17	Warrenton, Mo.	72	Home for the aged burned.
1958 12/1	Chicago, Ill.	95	Our Lady of the Angels parochial school burned. Victims were nuns and grade-school children.
1963 11/23	Fitchville, Ohio	63	Rest home burned.

FIRES

ire was stolen from heaven by the Titan god Prometheus and given to man. Fire warms us and cooks our food; it has given us vast mechanical power. Fire also makes ashes of our homes, cities, and forests, and of our very bones. It is our most common disaster. Even as you read this, fires are taking their toll all over the nation. Whether started by heating-system failures, lightning, or the tiny spark of a cigarette, fire is one of our worst killers.

However, this queen of catastrophes is not as fatal as it once was. Modern fire-fighting equipment and organizations, alarm and vigilance systems, strict building codes, and fireproof building materials have changed things. Like the smartest little pig in the story of the three little pigs, we always knew brick and stone were the best materials, but they were very expensive. Wood was something we had plenty of—and at the right price—and it was with wood that we built our settlements and towns and even our big cities until well into the 1800's.

It wasn't until the 1800's that our towns even began to be real cities. Boston, New York, Philadelphia, and other big towns did not rival London or other crowded old cities of Europe. Houses or clumps of houses were a good distance apart, often with ground for barns and stables. Though a fire might wipe out a small community, it did not burn down the whole city.

In the nineteenth century, the number of factories and mills increased greatly, and row houses and multiple-dwelling tenements were built to house the workers. Homes were set closer together. Sidewalks were constructed along the muddy streets, and almost all of them were built of wood. Even many of the early mansions of millionaires were wooden. If soft wood was used—such as resinous pine—a spark on a sidewalk was enough to set an entire city ablaze. And some cities were dependent on volunteer firemen. Thus it is not surprising that several cities were destroyed—New York, Boston, Baltimore, Jacksonville, and Chicago, to name a few. For the most part, city fires were slow ravagers, like rising rivers, and relatively few people lost their lives. In the Chicago fire of 1871, which holds the nation's fatality record for city-wide fires, fewer died than anyone could have guessed from looking at the ruins. More people have been lost in a single fire in a public building—such as a theater, school, church, or hospital—than in most city-wide fires.

The size of places for public meetings and amusement grew with the cities, and of course were built of the same materials. Crowds were confined in buildings with too few exits. Most lethal were the theaters with their fatal combination of curtains, flimsy scenery, and open-flame gas lighting. Even the hint of a fire could cause panic and stampede as deadly as the flames themselves. As many people have been trampled to death in such establishments as have succumbed to suffocating smoke or the fire itself. These fires called public attention to the need for many clearly marked fire exits, outside stairs and fire escapes, proper placing of lighting materials, prohibition of flammable materials, and building inspection. So horrible were the fires in large public places that they did more to inspire the search for new materials than the burning of entire cities.

However, the two worst fires in our history have been forest fires. Smokey the Bear notwithstanding, forest fires are not always the result of man's carelessness. Sometimes, they are nature's way of clearing out the old deadwood and making way for the new. But unwittingly we created many serious hazards. In the mid-nineteenth century, as we began to cut lumber and establish towns in the great forests of the West, we deforested large areas. This decreased humidity and caused a danger to the rest of the forest in dry spells. To clear areas, we used explosives and flammables, sometimes during droughts. We were careless and ignorant, and when nature herself set the flames amid the marsh gases and flammable pines, we could only be horrified as they swept over defenseless towns. It happened often, and there was little local fire-fighters could do against the advance of immense fires fed by thousands of acres of forest. The forest needed a police and fire-fighting force as much as any town or city did, and so the Forest Rangers were born.

Today our cities are no longer wood. Space between floors, fireproof doors and fireproof materials in walls have made the offices and apartments in multiple-dwelling buildings into separate compartments and one is not easily affected by fire in another. We have been warned—by fiction and film as well as by architects and fire experts—that the "towering inferno" could happen. But so far it's been the older, somewhat neglected homes and tenements that have claimed lives. Nor have we had a really immense fire in a theater, church, hotel or hospital since the 1940's. Of course, there have been smaller fires, mostly in older neglected buildings which seem to escape the eye of the fire inspectors. They happen often enough to be frightening, and it adds up.

But it does keep adding up to less, especially in our cities and forests. In those places, at least, we've insisted on trained fire-fighters. In our small towns and rural areas, even volunteers are expected to know something about the nature of fire and the latest equipment. Fire is a fiend which we'll never wipe out, especially since we must go on using it as a friend, but we can keep trying to cut down the death toll.

The burning of Boston, 1872. Washington Street looking toward Old South Church.

CAUGHT IN THE CANVAS HELD BY CITIZENS.

ESCAPING BY MEANS OF BLANKETS.

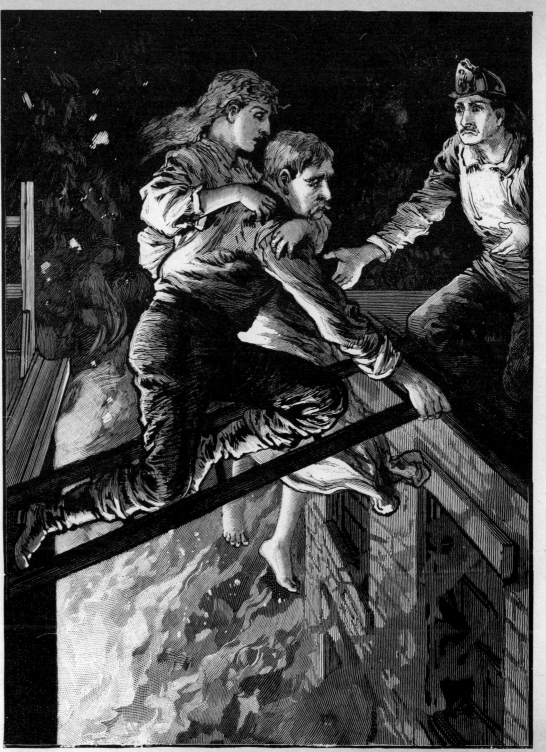

RESCUE OF WOMEN BY FIREMEN OF HOOK AND LADDER TRUCKS NOS. 1 AND 2.

THE OLD NEW YORK FIRE DEPARTMENT CELEBRATION.—DRAWN BY SCHELL AND HOGAN.

The Chicago Fire, 1871

Date	Location	Fatalities	Remarks
10/8	Chicago, Ill.	250+	Most famous fire in American history. Only found bodies were counted, but probably an equal number were killed and never found.

She was an old woman of 70, said the Chicago *Times*, and bent nearly double with the burdens of what appeared to be a fruitless life. She'd been on county relief for years, they said, until a neighbor revealed that the old Irishwoman was no pauper at all.

She owned not only a house, a barn, and the ground they stood on, but a milch cow who was a legend in the neighborhood. The cow was said to produce prodigious amounts of milk of such wonderful quality that the old lady was able to peddle it for wonderful profits. The county agent purportedly cut off her funds when he learned of this, and scolded her for having deceived him. Whereupon the old lady was said to have vowed her revenge on a city that would deny her "a bit of wood and a pound of bacon."

Here the story begins to vary a bit, even within the pages of the *Times* itself. No one could quite believe the old lady had set fire to the barn in a fit of pique. She wouldn't have done that to her wonderful cow. All of the newspapers, from Chicago to New York, claimed to have had a word with the woman, and told basically the same story, with minor variations. She'd gone to her barn, after dark, carrying a kerosene lamp. Some said it was to see to the welfare of her "pet"; others said she was there to milk it.

In any event, the cow, of a tempestuous nature not foreign to talented stars, was reported to have kicked over not only a bucket of the magic milk but the kerosene lamp as well — which spilled the kerosene that lighted the straw that burned the barn that set all of Chicago ablaze.

The *Times* never mentioned the old lady's name, but everyone knew where the fire had started. It was in an old barn on DeKoven Street, on Chicago's West Side. The barn, and the cottage in front of it, was owned by the O'Leary family — Patrick, Catherina, and their five children. The barn was Catherina's province.

At about 8:30 on that Sunday evening, a friend had dropped by to visit with the O'Learys. Catherina was in bed with a sore foot. Patrick and the friend chatted about the drought that gripped the Chicago area and the surrounding states (known then as the American West). For months it had not rained at

VOL. XV.—No. 774.]   NEW YORK, SATURDAY, OCTOBER 28, 1871.   [WITH A SUPPLEMENT. PRICE TEN CENTS.

Entered according to Act of Congress, in the Year 1871, by Harper & Brothers, in the Office of the Librarian of Congress, at Washington.

THE GREAT FIRE IN CHICAGO—GROUP OF REFUGEES IN THE STREET.—DRAWN BY C. S. REINHART.

all, and the city, built mostly of wood, including the sidewalks, was bone dry. There had been forty fires in the past month, and an immense fire down by the Chicago River only the night before.

Patrick was too weary to think much about it, so the friend left early. As he walked down the street, he noted that the wind had come up. He stopped for a moment to enjoy the breeze, lit a pipe, and sat down on the wooden curb to smoke it. He glanced back at the home of the O'Learys and noticed a red glare behind the barn. At first, he didn't know what to make of it, and then he realized what it was. The barn was on fire. He ran to sound the alarm.

By the time firemen arrived, three blocks of Chicago were ablaze. Numbed by their fire-fighting efforts of the past month—and particularly of the night before—the firemen were powerless. To add to the horror, the pleasant breeze from a moment ago turned into a gale wind, an unusual phenomenon even in the Windy City. The flames were uncontrollable and, despite all efforts of the firemen, street after street of the West Side caught fire.

In other sections of Chicago, people did not know what was happening. They heard the alarm, but there'd been many alarms in the past month. The people on the West Side, however, were engaged in a desperate struggle to cross the Chicago River to the North Side. They hired every vehicle in sight, hastily packed their belongings, and moved to reach the river before the fire consumed all the bridges and encircled them in flames. The streets were filled with screaming horses, howling dogs, crying mothers and children, and bellowing men. They nearly trampled each other to death as the fire cut off path after path to the river. In some areas, which the fire left untouched, people just sat in the streets watching. Then the wind shifted, and the fire came back to consume whatever it had left behind.

The wind shifted constantly, sending the fire back and forth like surf—the waves surged always forward, the undertow rolled back over old ground. Hysterical crowds in the streets shifted backward and forward with the flames. Men broke into all the bars and vast amounts of beer and liquor were consumed. At last, the waterworks burned, leaving firemen weaponless and the citizenry half baked and parched. It has been suggested that the more respectable among the drinkers were merely slaking their thirst. The drinkers, however, "spread out in all directions—a terror to all they met."

By midnight, even the looters and drinkers had stopped laughing at the flames. All were headed toward the river, and the safety of the North Side. Some unfortunates fell into the

CHICAGO IN FLAMES—THE RUSH FOR LIFE OVER RANDOLPH-STREET BRIDGE.—FROM A SKETCH BY JOHN R. CHAPIN.

heated river, never to be seen again, but most made it to the other shore.

At 1:00 P.M., the fire jumped the river, and the North Side began to burn. Some families, caught on their roofs where they'd been watching the blaze, perished. The county jail caught fire, and prisoners had to be released. They immediately began stealing clothing and disguising themselves for escape. Some made it, but not those on murderers' row. They were kept under guard by police.

Firemen, able to do nothing else, used explosives to keep the fire from reaching the South Side, which slept, ignorant of what was happening. The rest of the population was still engaged in the struggle for safety. Some headed toward "the Sands," a barren stretch of sand that bordered Lake Michigan, on the other side of town. "Throwing children and their crazy mothers" into carts, and grabbing whatever they'd managed to save, they hurried to the lake. But the Sands had some old wooden shanties standing on it, and people cast their belongings on the beach, thus providing even more fuel. Sure enough, the fire overran them, and a howling mob invaded the lake. Those who survived in the hot waters waved at nearby boats to pick them up. The boats wouldn't come near the shore. Finally, the mayor ordered tugs to pick up survivors and ferry them to safety.

At dawn, most of the West Side and North Side was in ashes. A few pockets — closely surrounded by burned-out areas — remained untouched. The number of people who had survived, however, some by merely avoiding the progress and various directions of the fire in the streets, was truly amazing. Fires still burned all over both sections, but they could be avoided. Although the fatalities could not be accurately counted yet, the guess was that not more than 200 had succumbed.

The worst was not over. At full daylight, the South Side, which had slept peacefully for most of the night, became an ocean of flames. The nighttime scenes were played out again —the drunks, the looters, the heroes, all surged back and forth in the streets, depending on the direction of the flames. Hovels and mansions alike went down. No place was really safe, with no fire at all. Then, twenty-seven hours after the O'Leary barn had gone up, rain fell on Chicago. The fire was over.

The rest of the nation responded to Chicago's plea for help.

FOR THE BENEFIT SUFFERERS CHICAGO
ONE TH...
US

Fugitives flee through Potter's Field to escape the flames.

A Chicago *Tribune* reporter wrote after the fire: "There remains only a sense of desolation and ruin, so great and terrible that one can linger no longer, but gropes his way back to the light and the homes of men."

But most people decided to stay and rebuild the "Garden City of the West." They had counted over 250 dead, and resigned themselves to the fact that about the same number of missing were also dead. Rich and poor helped each other, and both were exploited by the kind of high-priced help that seems to thrive on catastrophes. Horace White, editor of the Chicago *Tribune*, decided not to be critical. Anyone who stayed to help Chicago was O.K. As he put it, "It takes all sorts of people to make a great fire."

An enterprising young reporter from the Chicago *Journal* decided to visit the already legendary Mrs. O'Leary. He made his way over to DeKoven Street, and noticed with amazement that the O'Leary house was practically untouched by fire damage. There he met a lady—not so old or bent as the *Times* had said—but looking weary indeed.

"Are you the lady of the house?" he asked.

"Yes," she answered.

"Have you lived here long?"

"Going on five years," she replied.

"Do you own this place?"

"I do."

"Did the fire start in your barn?"

"It did."

"What was in it?"

"Five cows, one horse, and two tons of hay in the loft. We all knocked our living out of those blessed five cows," she added with spirit, "and I never had a cint from the parish in all my life, and the dirty *Times* had no business to say it!"

"How about the kerosene-lamp story?" the reporter asked.

"There's not a word of truth in the whole story. I always milked my cows by daylight, and never had a lamp or candle about the barn. I hope to die if this isn't every word of it true. If you was a priest, I wouldn't tell it any different."

Mrs. O'Leary stuck to her story. All the same, she became known in Chicago as "Our Lady of the Lamp." The rest of the world liked the legend and wouldn't give it up.

The London *Punch* wrote: "We suppose that the most costly pail of milk ever heard of was the pail which burned Chicago. The gallant Americans are the last people to cry over spilt milk or burned cities. Chicago will quickly *rediviva*. She has likely accepted the fact that she will soon be flowing again with milk—and honey—and has elected in her cheery way to call herself the Cow City."

Great Forest Fires of the West, 1871

Date	Location	Fatalities	Remarks
10/8	Michigan, Minnesota, Wisconsin	1,182	Simultaneous forest fires ravaged small towns in three states. Peshtigo, Wis., was hardest hit, but was typical of what happened during worst fire in U.S. history.

That dry October Sunday in 1871 must be the most incendiary day on record. At the very moment Chicago was ablaze in Illinois, little towns all over Michigan, Minnesota, and Wisconsin were also going up in smoke, and their populations were disappearing with them. These great forest fires of the West were so simultaneous that some writers thought they were a single huge, meandering blaze. Chicago may have captured the imagination of the world, but the one little town of Peshtigo, Wisconsin, lost more people than Chicago. Peshtigo—population 2,000—lost more people than any town, and by Monday morning it was no town at all.

Peshtigo was a bustling little town in 1871. It had lumber mills, gristmills, factories, a foundry, about a dozen stores, and some fairly busy hotels. The town was divided by the Peshtigo River, and some 350 homes graced its banks. Life was good, and to add to the town's potential wealth and growth, it was surrounded by some of the densest, grandest forest lands in Wisconsin.

Venturing into the forest was a risk that year, and had been from late summer on. For three months, there had been scarcely any rain, and the forest was dry as a bone. But the people were careful. They knew about forest fires, and about marsh gas that was as flammable as natural gas.

Someone heard that railroad workers had been burning felled trees a bit south of town. It was only a rumor, and on that Sunday afternoon, nobody saw any signs of the black, smoke-filled air that usually precedes a forest fire. No one saw anything unusual the entire afternoon. At nightfall, someone noticed a red glare in the sky to the south. Before anyone had time to wonder about it, a great wind began to blow and intense heat engulfed the town. There was a terrible roar, and like magic the entire town was in flames.

Within seconds, the only sounds in Peshtigo were the crashing of falling timber, the roar of exploding marsh gas and wood, and the shrieks of men, women, and children. Totally surrounded without warning, they hardly had time to think.

Women and children with flaming hair, men with blazing whiskers, ran for the river. But the fire that was swallowing the town had made a low bridge over the river. It was necessary to lie low, with only nose and mouth exposed, to keep from being roasted by the intense heat.

Those too far to run for the river watched terrified as houses caught fire like feathers and factories exploded. Some took shelter in a brick boarding house, hoping the sturdy walls would stop the flames. Nothing remained of them, not so much as a charred bone. Others headed for cleared farmland. The heat blasted rocks in their faces, and the fire fed on the little stubble and few trunks to be found in the open land. White ashes were the only evidence that anyone had tried to escape the fire there. A group of men had begun to dig ditches, but all that remained to show that they had ever been there were their shovel blades.

The town had become a furnace, an immense crematorium.

By morning the flames were gone, and Peshtigo was but a dying coal. Few structures were left; no one on land survived. Only those in the river were alive. About 150 had reached a marshy spot along the banks and had simply lain down in it; they were fine. More than 1,000, some badly burned, had spent the night up to their noses in the river. They were sick and injured and tired, and had suffered all night from the flames and sparks and flying debris over their heads.

An uninjured survivor was sent out to tell the world that Peshtigo was gone, and that the survivors needed help. By afternoon, they had been moved to the town of Marinette. By nightfall, it began to rain on the ashes that were left of Peshtigo.

During the next few weeks, the Governor of Wisconsin spent much time trying to divert some of the generous gifts for Chicago to the towns in his state that had suffered in the great forest fires of the West, the worst fire disaster in our history.

The holocaust at Peshtigo forces people to the river.

Brooklyn Theater, 1876

Date	Location	Fatalities	Remarks
12/5	Brooklyn, N.Y.	300+	"Flying" scenery hit gas lamp at Conway's Theater. Many theaters caught fire the same way, but this was worst of its time.

Reprinted from *Harper's Weekly*, December 23, 1876:

THE BROOKLYN THEATER

The terrible calamity of the Brooklyn Theatre [Conway's] is another of the warnings which are constantly thrust upon the public attention and as constantly unheeded. How many theaters are there in New York or in any of the cities and towns of the country which are better protected against such a disaster than the Brooklyn Theater? A few years ago there was some inquiry into the safety of the theaters in the city of New York, and some extraordinary facts were discovered, showing how imminent was the risk of life in every performance. Undoubtedly the situation is precisely the same in the great multitude of theaters now. They cannot be entered without serious peril. But a resolute public opinion would remove it entirely.

In the Brooklyn Theater the catastrophe was occasioned by the blowing of a "fly"—one of the light pieces of canvas stretching across the top of the stage and representing the sky or clouds—into an exposed gas burner. The light stuff fell in flames upon the canvas in the scenery below—and in fifteen minutes the burning roof fell in. The upper galleries communicated with the lobby, by which alone escape was possible, by a winding staircase. In this trap hundreds of human beings were caught and smothered.

Such events accuse our civilization. They show a sordid mind which despises human life. For the structure of places of public resort is a matter of public concern, and if we do not insist by stringent laws that such places shall not be built except with the most ample security against the most obvious dangers, it is we, the public, and we only, who are truly responsible.

There are hundreds and thousands of parents who never carry their children to a theater in the city of New York without the gravest apprehension. They may not know that the particular theater is exposed, but they know that all theaters are dangerous, and especially exposed to fire. The cyclone that lately swept over parts of Bengal and slew thousands of persons is not a tragedy so great as that of the burning of the Brooklyn Theater. The cyclone was unavoidable. It was

Vol. XX.—No. 1043.]   NEW YORK, SATURDAY, DECEMBER 23, 1876.   [WITH A SUPPLEMENT. PRICE TEN CENTS.

Entered according to Act of Congress, in the Year 1876, by Harper & Brothers, in the Office of the Librarian of Congress, at Washington.

Mob scene at the entrance to the Brooklyn Theater.

beyond human calculation and control. But there was not a life lost in Brooklyn that might not easily have been saved, and that ought not to have been saved.

This can be attained by law, and by law only; and to secure the law, something more is necessary than horror when three or four hundred human beings are needlessly suffocated.

Baptist Church, 1902

Date	Location	Fatalities	Remarks
9/19	Birmingham, Ala.	115	Panic and stampede in Shiloh Baptist Church was the killer. There was no fire at all.

The following is a news story that was published on September 20, 1902, the day after the disaster:

BIRMINGHAM, Ala., Sept. 20—The list of people who lost their lives in the panic at Shiloh Church last night is now reported at nearly 100.

In an awful crush of humanity, caused by a stampede in the Shiloh Negro Baptist Church at Avenue G and Eighteenth Street tonight, 73 persons were killed and as many more seriously injured. The catastrophe occurred at nine o'clock just as Booker T. Washington had concluded his address to the national convention of Baptists, and for three hours the scenes around the church were indescribable. Dead bodies were strewn in every direction, and the ambulance service of the city was utterly unable to move them until after midnight.

The church is the largest church for Negroes in Birmingham, and the pastor says that at least 2,000 persons were in the building when the stampede began. Instructions had been issued to allow no more to enter, but the Negroes forced their way inside the building and were standing in every aisle; even the entrance to the church being literally packed.

Just as Booker T. Washington concluded his address, Judge Billou, a Negro lawyer from Baltimore, engaged in an altercation with the choir leader concerning an unoccupied seat, and, it is said, a blow was struck. Someone in the choir cried, "They're fighting." Mistaking the word "fighting" for "fire," the congregation rose en masse and started for the doors. One of the ministers quickly mounted the rostrum and urged the people to keep quiet.

He repeated the word "quiet" several times and motioned his hearers to be seated. The excited congregation mistook the word "quiet" for "fire" and renewed the struggle to reach the doors. Men and women crawled over benches, fought their way into the aisles, and those who had fallen were trampled upon. The ministers tried again and again to stop the stampede, but no power on earth could stay the struggling, fighting mass of humanity. The screams of women and children added to the horror of the scene, and through mere fright many persons fainted, and as they fell to the floor, were crushed to death.

The level of the floor is about 15 feet from the ground and long steps lead to the sidewalk from the lobby just outside the main auditorium. Brick walls extend on each side of these steps for 6 or 7 feet, and this place proved a veritable death-trap. Negroes who had reached the top of the steps were pushed violently forward and many fell. Before they could move others fell upon them and in 15 minutes persons were piled upon each other to a height of 10 feet. This mass of struggling humanity blocked the entrance and the weight of 1,500 persons was pushed against it. More than 20 persons lying on the steps underneath the heap of bodies died from suffocation.

Two white men, who were in the rear of the church when the rush began, escaped and, realizing the seriousness of the situation, rushed to a corner nearby and turned in a fire alarm. The department came quickly and the arrival of the wagons served to scatter the crowd which had gathered around the front of the church. A squad of policemen also hastened to the church and, with the firemen, finally succeeded in releasing the Negroes from their pinioned positions in the entrance. The dead bodies were quickly removed and the crowd inside, finding an outlet, came pouring out. Scores of them lost their footing and rolled down the long steps to the pavement, sustaining broken limbs and internal injuries.

In an hour the church had been practically cleared and the sight which greeted the eyes of those who had come to aid the injured was sickening. Down the aisles and along the outside of the pews the dead bodies of men and women were strewn and the cries of the maimed and crippled were heartrending. In a few minutes the work of removing the bodies was begun.

The Shiloh Church is located just on the edge of the fashionable residence section of the city, and all the physicians living in that part of town went to the assistance of the injured.

During the stampede, Booker T. Washington and several other prominent Negroes were on the stage and were unwilling witnesses to the frightful catastrophe. None of those in the choir or in the pulpit was injured in the least. For a few minutes they attempted to restore order, but seeing their efforts were futile, they waited until the struggling crowd had advanced far enough for them to pick up the dead and injured.

Most of the dead are women, and the physicians say that in many cases they fainted and died from suffocation. A remarkable feature of the calamity is that no blood was seen on any of the victims. They were either crushed or died from suffocation.

Rev. Dr. T. W. Walker, pastor of Shiloh Church, said tonight: "Shiloh Church is a modern brick structure and has just been completed at a cost of $75,000. There are 4 entrances to the building and the main one is 16 feet wide. The deaths were caused by everybody trying to rush out of the main entrance at the same time. Inside the church not a bench was overturned and all those who were killed died in or about the entrance. The people up near the front of the church were not injured in the least."

Mayor W. M. Drennen said: "Most of those who were killed are strangers but their bodies will be cared for until identified and claimed by relatives."

Iroquois Theater, 1903

Date	Location	Fatalities	Remarks
12/30	Chicago, Ill.	602	Chicago's second great fire took place at Iroquois Theater. Worst theater fire in U.S. history. The actors helped save many lives.

Reprinted from *Harper's Weekly*, January 4, 1904:

On December 30, during a fire and panic at a matinee performance at the Iroquois Theater, Chicago, 602 lives were lost and 142 persons were injured. With two exceptions — the fire at the Ring Theater in Vienna, in 1881, when 875 lives were lost, and the burning of Lehman's Theater, in St. Petersburg, in which between 600 and 700 perished — the disaster at the Iroquois Theater is the most appalling in history. The fire was started by a defective electric-light wire, and spread quickly over the auditorium.

Mr. Bluebeard, the Drury Lane extravaganza, was being played, and an unusually large audience, made up mostly of women and children, filled the theater. An effort was made to lower the fireproof curtain, but it was unsuccessful. When the rush for safety began it was found that, although the theater had thirty exits, only one door, at the Randolph Street entrance, was open. People in the balcony and gallery had little chance of escape. Those who were not burned were crushed in the struggle at the exits and on the stairways.

The Iroquois Theater was only recently completed, at a cost of $500,000, and was opened on November 23, 1903. It was supposed to be of the most modern and improved construction, and was considered one of the safest theaters in the world. The building was inspected by the proper official, who reported on November 25 that it was completed and ready for use. Among other defects in equipment, however, some of the fire escapes were not in position, and the asbestos curtain, supposed to be fireproof, was almost entirely destroyed. The loss to the owners of the building is estimated at $20,000.

New Year's Day in Chicago was observed throughout the

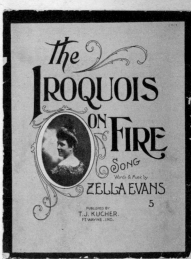

Top: View from the stage of the Iroquois Theater. *Left:* Searching for bodies after the fire was extinguished. *Right:* Another major catastrophe is commemorated in song.

city as a day of mourning. No bells were rung to celebrate the beginning of the new year, and all festivities were suspended.

On Friday, January 1, Mayor Harrison ordered an investigation of Chicago's playhouses. The conditions which were discovered resulted in an order to close nineteen of the city's theaters, because they were unprovided with an asbestos curtain. There were, moreover, other dangerous defects in some of the houses which the managers will be required to remedy.

Ohio School Fire, 1908

Date	Location	Fatalities	Remarks
3/4	Collinwood, Ohio	176	Children trapped by fire in school. Two teachers also killed.

Reprinted from *The New York Herald*, March 5, 1908:

174 CHILDREN KILLED IN BURNING SCHOOL

Cleveland, Ohio—One hundred and seventy-four children were burned or trampled to death this morning in a fire that swept through the village school in North Collinwood, an eastern suburb of this city. Two teachers lost their lives in a vain effort to restore order when the pupils, marching out in the belief that they were engaged in an ordinary fire drill, saw that the peril was real and broke from all restraint.

The big doors at the school's exits were built to swing inward. The leaders of the crowd of children which sought escape that way had no opportunity to pull them open, but were pressed tightly against the impassable barrier by the terrified followers. Both ends of the hall on the ground floor were choked by the struggling mass. Then followed a scene of horror. The frail bodies of children were transformed by terror, and with fatal strength they fought and trampled one another. It was at these exits, where the battle for life had been fiercest, that most of the bodies were found.

Starting about half-past nine o'clock in the basement from the overheated furnace, the fire gained tremendous headway before its presence was noted. The fire drill was started at once, and those in the rooms on the lower floors quickly moved out of the building. But when the panic-stricken little ones in the upper rooms attempted to make their way to the stairway, the jam of uncontrolled and fear-stricken children grew until but few were able to extricate themselves, and they perished almost within reach of safety.

The janitor, Fritz Herter, himself bereaved of three children,

FIVE OF THE CHILDREN WHO LOST THEIR FIGHT WITH DEATH AT COLLINWOOD SCHOOL.

says the doors were open, according to custom. Deputy State Fire Marshal Nathan Fiegenbaum made an inspection of the ruins after the fire and declared that the doors of the schoolhouse opened toward the inside and that the rear door was locked when the children reached it. At any rate, the congestion of fleeing children in the hallway barred the way, and the little ones went to their death totally unable to evade the flames.

Within three hours after the start of the fire it had burned itself out, and the work of recovering the bodies proceeded. The village fire department had only two engines, and neither, upon arrival after the alarm was given, was at all effective in stemming the flames.

The school was a two-story-and-attic brick building, constructed about six years ago. It was overcrowded with pupils and it was found necessary to utilize the attic for those of the ages between six and eight. Approximately 300 children attended the school, which had 9 rooms.

Janitor Herter could remember little of what happened after the fire started. "I was sweeping in the basement," he said, "when I looked up and saw a wisp of smoke curling out from beneath the front stairway. I ran to the fire alarm and pulled the gong that sounded throughout the building. Then I ran first to the front and then to the rear doors. I can't remember what happened next, except that I saw the flames shooting all about and the children running down through them screaming. Some fell at the rear entrance and others stumbled over them. I saw my little Helen among them. I tried to pull her out, but the flames drove me back. I had to leave my little child to die." Herter was badly burned about the head.

After the fire had practically burned itself out, the work of rescuing the bodies was begun by firemen and railroad employees from the Lake Shore shops. The railroad company turned over one of its buildings nearby to be used as a temporary morgue, and thither the charred and broken little bodies were removed as fast as they could be dug from the ruins.

They were placed in rows in the Lake Shore shop. Identifications were made only by means of clothing or trinkets. The fire had swept away nearly all resemblance to human features in the majority of instances. Distracted parents soon began to gather and the work of identifying the blackened and mangled corpses was begun.

The first identification was made by the mother of Nels and Tommy Thompson, aged six and nine years respectively. The heads and arms had been burned from both bodies, but the mother recognized the shoes on her children's feet. And so the disheartening work went on, accentuated now and then by a piercing shriek or plaintive moan as a loved one was recognized by clothing or token, such as a ring or necklace.

THE NEW YORK HERALD.

NEW YORK, THURSDAY, MARCH 5, 1908. —TWENTY PAGES.— BY THE NEW YORK HERALD COMPANY.   [COPYRIGHT, 1908.]

171 CHILDREN KILLED IN BURNING SCHOOL; TRAMPLE ONE ANOTHER TO DEATH IN PANIC

SCHOOL AT COLLINWOOD, OHIO (NEAR CLEVELAND).

L.S. AND M.S. SHOPS AND OFFICE BUILDING USED AS MORGUE.

AN ASSUMES BELLICOSE STAND TOWARD CHINA

Count Hayashi Threatens to Use Drastic Measures if Demand Is Denied.

CONFLICT CAUSED BY TATSU MARU SEIZURE

General That Mikado's Government Is Trying to Pick a Quarrel Over the Incident.

SERIOUS FEELING PREVAILS

Japanese Foreign Office Denies Having Given an Ultimatum or Having Made Demands in a Threatening Manner.

[SPECIAL CABLE TO THE HERALD.]

TOKIO, Wednesday.—The seizure of the Japanese steamship Tatsu Maru is assume a serious phase owing...

TO SURRENDER THE REFUGEES

Caught by Doors Opening Inward, Scores Are Borne Down in Fright by Their Comrades Fleeing from Pursuing Flames.

TEACHERS BRAVELY GIVE LIVES IN EFFORT TO SAVE THEIR LITTLE ONES

Fire Drill Started, but Fails When Children See That the Peril Is Real—Calamity Throws Whole of North Collinwood, a Suburb of Cleveland, Into Mourning.

FEARED MORE BODIES ARE IN RUINS, MANY INJURED IN HOSPITALS AND HOMES

Heartrending Scenes as Parents Seek Their Children in Piles of Dead—Mother Gets to Window to Rescue Her Boy—His Hair Burns in Her Hand and He Falls Into the Flames.

DECLARES BACK DOOR OF THE STRUCTURE WAS LOCKED

Man Who Lost Two Little Ones Declares Many More Could Have Been Saved if Egress Had Been Free—Janitor, Who Mourns Three Children, Says the Door Was Open.

[SPECIAL DESPATCH TO THE HERALD.]

CLEVELAND, Ohio, Wednesday.—One hundred and seventy-one children were burned or trampled to death this morning in a fire that swept through the village school in North Collinwood, an eastern suburb of this city. Two teachers lost their lives in a vain effort to restore order when the pupils, marching out in the belief that they were engaged in an ordinary fire drill, saw that the peril was real and broke from all restraint.

The fire doors at the school's exits were built to swing inward. The leaders of the crowd of children which sought escape that way had no opportunity to pull them open, but were pressed tightly against the impassable barrier by the terrified followers. Both ends of the hall on the ground floor choked by the struggling mass. Then followed a scene of horror. The bodies of the children were transformed by terror, and with fatal...

F. L. TUCKERMAN MARRIES ABROAD

A GROUP OF THE LITTLE VICTIMS OF THE COLLINWOOD FIRE.

1—Henry S. Kelly.
2—James Turner.
3—Morris Shepherd.
4—Walter Hirter.
5—Hugh McIlrath.
6—Henry Schultz.
7—Irene Davis.

MAGNITUDE OF ITS DISASTER

AND GRIEF AND IN HAND

The Greiners Starve While Mourning Over Their Losses.

The Goal Almost Attained by Hopeless Mother.

MANY OWN IN CHARNEL HOUSE

But Few of Death's Great Host Meet Recognition of Sorrowing Fathers.

Vulturelike, the Curious Gaze at Saddened Souls Laid Bare.

DRILLS NEGLECTED IN CITY SCHOOLS

Assistant Superintendent Says That One Principal Reports None.

Rigid Observance of Rule Will Be Enforced by Board.

CITY WILL LEARN DISASTER'S LESSON

Building Inspector Will Soon Recommend Changes in School Code.

Chief Wallace Now Suggests Fireproof Stairs and Floors.

PROBE WILL AWAIT RITES OF BURIAL

Collinwood Officials Will Drop Inquiry Until Graves Hold Dead.

Mayor Favors Selection of Expert to Fathom Blame.

Beginning

The Price of Milk Will Be

7c a Quart

Quality and service made Belle Vernon will be maintained

The Belle Vernon

Belle Vernon Milk

TAKING PICTURE PREVENTS PANIC

Children Thought Smoke Was From Flashlight; Marched Out in Order.

Fire in Grand Rapids School Comes at Opportune Time.

GRAND RAPIDS, Mich., March 4.—Grand Rapids today was threatened with a repetition of Collinwood's tragedy of yesterday on a much larger scale. Fire broke out in the laboratory of the Central high school while 1,200 pupils were in the midst of the morning work. The signal for the fire drill was given and the children marched out in perfect order.

Triangle Sweatshop Fire, 1911

Date	Location	Fatalities	Remarks
3/25	New York City	145	Fire in Triangle shirt factory, a sweatshop in Greenwich Village, brought changes in legislation concerning working and safety conditions in factories.

Building that housed Triangle Waist factory in New York's Greenwich Village.

They were young girls, pretty and cheerful, and not even the Triangle Waist Company could get them down. All other shirtwaist companies had given in to the Waistmakers' Union's demands that factories be closed a half day on Saturday to give workers a little time off. But not the Triangle Waist Company, the worst sweatshop in town. For them, Saturday afternoon was business as usual.

No doubt, the girls would have preferred to be elsewhere that Saturday afternoon in March. But they were immigrants, most of them, and their families depended on their paychecks. It wasn't so bad being together with other young girls, chatting and confiding between long bouts at the machines.

Not that the chatting or confiding could last very long. Their two bosses made sure of that. But the one place they couldn't keep watch on their charges was in the toilet.

To reach a toilet belonging to the Triangle Waist Company, the girls, who worked on three upper stories of the building, had to go through big steel doors at the end of the floors on which they worked, then go down many flights of stairs and out of the building. The bosses did not want the girls to use the elevators. It would be too easy, they felt, for the girls to carry stolen merchandise from the shop that way. In fact, the bosses didn't want the girls to use the toilets, either. To prevent what they called "interruption of work," the doors were locked at intervals when going to the bathroom seemed like an indulgence.

Inside the factory, the girls sat near each other at the closely placed machines, with oily rags and flammable leftover fabric beneath them. An ash from a cigarette could have set fire to the rags and fabric.

However it started, in minutes the whole top of the building was in flames. The girls ran for the doors, only to find them locked.

During the first few minutes of the fire, some girls managed to escape through the elevator shafts. But the shafts began to fill with smoke, and then they were filled with bodies.

The girls on the lower floors managed to escape. But on the eighth, ninth and tenth stories, they were trapped. A few escaped by rear windows to an adjoining roof. For the rest of the girls there was no place to go except the front windows. One by one, they began to jump, hurtling through the air and crashing on the street below. Like the young girls they were, some held hands and jumped. Women in the crowd on the street began to faint. Men wept and tried to break through the police barriers so they might try to save the girls. Even police and firemen wept.

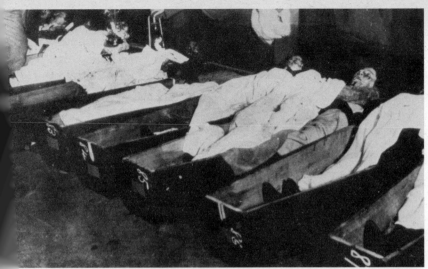

Most of the Triangle fire victims were young women.

The gutted loft of the Triangle factory. The shell of the fireproof building remained intact.

By the time it was over, the street was lined with charred corpses. Inside the factory, firemen found dead girls huddled under machines, and bodies were piled high in the elevator shafts.

A few days later, the Waistmakers' Union held a mass funeral for the victims. They were determined that these 145 girls would not die in vain. A movement was begun to change the safety and health regulations in all factories. The Triangle girls would never be forgotten.

Ohio State Penitentiary, 1930

Date	Location	Fatalities	Remarks
4/21	Columbus, Ohio	320	Ohio State Penitentiary inmates were trapped in locked cells of the west block.

In one way, it wasn't an accident at all, though nobody would know that for another year to come. It was a horror born of bad judgment, if not outright stupidity, and born in a place just waiting for a catastrophe to happen.

The Ohio State Penitentiary, where the writer O. Henry spent three of his unhappiest years, was notorious among penal institutions. Built to hold 1,500 convicts, 5,000 men were there in 1930. The buildings were old, without proper fireproof materials, and there hadn't been a fire drill in the prison in anyone's memory.

A new cell block was being built by the prisoners themselves, but it would not begin to relieve the overcrowding. The prisoners were in a rebellious mood, and one of the things they seemed to resent most—besides the conditions of their everyday lives—was the futile cell block they were building.

The mild April evening was pleasant, and for once, the prison tensions seemed in no danger of erupting. In the west block, which housed 800 prisoners, guards joked with inmates as they locked them in. Suddenly, there was a burst of flame that seemed to come through the northwest corner of the roof. The guards and prisoners looked at each other in amazement. The fire spread, and they heard alarms and sirens and shouting outside the cell block.

The warden's daughter, Miss Amanda Thomas, was among the first to realize what was happening. Organizing the guards, and arming them, she also called out the state troops. Thousands of prisoners were evacuated from their cells to the prison yard, where the troops kept them lined up. In anger, some prisoners cut the firemen's hoses.

If thousands were evacuated from the other cell blocks, none were from the west block. The men outside could hear the west-block inmates screaming and rattling bars, begging to be saved or killed. Why wasn't somebody letting them out? On the upper tiers of the west block, one guard, outside, saw "faces at the windows wreathed in smoke." With others, he "tried to get to them, but we could not move the bars. Soon flames burst into the cellroom and the convicts dropped to the floor. They were literally burned before our eyes."

NES AFTER THE MOST DISASTROUS FIRE IN PRISON HISTORY

INSPECTING THE DEBRIS OF THE OHIO PRISON FIRE IN WHICH MORE THAN 300 PRISONERS DIED: FIREMEN OF COLUMBUS AND RESCUE WORKERS Looking Over the Wreckage of the Cell Houses in Which the Convicts Were Trapped by the Flames Before Their Cells Could Be Unlocked.
(Associated Press.)

SEEKING TO FIX THE RESPONSIBILITY FOR THE TRAGEDY: GOVERNOR MYERS Y. COOPER (Sitting at the Head of the Table With His Hands Clasped) Questioning Warden Preston E. Thomas, Who Took Command of the Armed Forces Outside the Walls to Prevent a Prison Break While the Fire Raged.
(Associated Press.)

CLEARING AWAY THE WRECKAGE OF THE DEATH TRAP: PRISONERS Carrying Out the Charred Beams of the Four Cell Blocks, Where What Seemed at First Only a Trifling Blaze Quickly Developed Into One of the Worst Fire Disasters on Record.
(Associated Press.)

At Left—
AN AERIAL VIEW OF THE OHIO PRISON AFTER THE FIRE. At the Left the Gutted Roof of the Cell Blocks Marks the Scene of the Greatest Loss of Life in a Disaster Which Was Believed to Be of Incendiary Origin.
(Times Wide World Photos.)

THE HEROINE OF THE PRISON FIRE: MISS AMANDA THOMAS, Daughter of the Warden, Who Took Command in the Prison Outer Office, Ordered Guards to Their Posts, Issued Arms and Ammunition and Called in Troops, Remaining at Her Post Until the Situation Was Under Control.
(Associated Press.)

Why did the guards need to move the bars at all? Where were the keys? Thomas Watkinson, the guard in charge of the cells on the upper tier, where so many suffocated, refused to give up his keys. The other guards finally took them from him by force, and carried out prisoners for as long as they could. In another part of the west block, one of the guards was startled to discover that the cage door leading to the cells was locked. It was never kept locked. Had someone locked it after the fire began?

Together, inmate volunteers and guards entered the building and smashed locks with sledgehammers to release trapped convicts. Others broke down doors and carried burning but still-alive men outside. Nearly 500 men were saved. But for 315 men, trapped behind locked doors, it was too late.

In the days that followed, an indignant citizenry demanded an inquiry and got one. The fact that the alarm rang outside the prison, instead of inside, seemed to indicate to investigators a deliberate delay by someone in the prison to sound an alarm. Had someone been afraid of a break or a riot?

The question was never answered, nor could Warden Preston E. Thomas explain why there had never been a fire drill during his regime. He would soon resign and take a post elsewhere.

Whether the delay in sounding the alarm and the lack of fire drills had contributed to causing deaths in this fire, investigators could not say for sure. There was still Thomas Watkinson and his keys. The Board of Inquiry felt that no lives would have been lost on the upper tier if he had let out the prisoners.

It wasn't until a year later that the Board learned what had caused the fire. Two convicts confessed they had set it in the west block — with a candle they'd taken from chapel — as a protest against working on the new cell block. They received life sentences for manslaughter.

The local newspapers, the citizenry, and Warden Thomas himself insisted they were not really the guilty parties. It was the state legislature who bore the blame, they all insisted. The warden had begged the state for twelve years to relieve crowding and improve conditions.

Cocoanut Grove Fire, 1942

Date	Location	Fatalities	Remarks
11/28	Boston, Mass.	492	Fake palm tree at Cocoanut Grove nightclub caught fire; flames quickly spread in packed club.

The whole world seemed to be alive and well and raising hell in Boston that weekend. The town was filled with sailors from nearby bases, looking for girls. Soldiers on leave were doing the same thing. They were all having a last fling before returning to their bases, and to World War II. And the girls, caught in the man shortage of the war, didn't mind being found and taken out for a great Saturday night.

The atmosphere was frantic, with everyone looking for a super Saturday night. In Boston, a super Saturday night was synonymous with Cocoanut Grove, the town's oldest, most glamorous, and probably biggest nightclub. That night, over 800 revelers crowded the floors until 10:00 P.M., floor-show time. The band warmed up, the emcee got ready—and a girl went dashing across the floor with her hair in flames. She was screaming, "Fire!"

The remains of the entryway to the Cocoanut Grove nightclub, where the tiny revolving door was the only exit known to most customers.

Rescuers tried to revive the victims of the fire on the cobblestone street outside the nightclub.

Ringling Bros. Circus Fire, 1944

Date	Location	Fatalities	Remarks
7/6	Hartford, Conn.	168	Ringling Bros. and Barnum & Bailey Circus tent caught fire and trapped ringside spectators.

To this day, she is known as Little Miss 1565. She was one of the children up front in the big tent when the Ringling Bros. and Barnum & Bailey Circus played in Hartford on July 6, 1944. That's where children want to be—right up front—and those who'd gotten tickets for the first three rows counted themselves lucky. But the third act that day was different from what anyone had expected.

It happened right after the wild-animal act. Nobody saw it at first except the bandmaster—just a small spot of fire at the top of the tent. He began to play "Stars and Stripes Forever," the circus "disaster march" that warned everyone to go to their posts.

Remains of the circus tent after the fire.

The stampede in the Cocoanut Grove was incredible. Most of the customers knew of only one exit—through a revolving door. As hundreds of fake palm trees burst into flames, the panic became ghastly.

Some of the club's employees knew of a basement exit and managed to lead some patrons to safety that way. Others led people up to the second-floor dressing rooms where they could escape to the next roof and reach the street by a ladder. People jumped from windows into the arms of bystanders. Some managed to push through a glass wall to safety. But most were trapped in the flaming club itself.

The fire department appeared almost immediately, and within minutes they had the fire under control. But by then, the fire, the smoke, and the awful crush had taken their toll. Nearly 500 people were dead, and 200 were seriously hurt. No more than 100 had escaped with no injury at all.

The death toll would have been higher but for a relatively new medical technique that had just come into use—injections of blood plasma. Doctors claimed they had saved 150 shock victims from death with the plasma. And they'd saved many from infection with a new drug called penicillin.

Before he could finish the march, the flames were six feet high, and panicked children and parents were trampling through the tent. Those in the back of the tent jumped down from their bleacher seats and ducked out of the big flaming canvas top. Those in the middle began to climb over the bleachers, and some of them made it out. The ones up front had no place to run but to the center of the tent itself. There were exit runways, but the crowd was too great and the tent was burning too fast for many people to reach them. The entire tent was soon aflame and the poles were also burning and falling. Flaming canvas fell all around.

Within twenty minutes it was over. The tent and tent poles had burned away, leaving 168 victims, so many of them children. There might have been more, but doctors had used plasma immediately.

Later it was explained why the tent had burned so rapidly. Instead of being fireproofed, it had been waterproofed, with paraffin, applied with gasoline. That's the way the circus always did it. They never would again.

The next few days were spent identifying victims, and that's when the authorities discovered Little Miss 1565. A clearly recognizable, blonde, blue-eyed child, she was more a victim of the crush than of the fire. Yet nobody ever came to claim the dead child. Newspapers ran her pictures, there were broadcasts, circulars, investigations at public schools and Sunday schools. Nobody knew who she was.

The authorities buried her in a nonsectarian cemetery in Wilson, Connecticut, with a stone inscribed "Little Miss 1565." On the anniversary of the fire, July 6, a wreath is put on the grave.

The Big Top in flames. In the stampede, many children were trampled.

IMPORTANT AMERICAN BLIZZARDS

DATE	LOCATION	FATALITIES	REMARKS
1778 12/26	Rhode Island, Massachusetts	125	Death reports were sporadic, some deaths not reported at all, which was not uncommon.
1886 1/6–1/13	Midwest	70	Kansas hardest hit.
1888 3/12–3/13	Maine to Maryland	400	New York City and metropolitan area hardest hit in the Blizzard of '88. Snowfall was 20.5".
1940 11/11–11/12	Northeast, Midwest	144	Death rate was low for a storm as vicious as this one was.
1947 12/26	New York City and vicinity	50+	Not technically a blizzard, because temperature did not drop below 10°. But snowfall (25.8") exceeded that of '88.
1950 11/25	Northeast	100	"Pre-winter" blizzard was unexpected, caused much damage.
1957 2/15–2/16	Northeast	171	Not properly a blizzard. Temperature did not drop below 10° until it stopped snowing. But many people died from snow, wind, and cold.
1967 12/12–12/20	Southwest	51	Freak storm took fairly snowless area by surprise, caused death to livestock and other damage.

Train trapped in blizzard snowdrift on Dakota prairies. From *Frank Leslie's Illustrated Newspaper*, December 11, 1886, with story that commented: "Our picture gives a striking but unexaggerated idea of what the Western traveler may expect to encounter at this season of the year."

The first English attempt to found a colony in the northern part of the New World took place in Sagadahoc County, Maine, in 1607, about the same time as the establishment of Jamestown in Virginia and thirteen years before the *Mayflower* arrived at Plymouth Rock with the Pilgrim Fathers. It was unsuccessful because the blizzards of 1607 killed half the colony and drove the other half back to England. Actually, we don't know for certain that the snowfalls of 1607 were blizzards. To qualify as a genuine blizzard, snows must be accompanied by winds blowing at least 35 miles per hour, and temperatures must fall below 10° Fahrenheit; the Colonies did not have weather-measuring equipment until 1740.

The temperate climate of Europe had not prepared the colonists for the winters in northern America. Only the Alps and northernmost reaches of Europe knew such low temperatures and so much snow. In England, France, Spain, Holland, and Italy, blizzards like those of 1607 never occurred. Moreover, the early explorers did most of their traveling in spring and summer, and thus could pass on no information about Canadian and New England winters.

The colonists soon learned a great deal about those blinding snowstorms that would later be called blizzards. For one thing, they learned never to venture out into such storms, not even to close the barn door just a few hundred feet away. Blizzards are absolutely blinding, and during one it is easy to get lost permanently in your own front yard. It's not possible to tell how treacherous they are until you're out in the driving snow, and when you look out at them from inside a cozy room, they are even seductively beautiful. From the East Coast to the West Coast, the American North knows strange tales of people who went out in blizzards to fetch sick cows or to visit neighbors and who disappeared till spring, when the thaw melted the snow and revealed their frozen bodies only yards from where they started. There are also miraculous tales of surviving for up to twenty days in strange woods of evergreen and other trees, which acted as cover against the snow. It happened more than once, but in each case the person had

become lost near his own home and had wandered for some time until he found himself at last in a protective woods.

In the 1800's, we began to use the term "blizzard." There was an old English word for a snowstorm—"bleassard"—but it was not much used. The Germans in America referred to the deadly white bombardments as *"blitz,"* and the two words apparently meshed to form "blizzard."

By then, Northeasterners had learned to stay indoors during blizzards, and the deadly storms took surprisingly few lives. There always were—and still are—people who take chances, and so each blizzard causes some deaths. But from our early days, no blizzard that has been predicted by weather experts has taken many lives. Unpredicted blizzards are another story.

By the time Northeasterners became familiar with blizzards, pioneers were moving westward. As it turned out, the noncoastal Midwest and West were our real blizzard belt. The Dakotas, Minnesota, Wisconsin, and northern Illinois had blizzards that startled even the bold Scandinavians who settled there in large colonies. In time, they, too, learned to cope with predicted blizzards. They simply never went out in them if they could help it, and storing up food and fuel for an entire winter is still a rural habit. Thus there are surprisingly few deaths in an expected blizzard.

Today, our problems with blizzards are much the same as they ever were. Not even the change in our style of travel has altered them. You can become just as lost in a car as in a horse and buggy, and you can freeze as easily in a car. If you keep a car running for warmth, carbon monoxide may accumulate and kill you before you succumb to the freezing temperatures. As for road accidents in blizzards, the automobile has added a new menace to the old problem. Then, too, our large modern cities import almost all of their food and fuel from great distances, and a city cut off by impassable snow can suffer shortages that quickly result in starvation and freezing. So far, however, we have had relatively few catastrophic blizzards. But those which have come upon us unannounced have given us one or two of our most spectacular and deadliest disasters.

Blizzard of '78

Date	Location	Fatalities	Remarks
12/26	Rhode Island, Massachusetts	125	Death reports were sporadic; some deaths not reported at all, which was not uncommon.

In the third year of the American Revolution, 1778, it was generally thought that the British had the situation well in hand. They had superior weapons, more money for food and medical supplies, and were better clothed than the ragged Continental Army. However, the British had one enemy for which they were unprepared: the harsh, grim winters of the northern colonies. It was this climate that had been driving Englishmen back to England for 200 years, ever since they had first begun colonizing.

The experience of the English troops and Hessian mercenaries who occupied Newport, Rhode Island, was typical. On December 25, they observed Christmas Day. On December 26, the wind began to blow at over 40 miles per hour. The temperature dropped to below zero, and the snow began to fall and fall.

They did not know in Newport that all of New England was caught in its worst blizzard in over thirty years. To them it was simply the "terriblest" thing they had ever seen. The snow

Above: Sufferings in an 1864 snowstorm on the Michigan Central. From *Harper's Weekly,* January 23, 1864. *Right:* The perils of Union Square in the midst of the New York blizzard, 1888. From *Harper's Weekly,* March 24, 1888.

was thick and blinding. The wind swept it into drifts 10, 20, and 30 feet high. The low temperatures were numbing, and people familiar with the elements in those parts did not leave their shelters unless forced to do so.

The English and Hessians were unused to this kind of ghostly, howling storm. Some wandered out into it and were not seen again until the first thaw melted the huge drifts and uncovered their frozen bodies. In some of their encampments, fuel was low, and men simply froze where they were. When the blizzard was over, at least 50 Englishmen and Hessians were among the known dead. Many others were missing until spring.

Native Americans, loyal to the Revolution, called the blizzard the "Hessian storm," and hoped it was a divine blow at the enemy. But if God were taking a swipe at the enemy at Newport, He was giving Hell to loyal sons in other places.

On Massachusetts Bay, the wind whipped the water into an unprecedented fury. Although the falling snow was like a thick veil, Captain Magee, master of the American brigantine *Arnold*, decided to brave the elements to get his crew and passengers to their destination. He set sail, and soon after, being unable to tell land from water and not being able at any rate to control his sailing vessel in the high wind, he ran the *Arnold* aground. Of the 100 on board, 65 perished, including the captain.

All over New England the blizzard raged. In homes throughout the Boston area, families waited for those who had been out when the storm started. In farm areas, families waited for men who had merely stepped out to drive some livestock into the barn. For days after the blizzard, there were reports of missing persons and bizarre deaths. Two ministers had been found frozen stiff, buried in small drifts by the side of the road. A man shovelling his way through a road found three bodies beneath a twenty-foot drift. At Boston Neck, a group found a man and a team of four oxen frozen solid in the road, standing upright and looking ready to start forward at a moment's notice. They made a monument to the cold and severity of the storm, the worst in anyone's memory and certainly the most powerful since the colonists had gotten their first weather instruments in 1740.

Blizzard of '88

Date	Location	Fatalities	Remarks
3/12–3/13	Maine to Maryland	400	New York City and metropolitan area hardest hit in the Blizzard of '88. Snowfall was 20.5".

On Saturday, March 10, 1888, New Yorkers had a good laugh. On this sunny, mild day of a very mild year, they read the saga of "Snow Shovel Ed" in the *New York Herald*. Ed Meisinger, head buyer for E. Ridley's, a popular Manhattan emporium, had bought a carload of snow shovels at an auction, and they were delivered to the store on this gloriously warm day. Ed had bought them cheap, but who needed snow shovels when spring had come so early? Who had needed snow shovels at all during this gentle, snowless winter of 1888? The robins had already settled in from Maryland to Maine, and from Long Island southward, farmers had even started to plant. Spring was here, all right, and in New York the laugh was on "Snow Shovel Ed."

Monday morning, March 12, is known as "Blizzard Monday," and it holds a place in the annals of Northeastern American lore.

In truth, New Yorkers had stopped smiling by Sunday. The weather had turned dismal, and what had started as a spring rain on Sunday morning had become a steady torrent by afternoon. It was a dreary, boring Sunday.

Policemen rubbing snow on frozen ears during New York's Blizzard of '88.

DOWN-TOWN SKETCHES IN NEW YORK DURING MONDAY'S BLIZZARD.—Drawn by Charles Graham.

1. Wall Street in a Flurry. 2. The City Hall Park. 3. Abandoned Street Car. 4. Passengers leaving an Elevated Train by Ladder.

Charles Graham's eyewitness sketches of downtown New York during Blizzard of '88.

The local Weather Bureau was not bored. This downpour had not been predicted, and as it grew worse, they wondered why they were not hearing more about it from the National Weather Bureau in Washington. When they tried to contact Washington, they got no answer. They could not imagine why power and telegraph lines would be down. Was there flooding or high winds? It never occurred to them that a deep freeze had set in south of New York, and that Washington was being buried under the worst blizzard of the century.

They had to have a prediction for the next day's weather, so when both the temperature and barometer began dropping rapidly by nightfall, they played it safe and predicted the possibility of light snow.

Most New Yorkers slept through Sunday night and the wee hours of Monday morning with no notion that anything unusual was happening outside their windows. But some people knew what was happening—those, for example, who had taken Sunday night trains from upstate New York or New England to Grand Central Station. They were awakened in the dead of night when their trains ran headlong into huge snow-drifts. At first, as long as there was fuel for the heating stoves and food for their bellies, most passengers thought it was a lark to be in a blizzard. Some passengers began formulating plans for Blizzard of '88 clubs. It would be something to tell to their grandchildren. These lighthearted plans ended in earnest when the snows didn't stop and help didn't come as quickly as was expected.

On some trains, coal stoves had spilled when the engines rammed into the huge drifts, and the trains had caught fire. Passengers were left out in the open in very low temperatures. In some cases, towns were nearby, but not close enough for people who had to tramp through thigh-deep or waist-high snow. Some succumbed to heart attacks or fatigue, and were not found until the snow melted.

New Yorkers awoke Monday morning to stare in amazement at the "light snow" that had been forecast by the Weather Bureau. New York was almost unrecognizable under a deep blanket of snow, and the snow was still falling so thick you could scarcely see across the street. The temperature was down in the teens and moving toward zero. The wind was blowing a steady 40 miles per hour, often rising to 75.

For some reason, New Yorkers could not bring themselves to believe there was anything deadly in the storm. Children over 12 years old were bundled up and sent off to school. Businessmen and laborers, both men and women, went off to work. Every child who left for school that morning managed to get there intact. School was soon dismissed, and the children all made it home, some through drifts taller than they were.

Negotiating snow in high winds and low temperatures seemed to be natural to them.

Not so the men and women who braved the day. Most trains and streetcars were stalled. People tramped from station to station, looking for something that was running. The exertion caused more heart attacks. Working women dropped in their tracks from weariness. Snow covered the victims. People fell into drifts and were just too weary to struggle out of them. They lay there and froze.

New York City's business establishments began to close down. Suburban employees had not been able to come to work, and there were very few customers, anyway. The shoe stores did well selling $3.00 boots for $10.00, and at E. Ridley's, Ed Meisinger was selling his snow shovels for almost three times what he'd paid for them. "I just had this feeling," he'd tell customers who had read about "Snow Shovel Ed" only two days earlier.

By noon, the wind was close to a constant 75 miles per hour, and the snow was falling thicker and faster than ever. The wind pushed up drifts that reached to third-story windows. Stores, factories, and offices sent their personnel home, but no means of transportation was running, and most people had to go by foot. Some were afraid to leave their shelters. The salesgirls at R. H. Macy's huddled in the doorway, not knowing what to do. Macy's decided to open their bedding department and let employees stay the night.

Most employees began to trek home. Again people were overcome by fatigue. Frostbite was a hazard. Thousands of people were felled, and the fact that hundreds, not thousands, died was due in large measure to the efforts of New York's policemen.

The saloons were busy. Many hikers stopped at one bar after another all the way home. For some people, the bars were life-savers, but others drank too much and passed out in the snow. They had too much alcohol in them to freeze to death, but they were covered by the falling and drifting snow, and many smothered before the police found them.

By Tuesday morning, it had stopped snowing, and by Wednesday, the city had hired hundreds of temporary workers to help with the digging out. To encourage the diggers, one shopkeeper put up a sign: "Ten-carat diamond ring lost here under this snowdrift. Finders keepers!" Unfortunately, much more had been lost under the snowdrifts, and the mystery of many people's whereabouts was tragically solved with the digging.

By Friday, the digging was unnecessary. The warm weather returned and melted the snow away. Spring was back, but it revealed the frozen robins of the Blizzard of '88.

HARPER'S WEEKLY.
JOURNAL OF CIVILIZATION.

VOL. XXXII.—No. 1631.
Copyright, 1888, by HARPER & BROTHERS.
All Rights Reserved.

NEW YORK, SATURDAY, MARCH 24, 1888.

TEN CENTS A COPY.
WITH A SUPPLEMENT.

A STRUGGLE TO ANSWER A FIRE-ALARM DURING THE NEW YORK BLIZZARD.—DRAWN BY T. DE THULSTRUP.

Struggle to answer a fire alarm during New York's great blizzard. Fire is always considered a double hazard during a blizzard because it's impossible to get equipment through snow.

Storm Country, 1940

Date	Location	Fatalities	Remarks
11/11–11/12	Northeast, Midwest	144	Death rate was low for a storm as vicious as this one was.

The one thing Americans dreaded that year was war. World War II raged in Europe and Asia, but so far the United States had stayed out of the conflict. Then, on Armistice Day, which commemorated the end of World War I, the war was pushed off the front pages of the newspapers.

From Canada to the Gulf Coast, from the Rockies to the Appalachians, the entire nation was enveloped in an incredible storm. A cold wave from Canada penetrated even the far reaches of our subtropical South with temperatures well below freezing, while tornadoes spotted the Southland with death and destruction. In the North, howling 100-mile-per-hour winds caused even more devastation. From east to west, blizzards blanketed the earth, especially in the Midwest and West. Wisconsin, Colorado, Wyoming, Nebraska, Missouri, the Dakotas, Minnesota, Iowa, Illinois, and Indiana suffered below-zero temperatures and blinding snowstorms.

The date was November 11. It wasn't even really winter. Even in the Northwest, nothing this fierce ever struck so early. It took old hands by surprise. In North Dakota, where everyone knows about blizzards, people were so unprepared that they were forced to go out into the storm. Two men froze to death trying to drive some cattle in from a field, in full sight of house and barn. Some motorists, caught on the highway or on small roads, froze to death when their cars ran out of gas, while others were asphyxiated by carbon monoxide fumes when snows drifted to cover the exhaust pipes of nonmoving but still-running vehicles. A man coming home from a neighbor's in what he thought was merely heavy snowfall was found frozen stiff the next morning, not a quarter of a mile from where he had started.

All over the Midwest and Northwest, the stories were the same. If the South had tornadoes and the north blizzards and subzero temperatures, Illinois had all three. The early and unusual cold burdened heating systems so that many failed and caused fires. Whole families perished in them, caught, like Sam McGee, between cremation and certain death in the freezing cold outside. In Chicago, people trying to make it from local stores to nearby homes were felled by wind, or by fatigue from walking through the deep snow. They were covered by drifts and died just steps from their houses. At Grand Rapids, Michigan, some motorists who abandoned their cars in the treacherous snow were electrocuted by power lines that had been blown down in gale winds. Toppling brick walls in South Bend, Indiana, and in Milwaukee, Wisconsin, and crashing chimneys in Michigan, were as big a hazard as the snow.

For twenty-four hours, chaos reigned in the Midwest and Northwest. Then the snows stopped, the wind dropped—and so did the temperatures. The cold hindered efforts to clear roads and to dig out victims, and made delivery of food and fuel a problem. However, considering the size of the storm, the death toll was low; smaller storms had killed more people. For a few short days, the war in Europe and Asia had been forgotten, while we fought the battle of the elements at home.

Blizzard buries cars in Kansas City, Missouri, February 14, 1958. Kansas is a frequent victim of blizzards.

A trainman works to free the diesel engine of a Northern Pacific passenger train caught in a ferocious blizzard in New Salem, North Dakota, March 11, 1966. The train was snowbound for three days.

omer's *Odyssey* and Jason's legendary quest for the Golden Fleece hint that long voyages were common since the dawn of time," says an old desk encyclopedia. Men have always tried to propel themselves on water. Yet accurate records of long voyages are practically nonexistent. Sea trips took months or years, and without means of long-distance communication, it was impossible to tell if a ship had been wrecked or was still voyaging.

This situation existed well into the 1700's. The hazards of long journeys, in small wooden boats, powered by oar or sail, were many and varied. Survivors of wrecks told tales of hurricanes, of being becalmed or marooned, and of starvation when their ship ran out of food. But passenger lists were scanty and it was difficult to know who or how many lived or died. Cargo lists, on the other hand, were detailed. Marine insurance on goods has existed longer than on people.

The coming of the steam engine changed everything. From the time Robert Fulton successfully launched the *Clermont* on the Hudson River, in 1807, shipbuilders and shipowners became intensely interested in ship safety. Steam could run a boat much faster than manpower,

could propel much more weight, and was easier to control than the wind—most of the time. When the owners could ship people and goods up and down rivers and coasts in days instead of weeks, get to Europe in weeks instead of months, the shipping business was revolutionized.

By the 1830's, steamships were setting speed records everywhere. It was a new era, and large numbers of people started to travel. There were new waves of immigration from Europe. The endless journeys with their hardships and dangers were gone, but a new kind of marine disaster had been born. Fire was used to build up steam pressure in the boilers to keep the ship moving. Fires and exploding boilers became the terror of travelers. Ships were much bigger, too, and one catastrophe could leave hundreds—sometimes more than a thousand—dead. Saddest of all, perhaps, were the immigrant ships, with their human cargo.

During this period, people began to keep accurate records of fatalities. No means of mass transportation had ever existed before that could claim as many lives in one stroke as the new ships. All too often, the catastrophes were the result of unsafe conditions or negligent owners and captains who cared more for their profits and cargo than they did for their passengers. Owners and captains and whole crews began to be taken to task, put on trial and sent to jail for manslaughter if culpability could be proved.

Sails had been replaced by steam, and wood was being replaced by steel. Engines became safer. Good fire-

fighting equipment was required by law, and the courts were very strict about it. They were also strict about lifesaving equipment—lifebelts, jackets and some lifeboats were required. In 1904, when the *General Slocum* burned in the East River, claiming more than 1,000 lives, her fire-fighting equipment and life jackets were proved defective, her captain negligent. He was sentenced to prison for ten years, as was the president of the company, for manslaughter.

Also, the twentieth century saw the appearance of the huge luxury liner. It was designed for beauty, comfort, and safety. With the invention of the ship's radio, people felt safer than ever. Even if a ship should get in trouble, she could always contact a nearby vessel, and lives could be saved.

The sinking of the *Titanic* brought people down with a thud. No ship was that safe. Even the best—and she was the best—required the kind of vigilance you'd see on the most vulnerable vessel. All vessels were, in fact, vulnerable. That was the lesson, and safety laws applying to passenger-carriers became more stringent.

Today, we have even more safety factors. Radar is legally required on all large ships, and has taken much of the danger out of that old killer, fog. Among commercial carriers, collisions—once common—are rarely heard of. Ships are, indeed, safer than ever, and likely to remain that way.

IMPORTANT AMERICAN MARINE TRAGEDIES

DATE	LOCATION	FATALITIES	REMARKS
1831 7/9	North Atlantic, off Cape May, N.J.	263	*Lady Sherbrook*, immigrant ship, sank within sight of New World.
1836 11/21	North Atlantic, off Far Rockaway, N.Y.	60+	*Bristol* was caught in gale and wrecked within a half mile of shore.
1837 1/2	North Atlantic, off Hempstead Beach, N.Y.	108	Barque *Mexico* was caught in gale and sank.
1837 5/8	Mississippi River, south of Natchez	200	River steamer *Ben Sherrod* burned.
1837 10/9	North Atlantic, between New York and Charleston, S.C.	95	Packet *Home* wrecked.
1837 10/31	Mississippi River, south of Natchez	300	*Monmouth*, carrying 611 Indians, collided with *Trenton* and *Warren*. Most of the victims were Indians.
1838 4/26	Ohio River, at Cincinnati	200+	Steamer *Moselle* exploded.
1838 6/14	North Atlantic, off North Carolina coast.	96	Steam packet *Pulaski* exploded and sank.
1840 1/13	Long Island Sound	50	*Lexington* burned between New York and Connecticut.
1854 9/27	North Pacific, off Grand Banks, Alaska.	350	U.S. *Arctic* sank.
1854 11/23	North Atlantic, off Jersey coast.	300+	*New Era*, immigrant ship, was wrecked.
1857 6/26	St. Lawrence River, Canada	300+	Steamer *Montreal* carried 400–500 passengers; 125 survived.
1857 9/12	North Atlantic, between New York and Cuba	400	*Central America* sank.
1858 9/13	North Atlantic, between Hamburg, Germany, and New York.	471	*Austria* sank.
1860 9/8	Lake Michigan	300	Excursion steamer *Lady Elgin* collided with lumber ship *Augusta*. "Lady of the Lakes" suffered greatest fatalities.
1865 4/27	Mississippi River, 8 miles north of Memphis, Tenn.	1,400–1,700	Sidewheeler *Sultana* exploded and burned. Worst marine disaster in U.S. history.
1871 7/30	New York City	66+	Staten Island Ferry *Westfield* exploded while loading at N.Y. Battery.
1898 2/15	Havana, Cuba	200	Battleship *Maine* exploded in Havana Harbor. Sabotage was suspected but never proven.
1898 11/26	North Atlantic, off Cape Cod	157	*Portland* was wrecked in a storm.
1904 6/14	East River, N.Y.	1,031	Excursion steamer *General Slocum* burned with huge church party aboard. At least 400 children died.
1912 4/15	North Atlantic	1,500	British liner *Titanic* hit iceberg and sank. Hundreds of Americans perished. Worst Atlantic disaster.
1914 5/29	St. Lawrence River, Canada	1,024	*Empress of Ireland* sank after collision with collier *Storstad*.
1915 5/7	North Atlantic, off Ireland	1,198	British liner *Lusitania* sank after being torpedoed by a German submarine; 124 Americans died with her.
1915 7/24	Chicago River	800–900	Excursion steamer *Eastland* capsized in port.
1934 9/8	North Atlantic, 8 miles off Jersey coast.	134	Burning of the *Morro Castle* was bad by modern standards, bizarre by any standards.
1952 4/26	North Atlantic	176	U.S. destroyer and minesweeper *Hobson* and aircraft carrier *Wasp* collided. *Hobson* sank.
1954 5/26	Quonset Pt., R.I.	103	U.S. aircraft carrier *Bennington* exploded, burned.

DATE	LOCATION	FATALITIES	REMARKS
1956 8/26	North Atlantic	50	Italian liner *Andrea Doria* collided with Swedish liner *Stockholm*. *Andrea Doria* sank. Many Americans aboard.
1963 4/10	North Atlantic, 220 miles off Cape Cod	129	U.S. nuclear submarine *Thresher* apparently disintegrated in deep water.
1967 7/25	Off Vietnam	134	U.S. aircraft carrier *Forrestal* crippled by fire.
1968 5/27	Atlantic, off the Azores	99	U.S. nuclear sub *Scorpion* sank.
1969 6/2	China Sea	74	U.S. destroyer *Frank E. Evans* sliced in two by Australian carrier *Melbourne*.

Creek Indian Catastrophe, 1837

Date	Location	Fatalities	Remarks
10/31	Mississippi River, south of Natchez	300	*Monmouth*, carrying 611 Indians, collided with *Trenton* and *Warren*. Most of the victims were Indians.

This account is reprinted from *Steamboat Disasters and Railroad Accidents in the United States* by S. A. Howland, which was published in 1840 in Massachusetts:

LOSS OF THE STEAMER *MONMOUTH*,
on the Mississippi River, October 31, 1837 —by
which melancholy catastrophe three hundred
emigrating Indians were drowned.

The steamboat *Monmouth* left New Orleans for Arkansas River, with upwards of 600 Indians on board, a portion of the emigrant Creek tribe, as passengers. In travelling up the Mississippi, through Prophet Island Bend, she was met by the ship *Trenton*, towed by the steamer *Warren*, descending the river. It was rather dark, being near eight o'clock in the evening—and through the mismanagement of the officers and obscurity of the atmosphere, a collision took place between the two vessels; and the cabin of the *Monmouth* parted from the hull, drifting some distance down the stream, when it broke into two parts, and emptied its contents into the river. There were 611 Indians on board—only 300 of whom were rescued by the crews of the *Warren* and *Yazoo*. The *Trenton* lost her cut-water [bow stem]. The bar-keepers and a fireman were the only persons attached to the *Monmouth* who lost their lives.

The disaster is ascribed chiefly to the neglect of the officers of the *Monmouth*. She was running in a part of the stream where, by the usages of the river, and the rules of the Mississippi navigation, she had no right to go, and where, of course, the descending vessels did not expect to meet her. Here is another evidence of the gross carelessness of a class of men to whose charge we often commit our lives and property.

This unfortunate event is one in which every citizen of our country must feel a melancholy interest. Bowing before the superiority of their conquerors, these men were removed from their homes by the policy of our Government. Thus on their way to the spot selected by the white man for their residence—reluctantly leaving the graves of their fathers, and the homes of their childhood, in obedience to the requisitions of a race before whom they seem doomed to become extinct—an accident, horrible and unanticipated, has brought death upon *three* hundred at once. Had they died as the savage would die, upon the battle field, in defense of his rights, and in the wars of his tribe, death had possessed little or no horror for them. But, in the full confidence of safety purchased by the concession and the compromise of all their savage chivalry, confined in a vessel strange to their habits, and dying by a death strange and ignoble to their natures—the victims of a catastrophe they could neither foresee nor resist—their last moments of life (for thought has the activity of lightning in extremity) must have been embittered by conflicting emotions, horrible indeed: regret at their submissions, indignation at what seemed to them wilful treachery, and impotent threatenings of revenge upon the pale faces, may have maddened their dying hour.

Steamer Explosion, 1838

Date	Location	Fatalities	Remarks
4/26	Ohio River, at Cincinnati	200+	Steamer *Moselle* exploded.

This account is also reprinted from *Steamboat Disasters and Railroad Accidents in the United States* by S. A. Howland:

EXPLOSION OF THE STEAMER *MOSELLE*,
at Cincinnati, April 26, 1838, by which more than two hundred persons lost their lives.

The new and elegant steamboat, *Moselle*, [under] Capt. Perkin, left the wharf in Cincinnati (full of passengers) for Louisville and St. Louis; and, with the view of taking a family on board at Fulton, a mile and a half above the quay, proceeded up the river, and made fast to a lumber raft for that purpose. Here the family was taken on board; and, during the whole time of his detention, the captain had madly held on to all the steam that he could create, with the intention, not only of showing off to the best advantage the great speed of his boat, as it passed down the river the entire length of the city, but that he might overtake and pass another boat which had left the wharf for Louisville, but a short time previous. As the *Moselle* was a *new brag* boat, and had recently made several exceedingly quick trips to and from Cincinnati, it would not do to risk her popularity for speed by giving to another boat (even though that boat had the advantage of time and distance) the most remote chance of being the first to arrive at the destined port. This insane policy—this poor ambition of proprietors and captains, has almost always inevitably tended to the same melancholy results. The *Moselle* had but just parted from the lumber raft to which she had been made fast—her wheels had scarcely made their first revolution—when her boilers burst with an awful and astounding noise, equal to the most violent clap of thunder. The explosion was destructive and heartrending in the extreme—heads, limbs, and bodies were seen flying through the air in every direction—attended with the most horrible shrieks and groans from the wounded and dying.

A gentleman who was an eyewitness, thus remarked: "We have just returned from the scene of horror occasioned by the explosion; and the account heretofore published, instead of being in the slightest degree exaggerated, as has been intimated by a few, *falls far short of the dreadful reality*. The fragments of human bodies are now lying scattered all along the shore, and we saw the corpses of a number so mangled and torn that they bear scarcely any resemblance to the human form. We also saw several with their heads and arms entirely blown off; others with only a part of their heads destroyed, and some with their lower extremities shattered to an apparent jelly."

Explosion of the Moselle.

"Montreal" Disaster, 1857

Date	Location	Fatalities	Remarks
6/26	St. Lawrence River, Canada	300+	Steamer *Montreal* carried 400–500 passengers; 125 survived.

They were near the end of their journey to a new home most of them had never seen. Between 400 and 500 Scots and Norwegians had crossed the Atlantic to be in the New World. They landed in the city of Montreal. A short voyage up the St. Lawrence River would bring them to their final destination, Quebec, and the beginning of their new lives.

The steamer *Montreal* had been declared "unfit to carry freight" by several insurance companies. But her officers apparently thought her good enough to carry passengers, and on a Friday afternoon in June, she loaded up. There were 30 cabin passengers—the equivalent of first or second class on an ocean-going vessel. The 400-500 Scots and Norwegians made this last part of their odyssey the way they'd made the first—in steerage.

The steamer had gone about 12 miles when a passenger noticed smoke coming from the center of the ship. Immediately, everyone in the vicinity grabbed the fire-fighting equipment and tried to quell what seemed to be a small blaze. In minutes, it became apparent that the equipment was inadequate and the fire was spreading. A jolly boat was lowered, and was rushed and swamped by the now thoroughly terrified passengers. The steamer headed for the nearest shore and actually came within 150 yards of dry land, but before she could get any further, she struck something—a rock or sandbar—and stopped dead. The water was deep; only a reasonably good swimmer could make it to shore.

In 10 minutes, the entire steamer was aflame. As a newspaper of the period reported, "the scene which ensued beggars all description. There is no language copious and powerful enough wherewith man can express the terrific and heart-rending sight that met the eye of the beholder, from the first moment the flames burst out from midships." Minutes later, "an unaccountable explosion" added to the terror and confusion.

Rescue boats could not get near the flame-enveloped steamer, not even close enough to pick up those who jumped from her blazing deck. Mothers perished with babies in their arms. Men trying to save whole families of five and six would carry two children to safety, only to return and find their wives and other children gone. For two hours, those on shore and in rescue boats watched as adults and children burned and drowned.

The *Montreal* was totally destroyed. More than 300 of her passengers were dead. Most of them were immigrants, whose new lives were over before they had begun.

Steamer *Montreal* caught fire, then exploded. From *Frank Leslie's Illustrated Newspaper*, July 11, 1857.

Riverboat Explosion, 1865

Date	Location	Fatalities	Remarks
4/17	Mississippi River, 8 miles north of Memphis, Tenn.	1,400–1,700	Sidewheeler *Sultana* exploded and burned. Worst marine disaster in U.S. history.

The Civil War was over. Robert E. Lee had surrendered less than a month before and Abraham Lincoln had recently been assassinated. Defeat and mourning engulfed the nation, but not the boys in blue who had spent the last months, or even years, as prisoners of war. Nothing could dim their joy at being on the way home. And who could blame them? Certainly not J. C. Mason, captain of the riverboat *Sultana*, not even as he watched 2,134 undernourished Union soldiers swarm over every bare inch of his vessel. But he was alarmed.

The *Sultana* regularly plied her way up and down the Mississippi between New Orleans and St. Louis, carrying sugar, cotton, some 200 passengers and crew, and the crew's pet alligator—a creature so vicious it had to be constantly confined to a slatted crate. The Union soldiers that boarded her at

EXPLOSION OF THE STEAMER "SULTANA," APRIL 28, 1865.

Vicksburg were on their way to Cairo, Illinois, a trip that took several days. There was scarcely room for the ex-POW's to stand, much less sleep. Worse, whenever the boat docked or the alligator gnashed its teeth, everyone would crowd to one side of the boat to look, dangerously tilting the vessel. Then they'd retreat to set it level again. The motion was bad for the boilers.

Captain Mason breathed a sigh of relief when he put in briefly at Memphis. "I'd give up all the interest I have in this boat if we were safely landed at Cairo," he swore.

Eight miles out of Memphis, at two o'clock in the morning, there was suddenly a deafening roar as a boiler exploded and men and deck hurtled through the air.

They heard the explosion in Memphis. Seconds later, they saw the ship burst into flames. From along the shore, boats rushed to the rescue, but could not approach the blazing ship. Nor were those struggling in the water easy to find in the dark night. Some had landed in the water safely, on the same piece of deck they'd occupied on board.

From their boats, rescuers could see screaming women rush from their cabins in nightclothes, some with children in their arms. Children were thrown overboard in the hopes they would be saved. One woman carefully tied a lifebelt around her daughter's waist and threw her over the railing, but the child bobbed to the surface upside down, for the woman had fastened the lifebelt too low.

Flaming wreckage fell from the boat with men clinging to it. Men ran back and forth on the deck, some ablaze, looking for lifeboats that had been destroyed by the explosion. Others lay pinned under debris and called for death before the flames should reach them. To those struggling in the water, the captain threw planks, window shutters, and whatever he could find that was buoyant.

Before dawn, the fire burned itself out. Weary strugglers nearby climbed back on board and threw water on any live embers that remained. The shrieking had ended, but survivors called to each other through the night, trying to keep each other's courage up as the current moved them back down toward Memphis. At dawn, wounded men and women were seen floating all along the river on barrels, logs, doors, and shutters, skimpily dressed, if at all. They'd survived the night but some would not live through the next day.

In the burning of the *Sultana*, 1,400 people were known to be killed. Another 300 were missing. Among the missing was the crew's ill-tempered alligator, but his fate was known. A quick-thinking passenger had run him through with a bayonette and used his crate to float to safety.

"General Slocum" Burning, 1904

Date	Location	Fatalities	Remarks
6/14	East River, N.Y.	1,031	Excursion steamer *General Slocum* burned with huge church party aboard. At least 400 children died.

Reprinted from *Harper's Weekly*, June 25, 1904:

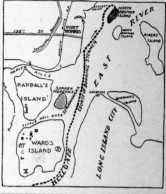

One of the most appalling marine disasters of recent years was the burning and sinking of the excursion streamer *General Slocum* at North Brother Island, East River, New York, on June 15. A conservative estimate of the dead and missing is 1,200. Up to 3:00 P.M., on June 16, 522 bodies had been recovered. These were mostly women and children connected with St. Mark's Lutheran Church of New York, under whose auspices the excursion was given.

Steamer *General Slocum* sinking off North Brother Island after the fire.

The *General Slocum* was chartered for the annual excursion of the Sunday school of St. Mark's German Lutheran Church, and left the foot of East Third Street about nine o'clock in the morning bound for Locust Grove, Long Island, where the excursionists were to spend the day. The number of tickets sold is reported to have been 988, but this did not include the children who were on board. Most of the excursionists were women and children. The *General Slocum*, commanded by Captain William Van Schaick and with two pilots on board, proceeded up the river as far as Hell Gate in apparent safety. It was not until the boat was opposite 130 Street that the first evidences of danger were noticed. According to the stories of some of the survivors, smoke had been noticed before this, but it was supposed to be coming from the kitchen on the lower deck, and no attention was paid to it. The first warning of peril came with the cry of Fire! from the forward deck, followed by an explosion and the appearance of a sheet of flame. Panic prevailed immediately, and the crowd of women and children, terrorized by the flames, which spread with great rapidity, crowded to the rear of the boat. It was then that what appears to have been an error of judgment was made in the management of the boat. Instead of running her ashore on the sunken meadows, the *General Slocum's* captain continued on up the Sound, the wind forcing the flames backward through the length of the boat with increasing rapidity. Then began a struggle among the panic-stricken excursionists. Many, frenzied by the oncoming rush of flames, threw their children over the rail into the water and jumped after them; others remained on the boat until they were forced overboard or until the flames were actually upon them. Apparently there was no attempt on the part of the deck hands of the boat to check the

fire or to restore order among the passengers; and according to the stories told by survivors, the boat's supply of life preservers proved to be worthless. The *General Slocum* by this time was opposite North Brother Island, where Captain Van Schaick planned to beach her. As she ran ashore the supports of the hurricane deck were burned away, plunging passengers on to the blazing deck below. Meanwhile the situation of the steamer had been observed, and river craft and boats from the shore went to her assistance. One tugboat put off from the pier at North Brother Island, and, going alongside the burning steamer as she grounded, succeeded in saving 155 lives. Rowboats and tugs by the score were hurried to the wreck and rescued many from the river. Shortly after the *Slocum* struck the shore at North Brother Island she drifted away downstream, bringing up finally on the beach at Hunt's Point, over a mile away, where she burned to the water's edge.

The news of the disaster spread rapidly, and from every hospital in the city ambulances, physicians, and nurses were sent to the scene, and prompt and efficient service was rendered to the injured who were taken from the wreck.

The burning of the *General Slocum* is the worst harbor disaster in the history of American catastrophes.

The *General Slocum* was launched in 1891, and suffered many mishaps.

One of the most serious of these accidents occurred on July 29, 1894, when she ran on a sandbar late at night when crowded with passengers. Many were injured in the panic that followed. She had had other mishaps of a more or less serious nature, the most recent before that of last week being a panic and riot on August 17, 1901.

Left: The fire after the collapse of the hurricane deck. *Right:* Bodies cast upon the shore of the East River.

VOL. 35. NO. 5.   LAST EDITION   TUESDAY EVENING, APRIL 16, 1912.   FOURTEEN PAGES   PRICE ONE CENT

ONLY 868 ESCAPE

1,350 SOULS GO TO BOTTOM WITH HUGE LEVIATHAN TITANIC

Notables on Wreck

"Titanic," 1912

Date	Location	Fatalities	Remarks
4/15	North Atlantic	1,500	British liner *Titanic* hit an iceberg and sank. Hundreds of Americans perished. Worst Atlantic disaster.

The parishioners of Rosedale Methodist Church, in Winnipeg, Canada, were surprised. Their pastor of long standing, Reverend Charles Gordon, had been acting oddly all through the Sunday evening service. Now, instead of ending as usual, he wanted them to sing the hymn that went, "Hear, Father, while we pray to Thee for those in peril on the sea." Winnipeg, though surrounded by lakes, was not near the sea. Hudson Bay was more than 500 miles away, the Atlantic and Pacific much farther. What was the pastor thinking?

Even the pastor wasn't sure. He had taken a nap before services and had dreamed something very strange. All he remembered was the sound of rushing water, a sense of great excitement, and a tumult of voices—many voices—all requesting the hymn. Some urge made him ask the congregation to sing the hymn.

The night was April 14, 1912. More than 2,000 miles away on the Atlantic, a ship the size of a village, with a population to match, was indeed in peril on the sea. The Rosedale parishioners would always believe that despite the distance, the imperiled had sent them a message. They had answered it as best they could.

Apprentice John Gibson and Second Officer Herbert Stone of the freighter *Californian* had been standing on deck watching the huge ocean liner for over an hour. They'd spotted her at

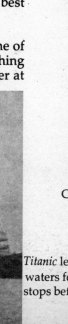

Captain Edward J. Smith.

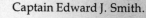

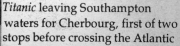

Titanic leaving Southampton waters for Cherbourg, first of two stops before crossing the Atlantic

The end of the *Titanic*. As passengers watched from lifeboats, she sank with all lights ablaze — and more than 1,500 people on board. From *L'Illustration*, April 27, 1912.

11:15 P.M., then her lights went out at 11:40. Now here she was at 12:45, lights ablaze, sending up white rockets. They tried to contact the ship. Failing to make contact by 2:00 A.M., when the rockets stopped and the big ship's lights began to disappear, Gibson and Stone reasoned that she was moving off and all must be well. But the fading lights had not moved off, they'd gone straight down—a tragic end to a voyage that had begun with such joy just four days before.

On April 10, 1912, at twelve noon, the *Titanic*—a brand-new luxury liner and the "leviathan" of the seas—left her berth at Southampton, England, while thousands of people cheered on shore. The "floating palace" was 4 city blocks long and 11 stories high, and was able to carry 3,000 people. On this, her maiden voyage, she carried 2,207, and her first-class passenger list read like a cross between *Burke's Peerage* and the *American Social Register*. Lords and ladies of Britain, together with America's richest, were among the tourist attractions for those on shore.

For four days, it was clear sailing for the *Titanic*. But on Sunday, April 14, as she neared Canada, iceberg warnings began to come in from ships in the vicinity. They were shown around to passengers as a source of great amusement. Nor did the big liner seem to slow down. Some said she was on her way to breaking a record for crossing the Atlantic. She would win the "Blue Ribband of the Atlantic" away from her rival, the *Lusitania*, if she did.

Iceberg warnings continued to come in—two from the *Californian*. The second was received ungraciously by the *Titanic's* radioman. Busy sending messages for passengers, he told the *Californian* to "shut up." The *Californian* had only one radioman. Busy and feeling a bit abused, he shut down the radio room before it became late, and the *Californian* received no radio messages until morning.

Shortly before 11:40 P.M., an iceberg was sighted and a warning was sent to the bridge. The *Titanic* was heading right for it. She swerved hard, but not in time. At exactly 11:40, there was a slight tearing sound.

Ice fell on the third-class deck and steerage passengers played in it like children in the snow. First-class passengers begged chunks for their drinks.

The commander of the vessel, Captain Edward J. Smith, and the ship's designer, Thomas Andrews, Jr., discovered that the berg had torn through five of the ship's watertight compartments. Had three or four been ripped open, had the *Titanic* hit the iceberg head-on, she might have had some chance of staying afloat. But the flooding of her first five compartments

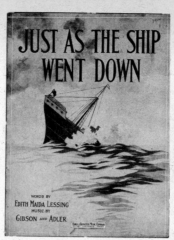

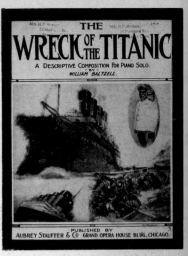

The tragedy was celebrated in music with at least three popular songs. Survivors insisted that the band did not play "Nearer My God to Thee" as the ship sank, but played ragtime through rescue operations then switched to "Autumn," an Episcopal hymn.

Carpathia, the Ship That Brought 745 Survivors to Port

Cunarder Carpathia, which arrived at scene of Titanic's disaster in time to prevent probable total loss of life.

1,595 Went to Death on the Titanic

TOTAL LIST		SAVED	
First Class	330	First Class	210
Second Class	320	Second Class	125
Third Class	750	Third Class	200
Officers and Crew	940	Officers and Crew	210
Total	2,340	Total	745

Of the members of the crew saved, 4 were officers, 39 seamen, 96 stewards and 71 firemen.

This division of victims and survivors by class status on board shows that the crew fared worst, as should be on a good ship. But some of the "crew" were actually musicians, operators of restaurant concessions, gym coaches, and so on. Class which fared worst was third, or steerage, which was treated shamefully.

AND LEADER

VOL. 35. NO. 8.   LAST EDITION   FRIDAY EVENING, APRIL 19, 1912.   TWENTY PAGES   PRICE ONE CENT

OFFICIAL DEATH LIST NOW 1,635;
J. B. ISMAY TELLS TITANIC'S FATE

ICEBERGS HAD BEEN REPORTED ADMITS ISMAY

White Star Line Director Is Called to Tell Senators of Titanic's Fate

COURTS FULLEST INQUIRY

No Women on Deck When He Entered Lifeboat, He Says

New York, April 19.—The story of how the Titanic met its fate was told today to the United States Senate investigating committee into the Titanic disaster by J. Bruce Ismay, managing-director of the White Star Line.

Mr. Ismay was accompanied by P. A. S. Franklin, vice-president, and Emerson E. Parvin, secretary of the International Mercantile Marine. Besides the committee, Representative Hughes of West Virginia, whose daughter, Mrs. Lucien P. Smith, was saved and whose son-in-law was lost was present. Another spectator was Truman H. Newberry, former Assistant Secretary of the Navy.

When asked the circumstances under which he left the boat Mr. Ismay replied, almost in a whisper:

"One of the boats was being filled. Officers called out to know if there were any more women to take. There were none. No passengers on the deck

J. Bruce Ismay

Managing director of White Star Line.

sank. Probably an hour and a quarter.

"Was there any attempt to lower the boats of the Carpathia to take on passengers after you went aboard her?" asked Senator Smith.

"There were no passengers there to take on," said Mr. Ismay.

Twenty Lifeboats on Titanic.

"How many lifeboats were there on the Titanic?"

"Twenty all together I think," said Mr. Ismay. "Sixteen collapsible and four wooden boats."

"It has been suggested," Senator Smith continued, "that two of the life boats sank as soon as lowered. Do you know anything about that?"

"I do not. I never heard of it and I think all the lifeboats were accounted for," Mr. Ismay said.

PORT SIDE OF SHIP RIPPED OPEN BY BERG

Incision Made Similar to That by Can Opener in Box of Sardines

20 SPEND NIGHT ON RAFT

Forced to Keep Others Off Because of Danger of Swamping

New York, April 19.—Col. Archibald Gracie, U. S. A., who jumped from the topmost deck of the Titanic as she sank and swam about until he found a cork life raft and then helped rescue those who had jumped into the water, told today of his experiences.

"The Titanic was struck by the berg on her port side," Colonel Gracie said. "She was ripped from near the middle boat to the bow, after the fashion of a can opener opening a box of sardines. The buttons were pressed immediately and the compartments closed as far as possible under the circumstances.

"The interval between the collision and the sinking of the ship was two hours and 22 minutes, timed by my watch, which lay open on the dresser. The watch stopped at 2:22 a. m. when I jumped into the water. I was awakened in my cabin at midnight.

Feared Being Boiled to Death.

"After sinking with the ship, it appeared to me as if it were propelled some great force through the

MRS. STRAUS REFUSES TO LEAVE HER HUSBAND'S SIDE

MR. AND MRS. ISIDOR STRAUS

HULL RIPPED BY ICE, BOILERS OF BIG SHIP BURST

Instant Panic Averted by Appeal of Captain to Manhood of Crew, Whose Discipline Proves Matchless

New York, April 19.—With the official passenger list of the Titanic, including the Roster of her heroic dead at the bottom of the sea, the total of those saved was today officially placed at 705 by W. W. Jefferies, General Passenger Agent of the White Star Line, although the latest revised list of survivors accounts for 745 persons.

Mr. Jefferies announced that Captain Rostron of the Carpathia, reports the number of survivors by cabins, as follows:

First class, 202; second class, 115; third class, 178; crew, 206; officers, 4; total, 705.

If the report of Captain Rostron is accepted as final, as Mr. Jefferies asserts it will be, the total number of dead increased to 1,635. It was announced at the White

---

would lower her into the water. There was no doubt—she was going to sink.

The captain told his radiomen to send for help at once. Then he instructed the crew to begin loading and lowering the lifeboats. "Be British, men," he admonished, for only the crew knew that there were not lifeboats enough for everyone.

Women and children were to go first, but many of the women were afraid of being lowered eleven stories in the flimsy-looking boats. They did not want to leave their husbands and grown sons behind, and since most of the passengers believed that the Titanic would never sink, the women were not easily coaxed into the lifeboats. Thus many of the boats were only partially filled when they were lowered to the water.

The insufficient number of lifeboats on the Titanic is blamed most often on the presumption that she was "unsinkable." However, she carried more lifeboats, proportionally, than most other ships at a time when no maritime laws required

enough lifeboats for every passenger. The fate of the Titanic changed those requirements.

In the "Marconi" room of the Titanic, the ship's radioman hoped to contact the one ship that could actually be seen. It appeared to be no more than ten miles away and had been there for some time. The international convention had just changed the traditional distress call from CDQ to SOS, and at 12:45 A.M., the "unsinkable" Titanic sent the first SOS in history. The effort was in vain, but the radioman had better luck contacting a number of other ships, all of which seemed eager to steam to her rescue. Most of them never got started. They called back to see if anyone else had arrived there yet, to ask if the Titanic was on her way to meet them, to inquire more about the nature of the damages. They seemed unable to understand the full extent of her peril—that she was unable to move and sinking fast—though the radioman made her position very clear.

1,595 GIVE THEIR LIVES FOR WOMEN AND CHILDREN

SURVIVORS TELL OF HEROISM OF

Astor and Butt Gain Fame Immortal; All Earth's Treasures Could Not

Trunk Pacific railway, who lost life.

After assisting the members of crew in filling up the first five b Major Puechen, who is an experi yachtsman, was assigned by the ond mate to take charge of boa 6. Major Puechen said he dec to accept such a post, not desir

One ship did understand. The small liner *Carpathia*, heading from New York to the Mediterranean, was 58 miles away. She changed her course and came as fast as she could.

By 2:10 that morning, it was clear the *Carpathia* could not reach the *Titanic* before she sank. All lifeboats had been lowered. It was every man for himself, the captain told his crew. Men whose fame, fortune, and status had not insured them against disaster prepared to die like gentlemen. At least all of the women and children were in the lifeboats, or so the men thought. They were surprised suddenly to see women and children coming up from the steerage deck. Third-class passengers had been woefully neglected and forgotten.

Those in the lifeboats saw the *Titanic* begin to upend. They heard furniture, glassware, and humans sliding down her decks as she came near to a vertical position. She hung there a moment, then glided under, lights still ablaze.

There was a mighty wail—"a tumult of voices"—as people thrown from her decks hit the icy water. A number swam to the lifeboats and pulled themselves aboard. Some in the boats wanted to go back to pick up anyone they could, but others were afraid that the boats would become overloaded and swamped. Fifth Officer Harold Lowell tried. Moving passengers from five half-empty boats into four, he took the fifth to pick up stray swimmers. He was too late. Nobody could survive long in water that cold.

It was past three in the morning when the *Carpathia* began shooting off rockets, searching vainly for the *Titanic*. She was not to be seen. Then they heard the cries of the survivors.

At 4:00 A.M., just before dawn, they saw them, in half-filled boats, and took them aboard. The survivors were quiet, said little more than that the *Titanic* had sunk. "We've just watched our husbands die," said a woman when pressed into conversation.

Not until the *Carpathia* began sending off rockets did the *Californian* even begin to realize what had happened. There was little they could do but promise to stay and search the area while the *Carpathia* took the survivors to New York. The world already knew the *Titanic* was in trouble, and newspapers had printed optimistic headlines about how everyone had been saved.

There was an inquiry with a few recriminations back and forth—but surprisingly few. New maritime laws were made that required every ship to carry an adequate number of lifeboats. The captain of the *Californian* was dealt with harshly for not going to the *Titanic*'s rescue. From now on, every sizable ship would be forced to keep their radios alive.

"Lusitania," 1915

Date	Location	Fatalities	Remarks
5/7	North Atlantic, off Ireland	1,198	British liner *Lusitania* sank after being torpedoed by German submarine; 124 Americans died with her.

The British liner *Lusitania* was torpedoed by a German submarine at a time when England and Germany were officially engaged in a war. She was not the victim of a natural calamity, nor was she done in by one of man's enormous but inadvertent mistakes. Or was she?

She was the "Greyhound of the Seas," the fastest, most luxurious liner afloat. Only the *Titanic* had threatened to rival her beauty and speed, but with that ship's tragic end, the *Lusitania* remained the queen of luxury liners.

Americans, especially the rich, had been traveling on the British liner for years. They saw no reason to stop because of World War I. America was not involved in the war, and the *Lusitania* was strictly a passenger ship. Surely the Germans would not harm a ship that carried women, children, and neutrals, such as the Americans.

The Germans, however, thought the *Lusitania* was carrying contraband—arms and explosives illegally purchased in the United States and bound for England.

On May 1, 1915, the day the *Lusitania* was to sail from New York to Liverpool, the German embassy placed an advertisement in New York City papers. It warned travelers that Germany was at war with England and that any ship flying the British flag was liable to destruction, no matter who was aboard. The zone of war, the Germans pointed out, extended to the "waters adjacent to the British Isles." It was understood to be a threat against the British liner, and a warning to Americans not to travel on her.

No American planning to sail on the *Lusitania* that day could have failed to see the notice. Local reporters roamed the ship's decks before she left, showing the ads to everyone and asking for comments. They'd even heard that millionaire Alfred Vanderbilt and theatrical producer Carl Frohman had received telegrams that specifically warned them not to go.

The Americans were concerned, even nervous. When Captain William Turner boarded his ship, all wanted to know if they should turn in their tickets. But Captain Turner had an urgent phone call waiting for him at the pier superintendent's office. He'd answer everyone as soon as he returned.

u of Circulation, '330 Rail-Exchange Building, Chicago.

BINGHAMTON PRESS
AND LEADER

VOL. 38. NO. 23.   LAST EDITION   FRIDAY EVENING, MAY 7, 1915.   TWENTY-TWO PAGES   PRICE ONE CENT

settled and cooler; probably local showers.

TORPEDO SINKS LINER

London, May 7—Lusitania has been sunk off Old Head, Kinsale, by a torpedo from a German submarine.   Assistance has been sent to her. The Lusitania sank at 2:33 this afternoon. The passengers are believed to be safe.

New York, May 7—The New York office of the Cunard Line announced this afternoon that the Lusitania had been sunk. The Dow, Jones & Co. ticker service in a report from London declares the Lusitania was beached and passengers and crew, according to Lloyds, were saved.

Liverpool, May 7—The Evening Express was officially informed this evening by the officials of the Cunard Steamship Company that the Lusitania had been torpedoed and that she had sunk this afternoon.

BIG LINER TORPEDOED OFF IRELAND BY GERMANS

View of bow of steamship Lusitania as she moved down New York bay on her recent trip to Europe.

When The Lusitania Went Down

By CHAS. M¢ CARRON and NAT. VINCENT

The popular song that commemorated the tragedy displayed little anger toward Germany but expressed a determination to sail on American ships rather than foreign vessels.

Captain Turner before his final voyage on the *Lusitania*.

LUSITANIA IS DESTROYED BY SUBMARINE

German Sea Raider Sends Cunard Liner Bound from New York to Liverpool, to Bottom Off Coast of Ireland

PASSENGERS BELIEVED TO BE SAFE

New York, May 7.—The Cunard Liner Lusitania, one of the fastest ships afloat, was torpedoed by a German submarine and sunk this afternoon off the coast of Ireland, 10 miles south of Kinsale.

She had aboard 1,253 passengers. She sailed from this port last Saturday, May 1, and carried, in addition to her own large passenger list, 163 passengers transferred to her from the Anchor liner Cameronia.

The news of her sinking was announced by the local office of the Cunard line and was based on cable advices received from the home office of the Company in Liverpool. Three dispatches, received in the order named, were made public by the line and read as follows:

"We received from the Land's End wireless station news of repeated distress calls made by Lusitania asking for assistance at once. Big list. Position 10 miles south of Kinsale. Subsequently received telegram from Queenstown that all available craft in the harbor had been dispatched to assist."

The second message to the local office read:

"Queenstown, 4:59 p. m.—Wire begins, about 20 boats of all sorts belonging to our line are in vicinity where Lusitania sunk. About 15 other boats are making for spot to render assistance."

The third cablegram was dated Liverpool and read as follows:

"Following received by Admiralty:

"Galleyhead, 4:25 p. m.—Several boats, apparently survivors, southeast nine miles. Greek steamer proceeding to assist."

Dispatches received here from London, Liverpool, and Queenstown confirmed the news. One of the mes-

of the liner and White House officials, while refraining from comment, were keenly anxious to learn if any American lives had been lost.

London Thinks Passengers Safe.

A dispatch from London this afternoon says:

"The Cunard Line steamer Lusitania, from New York May 1 for Liverpool, with 1,253 passengers on board, was torpedoed about 2 o'clock this afternoon at a point about 10 miles off Old Head, Kinsale, Ireland, and later went down.

"It is believed that her passengers are safe. No details of how they may have been lost, however, at hand.

"A message received here says: 'It is not known how many of the Lusitania's passengers are saved.'

"Relief was immediately sent out from Queenstown. If she floated a reasonable length of time before go-

sengers, according to information contained in a cablegram received by the Cunard Line from Queenstown. This message stated:

"Weather here beautifully fine. Wind southeast, light."

Of the 1,253 passengers aboard 290 were in the first cabin, 602 in the second and 361 in the steerage.

A London dispatch says:

"The Cunard line this evening announced that 20 boats were near the spot where the Lusitania went down.

"Sixteen more boats, the line says, have been dispatched to the scene for rescue work."

DISASTER IS MOST SERIOUS ONE THAT U. S. HAS FACED YET

News of Sinking of Lusitania by Torpedo Strikes Washington Like Bomb; Officials Realize Grave Import of Situation

Washington, May 7.—News of the torpedoing of the Lusitania struck official Washington like a bomb. All administration officials realized that the incident was

MOSLEM OFFICERS
LEAD REBELFORCES

PASSENGERS LAUGH AT WARNING TO LUSITANIA

Great Liner Sails from New York with Long List of Notables Who Refuse to Heed Advertisement

1,253 PERSONS ABOARD

Reports in New York Declare Steamer Was Afloat for 12 Hours After Torpedo Struck Her

New York, May 7.—The Cunard Steamship Co. announced this afternoon that it had received from its agents in England a report that the steamship Lusitania had been torpedoed off the coast of Ireland.

Officials of the line here announced that they would promptly make public any confirmation or denial of the report.

The Lusitania sailed last Saturday from New York and was due in Liverpool today.

A dispatch from London printed on the Dow Jones News Bureau ticker states that a report to the Lloyds says that Lusitania has been sunk off Kinsale, Ireland.

Afloat Over 12 Hours.

If the reports are true that the Lusitania was torpedoed at 2 o'clock this morning and that she did not go down until half past two this afternoon, a period of time which undoubtedly gave opportunity for efforts at the removal of passengers.

It is not known just how far from shore the Lusitania was when she was struck.

A dispatch from London set forth that assistance was sent to her.

Confirmation of the report was received in a dispatch dated Queenstown, 4:59 p. m., and reading as follows:

"Old Head, Kinsale, about 20 boats, all sorts, belonging to Lusitania are in vicinity where sunk. About 15 boats are making for the spot to rescue."

"Queenstown, May 7.—All available craft in harbor dispatched to assist.

Captain Turner fully believed that the phone call would instruct him not to sail. The Yank liner *America* was scheduled to leave for Liverpool that day and he expected orders to transfer his passengers to her immediately.

The orders did not come. The *Lusitania* was to sail as scheduled. When the Captain returned to his passengers, who waited to hear if there was any danger, he told them, "There is always danger, but the best guarantees of your safety are the *Lusitania* herself and the fact that wherever there is danger your safety is in the hands of the Royal Navy."

It was very reassuring. Nobody thought to ask whether the *Lusitania* was indeed carrying contraband. Some did note that while the *Lusitania* rarely carried cargo, she was this trip.

For five days, the *Lusitania* enjoyed a smooth and pleasant crossing. On the sixth day she came within the "waters adjacent" to England. The captain learned that the British ships *Centurion* and *Candidate* had just been sunk by German subs. Passengers were told not to light their after-dinner cigars out on deck in the dark. Their cabins were blacked out. Lifeboats were made ready. It looked to the passengers as if the war was on. Captain Turner tried to reassure them. There had been submarine warnings, but tomorrow, on entering the war zone, they'd be under the wing of the Royal Navy, and a ship, the *Juno*, was expected to meet and guide them to safety.

May 7 dawned on a lot of nervous people, not all of them aboard the *Lusitania*. According to Colin Wilson, in his definitive study on the subject, it began to occur to some in the British Admiralty and other high places that the *Lusitania* could be torpedoed. "What will America do if the Germans sink an ocean liner with Americans on board?" That was the question English officials were putting to American officials that day in London.

Some thought America would go to war against Germany, an answer the British wanted to hear. Afterward, a few began to wonder just how far Britain would have gone to get America into the war. The consensus was that she would not set up some 2,000 innocent people even to gain a powerful ally.

Captain Turner was troubled. The *Juno*, which he had mentioned to his passengers, was to have met the *Lusitania*. She was to have guided the big ship up the Mersey River to Liverpool. But the *Juno* wasn't there.

Now Turner received a message warning that German submarines were lurking in those waters. Then he received a change in plans. The *Lusitania* was not going up the Mersey. She was going to Queenstown, Ireland.

The *Lusitania* plunges to her doom.

An American victim of the *Lusitania*, in flag-draped coffin, carried through Queenstown, Ireland.

At two o'clock in the afternoon, the *Lusitania* was hurrying for Queenstown. All on board could see the Old Head of Kinsdale off the Irish coast ten miles away. They were so close to land. . . .

Then one of the watches saw a string of air bubbles, a rush of water, heading for the ship. "Torpedo!" he yelled.

It struck at 2:20 P.M.—with a dull thud, one of the survivors later said. In minutes, two of her compartments filled with water, and she began to list badly. For a moment, nothing else seemed to happen. It occurred to Captain Turner that his ship might not sink. Then there was another explosion and the ship started sinking again.

Had another torpedo struck? That was the prevailing belief for the duration of the war at least, but years later evidence proved it untrue. Some thought the boilers exploded. Again, that theory proved untrue. Then what caused the second explosion, which ripped through the *Lusitania*'s bottom?

The ship sank quickly. Lifeboats were readied in too great a hurry. The operation was chaos. One boat would be successfully launched only to have another dropped on it, crushing and killing passengers, swamping and sinking other boats. Of the *Lusitania*'s 48 boats, only 6 would make it to shore. Just 18 minutes after the second explosion, the *Lusitania* sank with "a terrible moan." More than 1,000 people went down with her.

The United States demanded that the Germans modify their submarine blockades. The Germans maintained that the *Lusitania* had been carrying contraband, but they did not want America in the war, and so they complied. Thus America did not join the war until two years later. The American people simply were not ready. Perhaps a favorite song of the day, "When the *Lusitania* Went Down," best expresses the popular American attitude:

A lesson to all it should be,
When we feel like crossing the sea,
American ships
That sail from our slips,
Are safer for you and me.
A Yankee can go anywhere,
As long as Old Glory is there.
Altho they were warned,
The warning they scorned,
And now we must cry in despair.

Many years later, when the Germans, English, and Americans were on speaking terms, the question of contraband came up again. It seems certain that the *Lusitania* was carrying contraband (firearms and explosives) and that the contraband caused the second explosion—the one that did in the *Lusitania*.

"Eastland" Sinking, 1915

Date	Location	Fatalities	Remarks
7/24	Chicago River	800–900	Excursion steamer *Eastland* capsized in port.

It happened in fifteen minutes—to a ship that never left her dock. Chicagoans who lined the South Clark Street Bridge and nearby streets could not believe it had happened at all. But rescuers lifted body after body from the river. People heard that 9 or 10 whole families were entirely wiped out, 300 or 400 were dead, but they hadn't heard the half of it.

It began one summer's morning, on a Saturday that was very special to the employees of the Western Electric Company. They had planned a day's cruise on the Chicago River. Early in the morning they trooped down to the docks where the excursion steamers lay basking in the sun. The *Eastland* was the first to load, and as a live band played gaily on her deck, more than 2,000 people boarded her. Crowds moved about her double decks, in the sunshine and fresh air, while others went inside to gossip, form parties of their own, and to calm overexcited children.

At 7:20, the gangplank was removed, and the boat began to move—strangely. Her decks seemed to slant. She stopped for a moment, then started again. This time, there could be no doubt. Her decks were slanting. Chairs, a refrigerator, over 1,000 screaming people went sliding down the eversteepening pitch. She was turning over.

Those outside were pitched into the river. If they were quick-witted and could swim, they headed for land immediately. Those too shocked or unable to swim drowned within sight of downtown Chicago. The hundreds inside the ship were trapped.

Police, firemen, and divers were on the scene within minutes. Rowboats were dispatched at once. They picked up 150 corpses in no time. Divers worked furiously to get inside the ship that now lay on her side. They managed to bring some people out alive, but not many. Men with blowtorches cut holes in the steel plate that stuck fifteen feet out of the water. Divers went in through the holes, but for the most part, it was too late. Rescue operations turned to body recovery, and by noon the count was over 600. The holes were repaired, the ship righted, and the count went past 800, with 22 families totally wiped out.

There were investigations, and the seaworthiness of the *Eastland* was called in question, but no blame or reason for her

mishap was ever arrived at. Chicago didn't want her anymore, however, and she was sold to the U.S. Navy, where she had a long and distinguished career under another name. Today, there are no excursion boats on the Chicago River.

THE EASTLAND'S DEAD 1,500; PRESIDENT CALLS FOR INQUIRY

Luxury Liner Disaster, 1934

Date	Location	Fatalities	Remarks
9/8	North Atlantic, 8 miles off Jersey coast.	134	Burning of the *Morro Castle* was bad by modern standards, bizarre by any standards.

For eight luxury-filled days this "floating hotel" had been their home. From New York to Cuba and almost back again, the *Morro Castle* had not disappointed anyone. This was their last night, and it should have been filled with music, dancing, and laughter, but from the moment they had sighted land, everything seemed to go wrong.

First there was a squall, with gale winds that tossed them about until over half the passengers were seasick. They gazed longingly at the lights of Asbury Park, New Jersey, shining in the distance.

For those not too green around the gills, the Captain's Farewell Dinner offered some hope, but not for long. Before the first course was served, the captain, Robert Willmott, collapsed. "Indigestion," someone said, as members of the crew carried him to his cabin. Soon after, there was an announcement. The captain was dead, of a heart attack.

Pall turned to distressing mystery when some of the passengers heard rumors that the captain had been deliberately murdered by poison. No one really believed it, but it did make some remember that the *Morro Castle* was a ship with a past. The year before, she'd been caught in a hurricane off Cape Hatteras and for two days had been tossed about, completely cut off from the world. She'd come through it, passengers and crew intact. Two months later, while harbored at Cuba, she was caught in some revolutionary crossfire and was shot up.

The smoking hulk of the liner *Morro Castle* with her stern 100 feet from the pier of the Asbury Park Convention Hall.

Nobody was hurt. She'd also had two fires in her hold, both of a suspicious origin, but no great harm had been done. Still, it did give you pause. Was the *Morro Castle* a jinx ship?

At 2:30 A.M., long after most passengers had gone to bed, a night watchman noticed smoke and sparks in the smoking room. First Officer William Warms, who had become captain, investigated and found a small fire in one of the storage lockers. Small as it was, the fire extinguishers could not quell it. The crew was roused and put to work with the latest and best in fire-fighting equipment. Nobody thought to awaken the passengers, perhaps because the fire seemed manageable.

Instead of dying, the fire spread, and by the time the general alarm was given, at nearly three, it was too late for some of the passengers below deck. A few were too seasick to help themselves; others were too drunk. Many, not realizing the danger, took time to dress while stairwells burst into flames and cut them off from the crew and the deck. Those who made it to the deck found more confusion there than help. Crew members were breaking stateroom windows on deck, pulling out passengers, and loading lifeboats willy-nilly. Frightened passengers were not helped into them. If you could climb in quickly—faster than the crew—you stood a chance. The boats were lowered in double time, most of them not a third full.

Most passengers were left to fend for themselves. Parents gave children to strong swimmers to take overboard. Many who couldn't swim jumped overboard rather than face the flames. They were still eight miles from the lights of Asbury Park, New Jersey.

The call for help did not go out until nearly 3:30. Chief Radio Operator George Rogers grew frantic as he waited for the orders to send an SOS, but apparently Warms thought the fire could be brought under control. The radio room was filled with fumes and almost aflame when Rogers finally sent the call for help. He had time for only one message. Help arrived a half hour later. Lifeboats from other ships and from shore had to plough through dead bodies to reach those still alive and struggling.

By ten in the morning, great crowds had gathered at Asbury Park and nearby Jersey shore towns. Some came to help, some to watch, and the scene took on a bizarre air as people began paying for spots from which they could clearly see the action.

Exhausted swimmers, who had made the eight miles from ship to shore, were wrapped in blankets and given hot food and coffee. Bodies were washed ashore and recovered. Ships and lifeboats had brought in the rest of the survivors, who received medical aid and comfort immediately and some were rushed to hospitals so quickly they never knew they had been

93d YEAR—No. 250

ENTERED AT THE BROOKLYN POST-
OFFICE AS 2D CLASS MAIL MATTER

DAILY EAGLE

★ NEW YORK CITY, SUNDAY, SEPTEMBER 9, 1934 ★

6 SECTIONS—72 PAGES

5 CENT

5 CENTS
IN NEW YORK CITY

10

FATE OF 133 UNKNOWN IN SHIP FIRE TRAGEDY

An air view of the windward side of the flaming Morro Castle taken off the Jersey coast (left) and (above) a life-boat with survivors of the Morro Castle shown as it approached the Monarch of Bermuda. The Monarch carried one dead woman and about 80 survivors into New York City.

Associated Press Photo.

...to Probe
...p Disaster

...ends Aide to
...k to Conduct
Investigation

...8 (AP)—Secretary
...merce Department
... Hoover, assist-
...Bureau of Navi-
...oat Inspection,
...once and per-
...investigation
...the Morro

...after th...

Survivor Thought Self Lost, Gave Son to Girl

Stranger Then Plunged 30 Feet Clinging to Youngster—Dr. Bregstein Now Awaits Word of Boy

By O. R. PILAT

Cut off by flames on a crumbling deck of the Morro Castle, Dr. S. Joseph Bregstein, well known Bay Ridge den- tist, early yesterday morning enthrusted his 8-year-old son, Mervin, to a stranger who seemed to have...

New Y...

Free Cab Rides For Survivors

64 Arrive on City of Sa- vannah—Women Shoe- less, Many Bruised

Sixty-four survivors were brought into port yesterday afterno... the City of Sav...

Saved

BROOKLYN AND LONG ISLAND
BREGSTEIN, DR. S. JOSEPH, 7825
4th Ave.
CARPENTER, MISS MADGE, 4108
171st St., Flushing.
COCHRANE, DR. CHARLES, 78 8th
Ave.
CLARK, WILLIAM F., Howard
Beach.
CONWAY, MISS ANNE C...
lyn, address...
DAN...

HOFMAN, MISS DOROTHY, Glen-
dale, address unknown.
NOTEBLOOM, MRS. KATIE.
REINZ, MARTIN, Brooklyn, address
unknown.
ROBINSON, MRS. MARY, 105 6...
134th St., Richmond H...
ROBERTS...

BODIES OF SIXTY ARE PICKED U...

8.

part of a financially successful spectacle.

The *Morro Castle* was towed into Asbury Park, where she lay smoking, with an occasional spark or flame licking up. So long as she lay there, the crowds came. More than 350,000 jammed the beach. Boardwalk concessions that usually opened only in summer reopened, and did a brisk $500,000 business.

Within sight of the boardwalk, 134 people had lost their lives.

The story of the *Morro Castle* went on for two more years. Though the cause of Captain Willmott's death was listed as a heart attack, many believed otherwise. The Ward Line, owners of the *Castle*, had been having labor problems. The dock workers at Havana had been very unfriendly. If they hadn't somehow caused the captain's death, as many believed, perhaps they'd sabotaged the ship, causing the fire, which still others believed. There was also a faction that believed the radioman, Rogers, had done the deed. He had a murderous temper, it was claimed, and had allegedly gotten into a row with Willmott, who was going to fire him. The allegations were not proved.

A court convicted Acting Captain Warms and his chief engineer of incompetence and neglect of duty, and they were sentenced to two years in prison. Nearly two years later, an appeals court cleared them on the grounds that had Captain Willmott maintained proper discipline aboard his ship to begin with, the crew would have functioned more effectively after his death.

"Andrea Doria," 1956

Date	Location	Fatalities	Remarks
8/26	North Atlantic	50	Italian liner *Andrea Doria* collided with Swedish liner *Stockholm*. *Anarea Doria* sank. Many Americans aboard.

An Italian boy stood on the deck, trying to smell land. The fog was so thick, it was impossible to see anything more than a few feet away. The ship had left Genoa eight days ago and was due to dock in New York City early tomorrow morning, so the boy knew that a place he thought was named Nantucket had to be out there somewhere. He peered through the fog and thought he saw something. Then he nearly fainted from fright. He saw something all right—something monstrous—the prow of an enormous ship heading straight for him.

A Brooklyn man was brushing his teeth in the bathroom while his wife sat in their cabin reading. They had packed their bags, then decided to turn in early, so they'd be fresh when they reached New York in the morning. The man thought he felt something and stopped brushing in surprise. Then he was down on the floor, struggling, while the ship shuddered and shook and ground to a halt. He lifted himself up and opened the door. His wife—the entire cabin—was gone!

A movie actress was talking with friends in the ballroom. The name Ruth Roman buzzed around the room. For a fraction

of a second everything seemed to stop, and everyone looked startled. Then there was a deafening noise of metal grinding and clashing, and people went sprawling and shouting. All the actress could think of was her three-year-old son, back in their cabin. Throwing off her shoes, she ran through the shaking ship to her cabin. Her son was asleep. "Dickie," she said, waking him, "we're going on a picnic." They headed for the deck.

It was just after 11:00 P.M. The *Andrea Doria*, headed for New York, had been struck by the *Stockholm*. The bow of the *Stockholm* was buried in the *Andrea Doria*'s metal vitals.

From the instant the *Stockholm* buried her nose in the *Andrea Doria* until she got it out minutes later, pandemonium reigned. Once she backed off, things quieted down to a manageable panic, if not calm. Lifesaving operations began. The ship was listing so badly, lifeboats could not be lowered. An SOS went out at once.

Part of the crew began freeing terrified passengers trapped in their cabins by wreckage. Some had seen husbands, wives, or children killed before their eyes. Colonel Carlin, who found his wife and cabin gone, was in a state of shock. Mrs. Camille Cianfarra, pinned by rubble to her bed, had seen her *New York Times* reporter husband killed instantly beside her. She shortly discovered that her daughter Joan was dead, her daughter Linda missing.

Responses to the *Andrea Doria*'s distress calls were immediate. The *Stockholm*, finding her bow out of joint but not inoperable, was on the scene. Sending out lifeboats, she took 500 survivors aboard. Soon after, the little fruit freighter *Cape Anne* arrived and carried 129 to safety. The *Ille de France*, on her way to Europe, turned around at once and arrived in time to rescue 750. The *Tomas* steamed her way to the *Andrea Doria* in time to pick up 150 survivors, the *Allen*, 77.

Of her 1,706 passengers and crew, 1,606 were alive and accounted for. But there hadn't been a disaster involving commerical liners as big as this for over twenty years, not in these waters. Shipbuilding knowledge, sophisticated equipment for fighting and preventing disaster, marine laws protecting passengers, had all come a long way. Commerical lines treated human beings like the precious irreplaceable cargo they were. What had gone wrong?

At 10:09 the next morning, the *Andrea Doria* sank in 225 feet of water. She had stayed afloat nearly 11 hours, ample time to get all survivors off safely.

An investigation into what had gone wrong was begun in New York. The fog had been murderously thick, and the two ships had been in a very crowded shipping lane, headed in opposite directions. By custom, not law, ships going in one direction generally stayed on one side of the lane, ships going in the opposite direction on the other. The *Stockholm* was not on the customary side headed for Europe. Italian and Swedish accusations turned the air in shipping circles blue. But investigators were interested in something far more important. Both ships had sophisticated radar equipment which should have warned each ship about the other's presence long before they came near each other. The equipment was working up

Dramatic sequence of photographs showing the slow sinking of the *Andrea Doria* in the Atlantic off the coast of Nantucket Island.

until the time the *Andrea Doria* sank. The *Stockholm's* was being monitored vigilantly until the moment the ships collided. Why had it failed?

There were theories but nobody ever found out for sure. It seems there are times, very few, when under certain conditions radar will fail. Like most areas of human endeavor, shipping was not yet disaster-free.

Of the 100 missing persons, 50 were found. Mrs. Cianfarra's missing daughter Linda had been located. She'd been scooped up by the *Stockholm's* bow, and had lain there, unconscious, until somebody found her.

Friends and family met the survivors at the pier, but 50 people were gone, killed by the impact of the collision.

The Coast Guard placed this 50-gallon drum on the spot where the *Andrea Doria* went down.

The shattered bow of the *Stockholm* shows the force with which the ship hit the ill-fated *Andrea Doria*.

Nuclear Sub Disaster, 1963

Date	Location	Fatalities	Remarks
4/10	North Atlantic, 220 miles off Cape Cod.	129	U.S. nuclear submarine *Thresher* apparently disintegrated in deep water.

The worst peacetime disaster in the history of the U.S. Navy began early on a spring morning, in a part of the Atlantic known as Wilkenson Deep. It was a fine morning, said the men aboard the submarine-rescue vessel *Skylark*—calm, clear, with just a hint of wind that was more like a breeze. They watched the big submarine *Thresher* surface at 6:23 A.M.

The *Thresher* was the Navy's pride, an anti-sub sub, built to seek and destroy enemy submarines. She'd just been overhauled, and the *Skylark* was guiding her through test dives in water 7,800 to 8,400 feet deep. There's always an element of risk in the testing situation, but the *Thresher* had gone through a series of tests the day before with no trouble. Today was expected to be routine.

Sometime after seven, the *Thresher* submerged, and was in constant contact with the *Skylark's* underwater telephones from that time forward. At 7:52, she reported that she was at 300 feet. At 7:54, there was another progress report. There were four more messages—at 8:25, 8:53, 9:02, and 9:12—the *Thresher* was near her test depth, which apparently was secret information.

The first hint of trouble came at 9:13. The *Thresher* was having some minor difficulties and was trying to surface. Four long minutes later, there was another message—garbled, strange, indecipherable. Something was certainly wrong with their communication system, and hopefully nothing more.

The *Skylark* waited and waited, but she never saw the *Thresher* again.

"Another Unsolved Mystery of the Sea!" headlines blared when the *Thresher* could not be found. So long as there was no conclusive evidence to the contrary, the public preferred to believe that the *Thresher* had simply vanished. Better to fantasize about 129 men on an adventure in an unknown realm than to think of them as irrevocably dead.

The Navy had no such illusions. Bathyspheres were immediately dispatched to the area. The *Skylark* scouted the vicinity all day. Along about dusk, she noticed a small oil slick on the water's surface, along with bits of cork and a red and yellow plastic glove of the type used by the crew of the *Thresher*. True, it was not proof positive, but the families of the missing 129 men were notified at once. However, the search for them and the investigation into the *Thresher*'s possible demise continued. Though the Navy thought they knew the answer to her ultimate fate, there was one mystery they wanted to solve: What had gone wrong?

They knew that the *Thresher* had some idiosyncrasies. Her periscope control, for example, was installed backward. *Up* meant *down* and *down* meant *up*. The same was true of some of her air-circulation valves—*close* meant *open* and vice versa. But the crew was aware of this and not likely to make a mistake. Submarine crews are the elite of the Navy and not given to errors. It was more likely, the Navy theorized, that some small pipe had sprung a leak, not obvious at first. At that depth and pressure, water would have filled the sub quickly, and sent it to the bottom, whole or in pieces, to be buried in the muck on the ocean floor, 8,400 feet below.

Nearly a month after the *Thresher*'s disappearance, the Navy thought it had its first clue to her whereabouts. A bathysphere had spied a great muddy mound in the vicinity where she'd last been heard from. They were convinced it was the *Thresher*'s burial mound. Three weeks later, a search party took a photograph of the ocean floor, which showed an area strewn with paper, metal sheeting, electrical cable, a book, an oxygen bottle, and a red and yellow shoe cover to match the glove found earlier.

It wasn't until August 29 that the Navy got what it considered proof positive, when a bathysphere came upon what it described as "an underwater junkyard" of hunks of plate metal, what looked to be submarine parts, pipe, and so on. A piece of piping was fished up as the bathysphere rose. On it were engraved the numbers 593—the *Thresher*'s numerical designation.

The hunt was abandoned on the grounds that further search was too risky to the underwater vessels involved. Considering the circumstances, the crew of the *Thresher* could not have survived, and the 129 men were presumed dead.

Mr. and Mrs. Neil D. Shafer lost two sons aboard *Thresher*.

U.S. nuclear submarine *Thresher*.

FEARFUL EXPLOSION IN FRONT OF THE WYOMING HOTEL, GREENWICH STREET, NEW YORK, ON SUNDAY, NOVEMBER 5.

From the time a gunpowder mill was first set up on these shores, in 1639—in case the need arose to blow up an enemy—we've been accidentally blowing ourselves to bits. From the time we first set eyes on James Watt's steam engine, in 1769—and started overloading the boiler in search of yet more power—we've been accidentally blowing ourselves to bits. From the time we first started seriously invading the bowels of the earth, about 1812—in search of nature's flammable resources—we've been accidentally unleashing violent forces capable of tearing us limb from limb.

An explosion, says *Webster's Dictionary*, is a "violent expansion of hot gases with great disruptive force and a loud noise." The *Encyclopaedia Britannica* tells you how to make your own. Get yourself a substance that expands and vaporizes—and/or changes chemically—very fast when heated or subjected to impact. Restrain it in a container, keep applying heat or force so that it keeps expanding and building up pressure inside, and when the pressure inside is greater than the pressure outside — bang! It's the story of the boiler overloaded with steam. Natural gas expands even more rapidly when it is ignited. Trap it in a container of any size, and a tiny spark will set it off. For gunpowder and its later forms, such as TNT, which expand when they change chemically, all you need is a good heavy blow.

Gunpowder was the first explosive and you might think it was responsible for the first accidental explosions in which great numbers of people were killed. However, although this volatile substance often caused deaths, in the early days it killed a few at a time. The first major disasters, in the early 1800's, were caused by exploding boilers on steamships and natural-gas explosions in coal mines. When such explosions involved only the ship and its passengers, or the coal mine and its workers, they are listed under marine or mine disasters. When a ship blows up in port, due to dangerous cargo rather than boiler malfunction, it's an explosion. We didn't have "dangerous-cargo" explosions until we started to have big trouble with gunpowder and to ship its more sophisticated and powerful progeny. They turned out to be our biggest killers in the long run, and we've suffered most from them during wars.

Unfortunately, from the time of the Civil War until recently, it was sometimes necessary to put our munitions factories—and more often, to load our munitions ships—in conveniently located, heavily populated areas. In one instance, at least, we came close to obliterating half a community, including the children. Today, however, the public is less sentimental about war and more vigilant about factories that use explosives of any sort. We use many potentially explosive ingredients in the manufacture of ultimately harmless products. But whether it's to be used for firearms or face cream, if explosive chemicals are involved, informed communities do not want them nearby.

Boiler explosions have not been confined to steamships, nor natural-gas explosions to coal mines. Boilers were used at an early date in factories to produce mechanical power, and factory explosions and subsequent fires were a real menace. Today's equipment is more reliable, but on a small scale, the exploding boiler is not dead.

Natural gas is piped into homes and large apartment buildings, and we've never been able to control leakage. Yet, there have been relatively few big explosions—with mass fatalities—caused by this substance. But there have been enough, and every year, homes and small buildings go up because of gas leakage. In New York City, no year passes without a gas main going off in one of the boroughs. In this chapter we deal only with large explosions, involving fifty or more fatalities, but in the small-scale, more-frequent accidents, gas is a big killer.

Our greatest progress in controlling explosions has been made in the most destructive area — the manufacture of explosives or products involving explosive materials. Even so, factory and plant owners are trying to argue their way back near the community. In the case of the nuclear plant, some people argue that we have fewer plant explosions now because equipment, personnel training, and safeguards are so much better than they used to be. That's true, but nothing is perfect. On any day, in any year, practically anything can happen, and often does. Would you want a nuclear plant in your backyard?

EXPLOSIONS

IMPORTANT AMERICAN EXPLOSIONS

DATE	LOCATION	FATALITIES	REMARKS
1862 3/29	Philadelphia, Pa.	50+	"Firework manufactory" of Samuel Jackson, produced cartridges. Gunpowder ignited. Records of fatalities incomplete.
1905 3/10	Brockton, Mass.	100	Boiler blew up in Grover shoe factory.
1917 4/10	Eddystone, Pa.	133	Explosion in a munitions plant.
1917 12/6	Halifax, Nova Scotia	1,400–3,000	Munitions ship exploded. Stupendous list of missing people—whole families perished. Fatality count closer to 3,000.
1918 7/2	Split Rock, N.Y.	51	Explosives accidentally detonated.
1918 10/4	Morgan Station, N.Y.	64	Munitions plant explosion.
1937 3/18	New London, Tex.	412	Natural-gas explosion destroyed Consolidated School. Worst school disaster in U.S. history.
1940 9/11	Kenville, N.J.	51	Hercules powder plant exploded.
1944 7/17	Port Chicago, Calif.	322	Two Navy ships loading ammunition caused explosion that leveled town.
1944 10/21	Cleveland, Ohio	135	Liquid gas tank exploded.
1947 4/16	Texas City, Tex.	561	Freighter *Grandcamp* blew up in port, causing a series of explosions that destroyed the city. Injuries were frightful.
1963 10/31	Indianapolis, Ind.	73	Explosion at the State Fair Coliseum.
1965 8/9	Searcy, Ark.	53	A missile silo exploded.

BOILER EXPLOSION AT THE MANUFACTORY OF LAZELL, PERKINS & CO., AT BRIDGEWATER, MASSACHUSETTS, ON THE MORNING OF JUNE 24.—FROM A SKETCH BY MR. W. C. WILBAR.

NEW YORK CITY.—APPALLING DISASTER—BOILER EXPLOSION ON THE STATEN ISLAND FERRY-BOAT "WESTFIELD," WHILE ABOUT TO LEAVE WHITEHALL LANDING, JULY 30TH.—SEE PAGE 373.

EXPLOSION OF A CARTRIDGE FACTORY, CORNER OF READE AND 10TH STREETS, PHILADELPHIA, MARCH 29, IN WHICH ABOVE 50 MEN, WOMEN AND CHILDREN WERE KILLED AND WOUNDED.—FROM A SKETCH BY C. M. JOHNS.—SEE PAGE 381.

Firework Manufactory, 1862

Date	Location	Fatalities	Remarks
3/29	Philadelphia, Pa.	50+	"Firework manufactory" of Samuel Jackson, produced cartridges. Gunpowder ignited. Records of fatalities incomplete.

Reprinted from *Frank Leslie's Illustrated*, April 19, 1862:

DREADFUL EXPLOSION IN PHILADELPHIA

Shortly before nine on the morning of Saturday, March 29, the citizens of that part of Philadelphia which adjoins the Moyamensing prison were aroused by a tremendous explosion, followed a moment after by another and more terrible shock. These were found to proceed from the firework manufactory of Samuel Jackson, of Tenth Street, immediately north of the prison, which now laid a mass of ruins. He had a few days before received an order for an immense quantity of cartridges, and had consequently employed an additional number of hands. At the time of the catastrophe the force consisted of 58 women and girls, 11 men and 9 boys, making 78 in all. The buildings used by Mr. Jackson were generally frame structures, but a single story in height, with a small brick edifice of the same size, and occupied a position in the middle of a lot, which was enclosed by a board fence. In this brick building there were three rooms. The magazine was small, and located but a short distance from it. The spot has been several times the scene of explosions.

On proceeding to the spot, a horrible scene presented itself. Around were scattered fragments of human bodies, lying close to the dead and dying. To add to the general horror the wreck remaining upon the ground took fire, and the horrified spectators who were first upon the ground saw men, boys and girls creeping from the ruins with their persons burned and blackened, and in some cases with their clothing on fire, writhing in agony despite the gallant efforts of the firemen.

All of the factory that was not blown to pieces was destroyed by fire, and in a very short time from the period of the explosion nothing was left but a few charred timbers, a shattered wall and a debris of Minie rifle balls, broken tools and machinery, and small portions of clothing. Just inside of the line of the building the body of a man was found. It was so shockingly burned and mutilated that it could not be identified at first; but it afterwards proved to be the remains of Edward Jackson, the son of the proprietor of the establishment.

There were but few persons who were killed outright by the explosion, and the bodies of most of these were blown to fragments. Heads, legs and arms were hurled through the air, and in some instances were picked up hundreds of feet from the scene. Portions of flesh, brains, limbs, entrails, etc. were found in the yards of houses, on roofs and in the adjacent streets. The walls of several houses in the vicinity had blood upon them where the fragments of the bodies had struck.

The head and part of the trunk of a man were blown into Passyunk Road, more than a block distant from the factory. A portion of the thigh struck against the rear wall of the tavern of Mr. Dougherty, No. 1324 Passyunk Road, leaving its bloody mark upon the brickwork, and then falling into the yard. The head, which appeared to belong to the same body, was thrown over the building and fell down in the same street. The skull was completely in pieces, its fragments being held together by the scalp, and the brains dashed out. The hair sprinkled with gray, and a short whisker, which had been scorched and singed, were all that were left to lead to the identification of the remains, which were supposed to belong to Mr. Yarnall Bailey, who was in the building at the time of the accident, and has not since been found. He was sixty years of age, and a native of West Chester.

The fragments gathered up were all removed to the First Ward Stationhouse, where they were soon after viewed by the coroner.

Shoe Factory Explosion, 1905

Date	Location	Fatalities	Remarks
3/10	Brockton, Mass.	100	Boiler blew up in Grover shoe factory.

Dr. David Rockwell, engineer of the Grover Company shoe factory at Brockton and keeper of its boiler, was not a happy man. Ordinarily good-natured, he had been irritable for the past few days "on account of the condition of the boiler," his wife claimed.

The boiler, practically brand-new, had been in and out of order for a week, slowing down factory operations considerably. By the week's end, Mr. Rockwell knew how he'd solve the problem. On Sunday night, he took out the new boiler for repair and replaced it with the old boiler, which had been retired because it was fifteen years old.

On Monday morning, workers arrived at the factory to find things humming as usual. They no sooner settled down to work than the humming turned to a mad vibration, and the vibration to a huge roar. Up through the building's four stories came the boiler. Those in its path were killed immediately. Others watched as it went straight up through the roof.

The flying boiler never stopped until it had demolished two other buildings outside the factory. It went straight through the house of David Rockwell, right next door, and without a pause went on another hundred feet and through the roof of a house "belonging to Mrs. Effie Hood."

But the Hoods and the Rockwells—except for David at the factory—managed to climb unharmed from the rubble that had been their homes. At the factory, however, the boiler had done much more than simply make its exit. The same explosive force that had wrenched it from its hiding place had also blown apart the large, four-story wooden building. One wall was torn away completely, and the three upper floors, filled with heavy machinery, began falling on helpless workers. The workers ran for the doors and windows. There were fire escapes and those on the top floors hoped to get out that way. But the explosion had ripped the fire escapes down. By crawling through the rubble, workers started to climb out, but stopped to help those pinned under beams and heavy machinery. Before all could escape, fire broke out.

Firemen and volunteer rescuers arrived quickly, but the workers pinned under rubble were trapped. Rescuers said that those trapped died like heroes, that they told the firemen and volunteers not to bother with them but to help those who had a better chance. Those with arms free helped lift women to safety, knowing full well they would die themselves.

All told, with the help of trapped victims, the volunteers managed to pull over 200 people from the fire, but at least 100 lost their lives.

Nobody ever discovered why the boiler exploded. David Rockwell was never seen again. Reported alive but wounded in one hospital, dead in another, he never was found.

Grover shoe factory in flames following the boiler explosion.

Nearby house of David Rockwell was demolished by the flying boiler.

5,000 IS DEATH'S TOLL IN HALIFAX DISASTER

Halifax Explosion, 1917

Date	Location	Fatalities	Remarks
12/6	Halifax, Nova Scotia	1,400– 3,000	Munitions ship exploded. Stupendous list of missing people— whole families perished. Fatality count closer to 3,000.

When telegraph operator Vincent Coleman saw the fire, he knew what it had to be. A ship was due to dock at Pier 8 this morning, a munitions ship. A ship in flames could mean only one thing—the fuse was lit on a bomb that could destroy Halifax harbor! He sent a message to a nearby city: "A munitions ship is on fire and heading for Pier 8. Goodbye."

The last anyone saw of Vincent, he was speeding for the door, in the hope, someone explained afterward, of finding his wife. Minutes later, Vincent, the flaming ship, and half of Halifax were gone.

It was just past 9:00 A.M. when the telegraph operator Vincent sent his message. By then, half the harbor knew about the burning ship. She was the French freighter *Mont Blanc* and carried 3,000 tons of TNT. The TNT was being sent to Europe to be used against the Kaiser. The *Mont Blanc* had come from New York to Halifax to meet the British cruiser *High Flyer*, which would lead her to Britain under cover of a convoy.

At nine that Thursday morning, the *Mont Blanc* reached the Narrows, the entrance to Halifax harbor. She steamed up the channel right on schedule. Suddenly, there was a great commotion, for the Belgian relief ship *Imo* was heading straight at them. She never stopped until she hit them. Quick maneuvering by the *Mont Blanc* kept the *Imo* from burying herself in the TNT. But the *Mont Blanc* was also carrying 2,000 tons of highly inflammable material, and fire broke out.

The freighter's crew attempted to quell the flames, then tried desperately to sink the ship. The fire drove them back. There was nothing they could do, and leaping into lifeboats, they rushed for shore and the woods beyond.

The crewless, flaming *Mont Blanc*, as though anxious to keep her rendezvous, drifted into the harbor and toward the piers.

As news of the burning ship spread, people poured out of buildings and scrambled up the hill for the city behind them. Firemen and Navy personnel ran for the water. There was another munitions ship in the harbor. If only they could sink her, if only they could sink the *Mont Blanc*.

One brave soul did manage to board the other munitions ship and sink her. A group of sailors from the *High Flyer* boarded the *Mont Blanc* and tried every way they knew to send her down. They worked frantically, racing against time.

At 9:15, they lost the race. With one gigantic blast, the *Mont Blanc* vanished and everything in sight began to crumble.

It lasted ten seconds. Everything along the harbor just fell. Inside a sugar refinery, at least a hundred people were killed. The railroad station collapsed and hundreds of commuters were killed. Those who had scrambled up the hill to the city thinking they would be safe were in for a shock. Houses crumbled around them, killing mothers, small children, and sometimes whole families. Office buildings toppled, trapping and killing men inside. Schools disintegrated, and more than 500 children were killed. People lay all along the streets, some dead, some unable to move. In the Richmond area of Halifax, more than two and a half square miles were totally devastated by the blast. After the explosion came the fires, which destroyed anything that had been left behind.

Vincent Coleman's last message paid off. As early as 9:30, 15 minutes after the blast, help began to arrive from neighboring towns. There were doctors, nurses, the Red Cross, people to help fight the fires. By noon, a driving snow began to fall. It checked the fires, but made rescue work difficult. People lying in the streets became snowy mounds, and it was hard to tell the humans from the snow drifts, much less the living from the dead.

By late afternoon, more help had arrived from Boston and New York. Emergency hospitals had been set up for the living, morgues for the dead. It was days before all the dead were recovered, and so little was left of some that an accurate count of fatalities was impossible.

One of the fine homes in Halifax that was destroyed by the explosion in the harbor.

School Explosion, 1937

Date	Location	Fatalities	Remarks
3/18	New London, Tex.	412	Natural-gas explosion destroyed Consolidated School. Worst school disaster in U.S. history.

It was nearly three o'clock when W. C. Shaw, Superintendent of the Consolidated School at New London, stepped out for some air. In minutes, the school day would be over. The grade-school pupils had already been released. About 700 seventh to twelfth graders remained inside.

Shaw was enjoying the sun that shone down on the school and on the nearby oil derricks that surrounded it. If he thought it was an odd landscape, he never said so. After all, East Texas oil taxes had built this place — "the finest rural school in the country." The oil derricks seemed as natural as the women's voices that came from a PTA meeting in the separate gymnasium 300 feet away.

"450 died here" is chalked on the blackboard of the demolished Consolidated School by one of the students who survived. The blackboard was all that remained standing after the roof and walls were blown away.

Smoking ruins of the Consolidated School at New London, Texas, after the explosion.

Then Shaw heard something that he could never quite describe afterward. It came from the direction of the school. "It was unbelievable! The roof just lifted up! The walls fell out — and the roof fell in!"

The Consolidated School seemed to have burst, and coming through the roof like projectiles were the bodies of children.

Mothers ran out of the gymnasium in time to see children falling through the air. Some landed unharmed. Others lay where they'd been hurled "like rag dolls." Many were unidentifiable, some decapitated. A few children managed to escape the falling walls, and there were tearful reunions. But most mothers stood there for a long moment looking alone and bewildered. Then they heard cries beneath the huge heap that had been the school. Screaming, the women rushed to the heap and clawed at it with their bare hands.

From across the oilfields, men came running. Like the women, they began tearing at the pile. Only when someone heard something falling inside did the digging stop for a moment. They couldn't keep tearing at the pile this way. It might cause more damage, make something fall and crush a child. They had to be more methodical.

The first thing they did was to remove parents who had become hysterical. All work was suspended, and 3,000 men volunteered to dig. The area was cordoned off, and spotlights were brought in. All night long, the men dug through the pile. Bricks were lifted one by one. The smallest piles of debris were searched for dismembered parts. There were some survivors — a weeping girl sheltered by a desk, who had seen friends and teacher blown away; a teacher sheltered by a fallen bookcase. But the number of sheet-covered bodies grew and grew.

By 2:00 A.M., 400 bodies had been recovered. Survivors and victims were sent to neighboring towns all over the country. Parents began the long trek from town to town, hospital to morgue, to see if they could find their children. The dead were almost totally unrecognizable, and parents did not know how to identify them. An appalled world tried to comfort them. President Roosevelt sent doctors and nurses and the Red Cross. Mrs. Roosevelt sent telegrams. Even Adolf Hitler was moved to send his personal condolences.

By Saturday, 412 bodies were recovered. New London, Texas, had lost a third of its youth and most of its teachers. The 10,000 people who had jammed the area, some to help, some to sightsee, went home. The press, among them a young reporter named Walter Cronkite, went home. In the Pleasant Hill Cemetery, graves were being dug in haste.

On Sunday, there was a mass funeral. If fainting mourners were asking why, so was an official court of inquiry.

In a few days, they had their answer. Superintendent Shaw, himself, gave it to them. Still in mourning for his son Sam, one of the victims, Shaw told them that the janitor had installed a connection to take natural gas for free from a nearby oil waste line. It saved the school about $250 to $350 in heating bills each month. Unlike commercial gas, it had no odor. No expert had been called in, and apparently the gas had leaked without anyone's knowing it. A small spark or flame had set it off into a huge explosion. East Texas oil built the school, but East Texas gas brought it down.

Port Chicago Explosion, 1944

Date	Location	Fatalities	Remarks
7/17	Port Chicago, Calif.	322	Two Navy ships loading ammunition caused explosion that leveled town.

Monday night was always a good movie night in Port Chicago. On the Monday of July 17, they were showing a war movie with a big bombing scene everyone wanted to see.

It was about 10:17 in Port Chicago when the movie heroes battled their way through enemy planes and antiaircraft fire. At 10:19, they reached their target. The audience held its breath as the planes dropped their loads. At that moment, the theater wall blew out.

The frightened audience made their way outside. What had struck?

Port Chicago was a sleepy little coast town until World War II, when the Navy moved in and took over the port as a loading base. Port Chicago became a little boom town. Some people weren't crazy about the idea, but everyone had to do their bit for the war. Others liked the extra money and jobs the Navy brought in. Of course, loading ships with munitions and explosives could be dangerous.

On the Monday night of the explosion, about 250 Navy men were loading two munitions ships. At 10:19, they blew up with a force that raised the seismograph at the University of California at Berkeley. Every building within a 2- to 3-mile radius was destroyed or damaged, including the Port Chicago Movie Theater. Close to 1,000 civilians were injured. More than 300 people were killed.

The Navy pointed out that most of the dead were their own personnel—men who had been loading the boat. There had been one or two civilians, but nobody who lived in Port Chicago. Residents weren't so sure they hadn't been just plain lucky.

The left wall and the screen of this Port Chicago theater were crushed by the force of the explosion in the harbor. Fortunately, everyone managed to escape with only minor injuries.

The owner of this Port Chicago grocery store cleans up after the explosion broke every window and toppled all the goods from his shelves.

The blackened, twisted hulls of the two munitions ships that collided and caused the harbor explosion are barely visible above the surface of the water.

Texas Tragedy, 1947

Date	Location	Fatalities	Remarks
4/16	Texas City, Tex.	561	Freighter *Grandcamp* blew up in port, causing a series of explosions that destroyed city. Injuries were frightful.

Everybody loves a fire, so long as it isn't theirs. Fire-watchers, lining the Texas City docks that Wednesday morning, never dreamed the big smudgepot they stared at could affect them in any way. It wasn't even a blaze, just smoke rising from the French freighter *Grandcamp*—the only cloud in a perfect blue sky. The ship's crew, local firemen, and

The Monsanto Chemical Plant in flames after the nitrate-laden ship exploded.

HUNDREDS AS EXPLO

longshoremen were pouring water down her hold and would probably have the fire out before anyone saw a lick of flame.

The firemen weren't so sure. The *Grandcamp* was loaded with tons of ammonium nitrate fertilizer, which was highly explosive. They'd been shocked, on boarding the ship at 8:00 A.M., to learn that the crew had been smoking all over the place, with no thought of caution. The crew was shocked, too. Nobody had told them their cargo was explosive.

By 9:00, the ship was still smoldering, and firemen were worried. The *Grandcamp* was docked 700 feet from the immense Monsanto Chemical Company plant, where 800 people were working. If the ship blew, what would happen to the plant? What, in fact, would happen to all the plants, oil tanks and refineries, smelters and granaries that lined the waterfront and made Texas City, a World War II boom town, into the nation's postwar "Port of Opportunity"?

The firemen decided to move the ship into Galveston Bay, and they quickly made plans to do it. But they weren't fast enough.

At 9:12, there was an earsplitting blast. The *Grandcamp* was gone. Fiery hunks of metal flew in every direction. Two planes overhead were struck by flying steel and came hurtling down. The fire-watchers got their flame. A great wall of it headed straight across the oily waters for the Monsanto plant. It was the last thing most of them ever saw.

The flames took one minute to reach the Monsanto plant. It went up like a nuclear bomb. The fire-watchers vanished. Arms, legs, and clothing were scattered for half a block around. Monsanto workers—bloodied, some maimed—struggled past collapsing walls for exit doors, while flames raced toward the other buildings on the waterfront. "I saw

DIE, THOUSAND MAIMED
SIONS RAZE TEXAS CITY

people walking around the streets with arms and hands torn off," said eyewitness Joe Sula. "One had half his face torn away, but he was still on his feet."

The blast was felt a mile and a half away. Office workers were thrown from windows. Roofs, doors, and windows were blown out or twisted grotesquely. Houses fell like playing cards. The manager of the White House department store was blown through the post office door. Shoppers staggered out of the crowded stores in a daze, some carrying terrified or wounded or dead children. One man down at the docks was blown clear into the bay, swam back, went straight home, and began repairing his swaying house immediately. Workers poured from office buildings with eyes and ears bleeding from the shock, only to be met by shock after shock.

The whole waterfront was going up. The heroic souls who had rushed down there to help save lives were going with it. It felt like the whole town was going with it. Mass hysteria gripped the city. One telephone operator kept her head long enough to contact nearby Houston. "For God's sake," she wept, "send the Red Cross."

By noon, the sky was black as night. The blasts had stopped, but the waterfront raged with uncontrollable fires. Help had arrived, and so had the press. "There isn't an unbroken window in this town," wrote reporter Bud Meyers. "People are running in every direction, many of them showing blood through their clothing. . . . A towering fire has broken out among the oil tanks and refineries. The heat of the flames burns my cheeks—even from this distance. It seems an impossible task to get any closer to the scene than I am now—about a mile and a half away."

Public buildings still standing were set up as hospitals and morgues. Doctors, nurses, and undertakers worked continuously. But a new peril threatened the city. Huge tanks of butane gas stood along the waterfront. If this poison gas were released, the city would be asphyxiated. An evacuation program was put into operation, but many stayed to help those who couldn't be moved and to find survivors, as well as to recover the bodies of victims.

By midnight, most of the big waterfront plants were completely destroyed. People began to wander back to town, and some went down to the waterfront to continue the heroic work others had started before them. Police begged them not to. The *Grandcamp*'s sister ship—the *High Flyer**—was still in port and carrying the same cargo. Now she was aflame.

At 1:11 A.M., the *High Flyer* exploded. There were more dead, more limbless, and the roads out of Texas City were once again jammed. The major companies announced they would not abandon Texas City. Her location on the bay, with access to the Gulf of Mexico, was too good. They'd rebuild. Eventually, people came back to the town.

*Same name, but not the same ship as the one that collided with the *Mont Blanc* at Halifax in 1917.

IMPORTANT AMERICAN RAILROAD DISASTERS

DATE	LOCATION	FATALITIES	REMARKS
1856 7/17	Camp Hill, Pa.	66	Two Northern Penn trains collided head-on. First of the big rail disasters.
1864 6/29	St. Hilaire, Canada	90	Train ran through open switch.
1864 7/15	Shohola, Pa.	65	Two trains collided.
1876 12/29	Ashtabula River, Ohio	91	A bridge, of Howe Truss design and already considered unsafe, collapsed over river while the Pacific Express was crossing. President of rail line later committed suicide.
1887 8/10	Chatsworth, Ill.	81	Burning bridge collapsed while Toledo, Peoria & Western train was crossing.
1888 10/10	Mud Run, Pa.	50+	Locomotive hit standing train of Temperance Leaguers on way home from big camp meeting.
1896 7/30	Atlantic City, N.J.	60	Train derailed.
1903 12/23	Laurel Run, Pa.	75	Train crashed into fallen timber.
1904 8/7	Eden, Colo.	96	Train derailed.
1904 9/24	New Market, Tenn.	56	Train derailed.
1906 12/30	Washington, D.C.	53	Train derailed.
1910 3/1	Wellington, Wash.	118	Two snow-bound Great Northern trains, with passengers stranded aboard for a week, were swept into canyon by avalanche.
1910 3/21	Green Mountain, Iowa	55	Train derailed.
1918 6/22	Ivanhoe, Ind.	85	Circus train was rammed from behind. Townsfolk panicked when they heard wild animals had escaped, but animals were on an earlier train.
1918 7/9	Near Nashville, Tenn.	100	Local train and late express collided head-on.
1918 11/1	Brooklyn, N.Y.	100	Train derailed at Malbone Street Tunnel.
1925 6/16	Hackettstown, N.J.	50	Train derailed at highway crossing.
1943 9/6	Philadelphia, Pa.	80	Congressional Limited derailed at Frankfurt Junction.
1943 12/16	Lumberton, N.C.	72	Two trains collided.
1944 12/31	Near Ogden, Utah	50	Two trains collided.
1950 11/22	Richmond Hill, N.Y.	79	Standing commuter train of the Long Island Railroad rammed from behind by another commuter train.
1951 2/6	Woodbridge, N.J.	84	Commuter train plunged through overpass. Worst commuter-train disaster in U.S. history.

They were called "iron horses," and sometimes "iron monsters." Big, clumsy, and imperfect in their newness, they regularly fell off their flimsy tracks, tumbled down steep grades, hurtled off bridges, went through open drawbridges, and collided with each other head-on. The steam-driven locomotive had been introduced in 1803, and by the late 1820's it was serving the public in a regular way.

These early trains traveled at speeds of 10 to 18 miles per hour, and though the head-on meeting of two iron monsters — rearing up like battling behemoths — was a fearful sight, it did not result in large numbers of fatalities. At those speeds, even tumbling down a hill or falling through a small bridge into a creek was more inconvenience than tragedy. The wooden passenger cars splintered around their passengers, so no one was trapped. People picked themselves up, dusted themselves off, and waited for the replacement train to come along. There were occasional deaths, but with short runs and little traffic, rail travel was considered safe.

In the 1850's, all this changed. More track was laid, runs became longer, and traffic increased — and so did speeds. Trains ran from 35 to 50 miles per hour, and impacts and tumbles became deadly. Perhaps if other things had changed along with the new speeds and new mileage, it might not have been so bad. But the poorly laid track remained the same. It froze and snapped in winter, lay buried under mud in spring, and expanded and buckled in summer. Death-dealing derailments were common.

Despite increased traffic, most train roads were one-track beds — one track for all trains going in both directions. With very careful scheduling, it worked most of the time. There were multiple tracks in depots, and some sidings along the way, where one train could wait for another to pass, if it knew the other was coming. Of course, schedules sometimes went awry.

The wooden passenger cars offered riders little protection against impact at 35 to 50 miles per hour, and train brakes were almost nonexistent. If an engineer had to stop suddenly because he saw a standing train in front of him, he had to throw his engine into reverse, while the brakeman had to run from car to car setting primitive handbrakes. It took time, to say the least. Rear-end collisions and telescoping (one car running inside another) were as much a menace as head-on collisions, perhaps more so.

The first big rail disasters occurred in the 1850's. In the two previous decades, half a dozen people may have been killed in a wreck. Now the numbers jumped—a dozen, over 20, then 32, 46, and finally, 66. The public was incensed. Newspapers attacked railroad owners as "butchers" and wrote about the gross carelessness and cheap equipment of the railways. Despite the public outcry, railroads became the accepted means of rapid mass transportation, especially to landlocked areas.

During the Civil War, train travel increased even more. Double tracks were laid, and although tempered steel rails—as opposed to thin iron ones—had been introduced, the railroad companies were slow to adopt the new rails. George Westinghouse invented an airbrake, but it wasn't required as standard equipment until the turn of the century. However, the trains of the 1860's became longer, and the cars became fancier. They were illuminated by lovely kerosene lamps, and heated by cozy little open-fire stoves. Thus fire was added to the dangers in rail accidents. Frequently, more passengers were burned or smothered to death than were killed in the actual wreck.

By 1870, everyone knew that wooden railroad bridges were unsafe. The newer Howe Truss bridges (sometimes

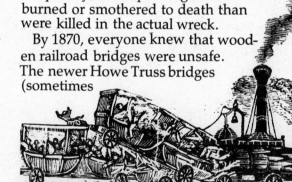

a combination of wood and iron, sometimes all iron) were also considered unsound. The railroad companies, "more interested in economy than safety," said their accusers, were very slow to change to newer and better designs.

In the 1880's, steam heating was installed in a few cars, and some steel cars were built, but even into the twentieth century, wooden cars and gaslight were used in some instances. Automatic signals were in use during the eighties, but for some reason, crews ignored them with insane frequency. Telegraph systems were available, and wired messages about traffic conditions along the track would have promoted safety, but companies were reluctant to spend the money for them.

By the end of the century, the Federal Government became concerned, and the Interstate Commerce Commission was formed to investigate rail accidents. The companies were required to report all collisions and derailments to the commission.

After the successful use of steel cars in the New York City subway, in 1904, railroads started to change over to steel cars in earnest. By now, trains could go 90 to 100 miles per hour. Accidents were frightful, and continued to be until after World War I. The railroad companies came to realize that investments in better materials and safety devices would increase their revenues. Safety records improved until the end of World War II, when the passenger railroad began to take a beating from cars, low-fare buses, and fast airplanes. Only the commuter trains maintained full-scale business. It was during this period, the early 1950's that we had the two worst commuter-train disasters on record. We have not had a major rail calamity since then, and that was 25 years ago. Has rail become the safest way to travel?

Some people say the decrease in traffic is the reason for the decrease in rail catastrophes. Some say safety devices and improved equipment are the reasons. But if the energy crisis continues to raise the cost of operating cars, buses, and planes, rail may again become the most efficient—and, hopefully, safest—way to travel.

Camp Hill, Pennsylvania, 1856

Date	Location	Fatalities	Remarks
7/17	Camp Hill, Pa.	66	Two Northern Penn trains collided head-on. First of the big rail disasters.

Most of them were children and teenagers from St. Michael's Catholic Church and School, in Philadelphia. They had arisen from bed at 4:00 A.M. to go on a picnic in the country. The Church had arranged an excursion for them to Fort Washington, Pennsylvania, about 15 miles away.

The spirited Irish-American youngsters numbered 1,500, and they crowded the depot where they awaited the train that was to carry them off at 5:00 A.M. In the end, two trains were needed to carry the crowd, and that delayed things a bit.

It was the day of the single track—one track to accommodate trains going in both directions—and keeping to schedule was a matter of importance. Multiple tracks and switch sidings existed, mostly in depots, so if a train knew another was coming, it could wait on a side track until the other had passed by.

A regular train left Fort Washington for Philadelphia every morning at 6:14. But no one seemed concerned. Everyone at Fort Washington knew the excursion train was coming, even if it was a little late. The regular train was due to stop at the Camp Hill depot, not far from Fort Washington, where they would know to look out for the excursion train.

The excursion train pulled out a half hour late, but the children were hardly troubled by that. When the first train pulled out at 5:30 A.M. with 600 youngsters aboard, all was laughter, jokes, and singing.

Conductor Alfred F. Hoppel was troubled. Perhaps he was thinking about the regular train and wondering if it would wait at Camp Hill. Deciding to make up for lost time, he urged the engineer to put on steam, and when they reached the outskirts of Camp Hill, they were clipping along at a smart 35 miles per hour.

There was a curve they had to negotiate at Camp Hill, but nothing that couldn't be handled at this speed. Only stopping would be a problem.

The engineer was already into the curve when he saw it. Another train—the regular from Fort Washington—coming around the bend. It had not waited, and the curve had hidden it from view until it was almost on them.

There was no time to slow down or even to blow a whistle. In a moment, the two trains collided with a fearful crash. The regular train, going slower, gave a shudder and just settled down. The excursion train fell to pieces. The first three cars were completely crushed, and the next two badly wrecked. In no time, sparks and flames from the dying engine set fire to the big pile of wrecked wooden cars.

Passengers from the regular train, and children who had escaped from the back of the excursion train, ran to help the youngsters caught in the first five cars. They did manage to save children from the fourth and fifth cars, but freeing them from the three crushed cars in front was almost impossible. They wept as they worked, but could save only a few children in those cars. In minutes, the splintered cars became a bonfire, and 66 helpless children were cremated inside.

The first of the great rail disasters occurred at Camp Hill, Pennsylvania, July 17, 1856.

The public was outraged. From the beginning of the 1850's, rail accidents had been getting more frequent and more fatal, but this was the worst. What had happened was very simple. The regular train reached the Camp Hill depot at 6:18. With no sign of the excursion train, Conductor William Vanstavoren, had a decision to make. He could wait until the excursion train arrived, or he could take a chance and go on to the next depot — and the next, so long as he didn't see the other train. The excursion train might be very late, and delays, the railroad companies frequently pointed out to their employees, cost money. Mr. Vanstavoren decided not to wait. The trains collided only minutes after the regular left the Camp Hill depot. Shortly after it was over, Mr. Vanstavoren hurried to his home. Filled with guilt and remorse, he committed suicide.

The newspapers did not think it was so much the conductor's fault as that of the company which hired him—the Northern Pennsylvania line — and forced him to make decisions of which no man was capable. If the line had invested in a telegraph system so that the excursion train might have wired ahead to say how late it would be, such a blind decision would not have been necessary.

Ashtabula River, Ohio, 1876

Date	Location	Fatalities	Remarks
12/29	Ashtabula River, Ohio	91	A bridge, of Howe Truss design and already considered unsafe, collapsed over river while the Pacific Express was crossing. President of rail line later committed suicide.

All day the wind had howled. The snow was falling so thick and fast, you could scarcely see. But the Pacific Express was a luxury train, and it was cozy to sit inside near the stoves that warmed the cars, while the elements raged outside. The train could only creep along through the snowdrifts and was close to three hours behind schedule, but everyone took it in stride. The extra time gave people an opportunity for a little more socializing.

Mr. Charles C. Carter, of Brooklyn, New York, for example, had retired to the palace car after dinner and had engaged in a game of cards with three other men. They were well into the game when they noticed that the train was slowing down. It was pitch black outside, but they knew they must be near the Ashtabula station. First, though, they had to cross a 150-foot bridge that spanned the Ashtabula River, 60 feet below. The engineer would be careful crossing it on such a windy, snowy night as this.

ASHTABULA'S HORROR.

Details of the Dreadful Calamity on the Lake Shore Road.

The train had slowed to 12 or 14 miles per hour when Mr. Carter heard the sound of window glass breaking. Before he could turn to look, he had the sensation that he was falling. The whole train was dropping through the air. Gripping the sides of his chair and sitting as quietly as he could, he fell and fell.

The train landed with incredible impact in the middle of the shallow but freezing waters of the Ashtabula River. Miraculously, Mr. Carter was still intact. He realized at once that two of his fellow card players were dead. The third, a Mr. Shepperd, seemed to have a broken leg. The front of the palace car was ablaze, and the flames were spreading rapidly to the back. The river waters were too low to have any effect on the fire.

Dragging Mr. Shepperd along as best he could, Mr. Carter made his way out of the car. Then he heard a woman cry for help and he went back in and pulled her out. There was no time for more. The fire was overwhelming. The cars went up like torches, ignited by the cozy stoves that had warmed them.

The howls of those trapped inside the cars were piteous, and the able-bodied survivors tried bravely to rescue them, but there were so few to help. Word had been sent to the town of Ashtabula, where a rescue party was immediately assembled, but the blizzard kept them from getting to the bridge in time. Those living nearby, however, ran through the storm to help. One man had to use force to drag out a woman who was unwilling to leave her little daughter. He set the woman down on the ice and went back for the daughter. The child, only three or four years old, was caught in the splintered wood of the car and couldn't free herself. By the time he got back, it was too late. Enveloped by flames, she could only cry, "Help me, mother," until the fire stopped her cries.

Within 15 minutes, the entire wreckage was a burning mass.

There was nothing to do but listen to the last horrible shrieks of pain. More than half the train's 172 passengers perished.

The train—eleven cars pulled by two locomotives—had been strung out across the entire length of the bridge when it went. The engineer in the first locomotive heard the bridge snap just as he had almost made it across. He put on speed, hoping to carry the train to safety, but the second engine became uncoupled from the first. Down it went with the big iron bridge and the eleven cars behind it.

At dawn, the twisted, tortured ruins of the train, tangled with ruins of the bridge, were seen to be spread from one base of the bridge to the other. They were still smoking. A reporter for the *New York Herald* wrote: "I have just returned from the ruins and have seen the smoldering remains of at least a dozen bodies, only one of which bears any resemblance whatever to a human being." It took days to remove all the bodies from the layers of rubble, and some were never identified.

What had gone wrong? Why had the bridge given way at that moment? The eleven-year-old bridge had long been considered unsafe by at least one railroad official. His superiors, however, claimed that the bridge had recently been tested with no less than six locomotives. What's more, it had a double track, and had not collapsed with two trains on it at the same time.

Perhaps the weight of the snow, the low temperature, and the gale winds had made the Pacific Express the last straw.

The Ashtabula disaster. From *Harper's Weekly*, January 20, 1877.

Chatsworth, Illinois, 1887

Date	Location	Fatalities	Remarks
8/10	Chatsworth, Ill.	81	Burning bridge collapsed while Toledo, Peoria & Western train was crossing.

The engineer was standing
With eye upon the track
And hand upon the throttle—
While shades of night were black.
They reached the town of Chatsworth
And rushed on through the gloom;
Oh, could someone have warned them
Before they reached their doom!

—From the ballad
"The Bridge Was Burned at Chatsworth"

Doom was the last thing on anyone's mind the night the Toledo, Peoria & Western train pulled out of Peoria, Illinois. Everyone was in a holiday mood — 800 people from northern and central Illinois, as well as a few from Iowa and Wisconsin. They were headed for Niagara Falls. The special excursion train carried young honeymooners, old couples on their second honeymoon, and many families who wished to visit one of the wonders of the world. There were even some unmarried couples who planned to do the deed in Niagara itself. No doubt they were all glad for a chance to trade the hot days of a Midwestern August for some cool northern air.

It was a joyful crowd, and even though it was after 11:00 P.M., many people were still up, chatting in the kerosene-lit coaches. In one car, a group of young men sang hymns.

Only Engineer Hitchcock seemed worried. The train was powered by two locomotives, and he was in charge of the second. Just before the train had pulled out of Peoria, he'd told the dispatcher, "This is a dangerous trip." There was no time to elaborate.

It was past 11:30 when the T.P.&W. passed through the sleeping town of Chatsworth. Two miles beyond the town was a culvert, a deep ditch that was always dry in August. It was spanned by a little wooden railroad trestle, not more than 15 feet across.

In the first locomotive, Engineer Sutherland kept the speed at about 35 miles per hour. A knoll ahead was blocking his view, but he thought he saw a light bobbing in the distance. A little brush fire, he thought, not too unusual at this time of year. As he pulled over the knoll, the fire got bigger.

"My God!" he yelled to his fireman. "The bridge is burning. Jump for your life."

The wreck at Chatsworth. Engine Number 13 fell through a burning bridge and rolled into a culvert, dragging the rest of the train behind it.

Nine coaches tumbled into the big ditch after Engine 13, in a deadly telescoping of cars.

Detail of the collapsed bridge.

Examining the wreck
at Chatsworth.

He was almost on the bridge by then, too late to stop. He opened up the throttle to full speed ahead in a last effort to pull the train over to the other side.

Sutherland made it. In the second engine, Hitchcock opened the throttle, too, but it was too late. The bridge gave way beneath him. Engine No. 2 went hurtling down into the ditch, and the passenger cars came like a great kite tail behind it. The big locomotive landed on its side, wheels spinning in the air as the passenger cars fell on top of it and splintered themselves on its huge bulk.

How many died on impact is unknown. One little boy, terribly injured himself, described his mother's head rolling down the aisle. The hymn-singers were crushed before the eyes of those who were listening to them. Two cars rammed together, folding each other in like accordians and killing everyone inside. And then the broken kerosene lamps set the wreck on fire.

The smashed kerosene lamps spilled oil on the wreckage and the people pinned beneath the broken rubble. Flames spread while the uninjured tried to free trapped and shrieking victims. A brakeman and a sobbing passenger ran the two miles back to Chatsworth to wake the town. Volunteer firemen were collected and rushed to the wreck. Peoria was notified by wire, and began collecting a trainload of doctors and nurses. News went up and down the line to nearby towns, which responded immediately with help.

While the firemen struggled, fairly successfully, doctors moved through the wrecked cars doing what they could for the suffering. That mostly meant administering morphine to ease pain. Behind the doctors came volunteers, extricating anyone they could. They dug out the injured—tearing screaming mothers from dead children—and carted 372 wounded people to the Chatsworth Town Hall. The dead numbered 81,

among them Engineer Hitchcock, still in his locomotive, hand on the throttle, his "dangerous trip" over.

Before the night was out, every space in the Chatsworth Town Hall was covered with the bodies of the dead, dying, and wounded. Local volunteers watched helplessly as one woman died atop a piano, another on the hall's stage.

By morning, relief had arrived from Peoria, and the rescue operations were complete. A special train would carry the injured back to Peoria, and as close to their homes as possible if they could be moved that far. A special train would carry the dead back as well. But it was left to the living to discover just how unnecessary their calamity had been.

Earlier on the day of the disaster, a railroad gang had been burning weeds along the track near the little bridge. The foreman of the gang had warned them to put the fires out — to make sure they were out. Augusts are dry in Illinois.

The gang thought they had put out the weed fires, but no one double-checked them. Apparently, some weeds were left smoldering near the little bridge. The bridge caught fire. It was such a little fire really, but it cost 81 people their lives.

Wellington, Washington, 1910

Date	Location	Fatalities	Remarks
3/1	Wellington, Wash.	118	Two snow-bound Great Northern trains, with passengers stranded aboard for a week, were swept into canyon by avalanche.

Reprinted from *Harper's Weekly*, March 19, 1910:

THE NORTHWEST'S RAILROAD DISASTER
By Paul Hedrick

One hundred and eighteen persons were killed in the worst railroad accident in the history of the Northwest, on the morning of March 2, when an avalanche swept down the mountainside at Wellington, at the west portal of the Great Northern Railway Company's Cascade Tunnel, and carried two trains to the canyon depths 400 feet below.

The trains had been imprisoned at Wellington for almost a week when the snow and ice pack on the mountainside, accumulated during ten days of the worst blizzard of record in Washington, broke loose, and, with terrible force, drove downward to the narrow ledge a half mile west of the westward tunnel entrance, on which stood the stalled trains.

Here were the sleeper, two passenger coaches, baggage,

and mail car and diner of the Spokane local, westbound. On an adjoining track were the four mail cars of the Great Northern fast mail; and the equipment also included four new electric locomotives, two steam locomotives, and the private car of Division Superintendent J. H. O'Neill.

Both the mail and the Spokane local had been blocked between mountain slides near Cascade and the eastern portal of the Great Northern tunnel ever since February 22. The day following, the two trains, by order of Superintendent O'Neill, were taken through the tunnel to Wellington. Half a mile west of the big bore was a narrow ledge, and there the trains were placed, in a point believed to be safe from the recurring snow slides. These avalanches came frequently during the seven days the passengers were imprisoned at Wellington, and added to the horror of their plight. From the tracks the men, women, and children saw within a few hundred yards huge bodies of snow and ice slide with a deafening roar from the steep mountainside, and, carrying great boulders and trees with them, descend with terrifying velocity to the canyon below.

The passengers at first entreated the superintendent to take the train back into the tunnel; but the fear that slides would block the tunnel's mouth and so imprison them, made them decide to stay where they were. O'Neill had summoned help from Everett, division headquarters, 60 miles away, but no relief train could get farther than Scenic Hot Springs, 9 miles west of Wellington, and 1,500 feet farther down the mountain.

Two parties of men left the beleaguered trains on Sunday and Monday, and made their way, constantly menaced by death-dealing avalanches, to Scenic. O'Neill was in one of these parties. Everything the operating department of the Great Northern could do was done to get help to the marooned trains. The road on the east slope of the Cascades was blocked with slides, so there was no possibility of help from that quarter.

The passengers spent the days in games and amusements, striving to cheer the women and children; but the nights were filled with horror, for the snow slides increased in frequency, and the strain was beginning to tell on all.

It was 1:45 in the morning of Wednesday, March 2, when the snow pack broke loose from the top of the mountain, 2,000 feet above Wellington. The time is made certain by the fact that the watch of one of the engineers, found on his body, had stopped at that hour. The avalanche carried away some of the houses and shacks in the straggling village of Wellington. The little hotel housed some of the trainmen and engineers of the electrical department; and these, aroused by the awful roar of the avalanche, rushed out to find that the mail and passenger trains had disappeared.

Digging for the dead in a sleeper car, after the avalanche at Wellington.

Steam pipes from one of the cars were twisted around a tree trunk by the terrific force of the avalanche.

Remains of the locomotives from the two trains.

Rescue crews were organized, and a courier dispatched to Scenic Hot Springs in the canyon below. Two days later the work of digging out the dead had progressed far enough to make it possible to determine the number of lost as 118. Many of the rescued were seriously injured. According to Superintendent O'Neill, it will be weeks before the last of the bodies will be recovered. The undertakers, who made their way up the mountain to the scene of the disaster, could find no means of getting out the dead, until, several days after the avalanche, improvised toboggans and sleds were employed, and the bodies were roped down the mountainside to Scenic, over a straight drop 1,000 feet high.

Hagenbeck-Wallace Circus Train Wreck, 1918

Date	Location	Fatalities	Remarks
6/22	Ivanhoe, Ind.	85	Circus train was rammed from behind. Townsfolk panicked when they heard wild animals had escaped, but animals were on an earlier train.

It was the kind of train a child dreams about. In fact, clown Joey Coyle's two kids had just come aboard to join him, and they thought it was heaven. There they were, riding the rails with Rosie Rosiland, equestrienne; Arthur Derrix, the Belgian Strong Man; Nellie Jewel, the beautiful animal trainer; the Rooney family and the world-famous Cottrells, bareback riders; aerialist Robert Ellis and his wife; and the Donavans, elephant trainers. They might be just co-workers to baggy-pants father Coyle, but not to his kids. These people belonged to the Hagenbeck-Wallace Circus, a big show in the Midwest. It even featured "100 Dancing Girls, Count Them."

Joe Coyle traveled with the circus so much, his children never saw enough of him. When their mother decided they'd travel with the circus a bit, it was a very special occasion.

On the night of June 21, the second section of the circus train left Michigan City, Indiana, for Hammond, Indiana, where the circus would open the following night. This train carried most of the human passengers of the circus, while the first train carried the animals.

By 3:00 A.M., everyone had gone to sleep. That's when something went wrong with the train. They were near the little town of Ivanhoe, and the engineer pulled off onto a switch. His last four cars were still on the main track, but the night was clear, and his flagman went around to the rear and set signals

that could be seen for miles. The flagman set off all his lights and flares; this caused signalmen up the line to set up automatic caution and stop signals. From where he stood, the flagman could see a big red stop signal quite far back. Suddenly, he saw the great white beam of a locomotive going right through the red signal.

The flagman could not believe his eyes. The train had completely ignored the signal. It was too late to try and rouse everyone on the circus train, so he grabbed his red lantern and ran up the track toward the onrushing train, swinging the lamp in a wide arc. The engineer would have to be blind not to see him. But the train never slowed down. In desperation, the flagman jumped from the tracks and tossed a small, fizzle-type red flare into the engine's cab as it passed. But the engineer never slowed an instant.

The flagman watched as the huge engine slammed into the wooden cars of the circus train. The last three cars were demolished, the fourth was badly damaged. In the last car, nobody knew what had hit them. Then the old circus cars, still lit by gaslight, caught fire. The injured were desperate, for there were very few to help the trapped out of this train. The locomotive which had run into them was carrying an empty troop train. Only the engineer and fireman were aboard.

Some lucky ones got out. Arthur Derrix, the Belgian Strong Man, didn't make it, nor did the aerialist Ellis or the elephant-training Donavans. When it was over, gone too was Rosie Rosiland, the Rooneys and the Cottrells, Nellie Jewel, many of the 100 dancing girls, and a number of clowns, riders, and trainers. Joe Coyle had escaped, but not his wife or the kids who had thought this trip was heaven. Joe wept, "I wish I could have died with them."

Survivors were taken to Hammond, their original destination. Many were hospitalized. Circus manager Charles Dollmer checked the living against the names on his payroll. In some instances, it was the only way to identify the dead, some of whom had been burned beyond all recognition.

The authorities in Hammond were very anxious to question Engineer Alonzo Sargent and Fireman Emil Kraus, the only two men aboard the empty troop train that had rammed the circus train. It was wartime, and the authorities were sure spies had drugged the two men, or why hadn't they stopped at the appropriate signals?

Sargent, it turned out, had been drugged, but he'd done it himself, without realizing it. Earlier in the evening, he had taken kidney pills which apparently left him drowsy. As for Kraus, he was new on the job and unfamiliar with the signals. Both men were charged with involuntary manslaughter.

Long Island Railroad, Richmond Hill, N.Y., 1950

Date	Location	Fatalities	Remarks
11/22	Richmond Hill, N.Y.	79	Standing commuter train of the Long Island Railroad rammed from behind by another commuter train.

On the eve of Thanksgiving, 1950, New York's Long Island Railroad Station was so crowded you could hardly move from one end of it to the other. Any last-minute dash to catch a train—a dash for which Long Island commuters are famous—was impossible. The 6:09 for Hempstead pulled out miraculously on time, but many regular commuters were left behind.

The 6:09 was packed, yet everyone had a seat. Now that the train had taken off on time, even the commuters joined in the holiday air.

In fifteen minutes, they reached Richmond Hill, just outside Jamaica, Queens, first stop for this train. They slowed down as usual before pulling into Jamaica, and then ground to a halt.

"Oh, no! Not again!" The cry went up and down the train like an old song. There was going to be a delay after all, wouldn't you know? Most of the commuters never heard the enormous locomotive coming up behind them.

The 6:13 for Babylon had left the station on time, too, and was having no problems along the way, except it was so crowded some passengers had to stand. Engineer B. J. Pokorny saw clear signals ahead, and it looked as if he was going to have his passengers at their respective destinations on time. Even as he headed into Richmond Hill and the approach to Jamaica, the signals were all go-aheads, and Mr. Pokorny went ahead at about 35 miles per hour. He apparently never saw the 6:09 until he was almost on it.

It was the most awful sound anyone in the area had ever heard. There was a great clashing and screeching and squealing of metal ground into metal as the mammoth engine of the 6:13 telescoped into the last train of the 6:09, crumpling and twisting the steel cars before it.

The last car of the 6:09 was nearly silent — and ghastly. Strewn in the aisles were the bodies of passengers, some missing limbs. Strangely, in spite of the impact, many of the passengers sat right where they had started the trip less than twenty minutes before, and gazed out of broken windows with sightless eyes. From the back, some of those seated bodies seemed to be slumped forward, as though their heads were bowed. On one, there was no head. Only the soft, mindless whimpering of one or two survivors stirred the thick silence of the car.

All through the night, police and doctors pulled survivors and victims from the wreck. By morning, they still hadn't found the body of Engineer Pokorny, so deep had the impact buried him in his engine.

The public demanded an explanation. Less than a year before, the Babylon train—same route and schedule as this one—had derailed, killing 32 people.

The investigation was brief and simple. The brakes on the 6:09 had grabbed (that is, become stuck) so that the train could not move. It had a go-ahead signal, and the engineer had tried frantically to disengage the brakes and get her moving. Before anyone had realized what was happening, the 6:13 had come along. At 6:26, it was all over.

Less than three months later, a New Jersey commuter train, owned by the Pennsylvania Railroad, jumped a rail and claimed even more victims. The circumstances were different, the error was different, but the Pennsylvania Railroad was in trouble. It was time to take safety seriously, and they did. Both commuter lines benefited, even after the Pennsy no longer owned the Long Island Railroad. Trains are still late, and commuters still grumble, but things have otherwise been fairly quiet on these two lines.

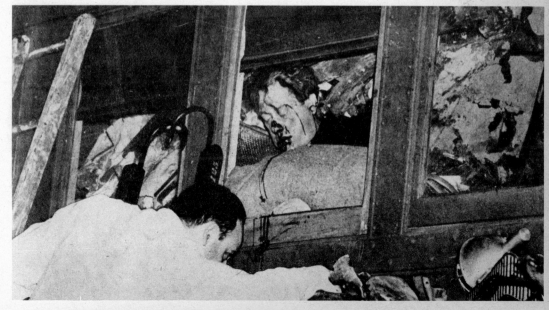

Injured man in window survived the LIRR accident; rescue worker in foreground is searching for the body of a trapped victim.

Wind and water in progress, as 130-mile-per-hour hurricane lashes against Providence's Washington Park Yacht Club.

IMPORTANT AMERICAN HURRICANES

DATE	LOCATION	FATALITIES	REMARKS
1775 9/2–9/9	North Carolina to Nova Scotia	4,170	The span between dates indicates time span between hurricane's destinations. This "hurricane of Independence" may be the worst ever to hit the Eastern Seaboard—if records are correct.
1856 8/11	Last Island, La. (also known as Isles Dernieres)	400	Island was destroyed, but nobody knew about it for days. Word trickled back, then newspapers in New Orleans began getting letters from survivors and visitors.
1893 8/28	Savannah, Ga., Charleston, S.C., Sea Islands, S.C.	1,000+	Charleston was devastated, but hardest hit were the Sea Islands off the South Carolina coast. Inhabited mostly by black farmers who grew, among other things, the best cotton in the world. Of the 1,000 known dead, 975 were black. The death toll was probably much higher.
1900 9/8	Galveston Island and Texas Gulf Coast	6,000+	List of 6,000 dead in the "Galveston Horror" was for city of Galveston only. More died in other towns on Galveston Island and the Texas mainland.
1909 9/14–9/21	Louisiana, Mississippi	350	
1915 8/5–8/25	Louisiana, Texas	275	Storm tide was the killer.
1915 9/22–10/1	Gulf Coast	250+	A bad year for Louisiana. In a large area of the state, 90 percent of buildings were destroyed.
1919 9/2–9/15	Florida, Louisiana	287	
1926 9/18	Miami and Moore Haven, Fla.	243	Hurricane turned Miami from a boom town into a solid, well-built city, and the most hurricane-conscious place in the world.
1928 9/16	Southern Florida, Puerto Rico	2,000	Worst damage was in Lake Okeechobee area.
1935 9/2	Florida Keys	408	Among highest winds ever recorded for a hurricane—up to 250 m.p.h.
1938 9/21	Long Island, New England, Montreal	600–700	"Hurricane of '38." Damage estimated from $50 million to $500 million. Problem was that New Englanders, who'd never seen a hurricane, had no insurance, and thus no claims were recorded.
1944 9/12–9/16	North Carolina to New England	389(?)	Various sources give different death tolls—one as low as 46. But the storm was bad and fatalities probably numbered closer to the higher figure.
1947 9/4–9/21	Florida and Gulf Coast	51	
1954 8/30–8/31	Eastern Seaboard	68	Carol
1954 10/12–10/16	Eastern Seaboard, Haiti	347	Hazel. Most of the fatalities were on Haiti. About 100 died in the States.
1955 8/18–8/19	Eastern Seaboard	400	Diane. Caused more material damage than any storm before it.
1957 6/27–6/30	Louisiana, Texas, Alabama	390	Audrey. Small, intense hurricane with winds up to 180 m.p.h. For a June storm, the intensity was extraordinary.
1960 9/4–9/12	Texas to Alabama	148	Donna
1965 9/7–9/10	Florida, Mississippi, Louisiana	74	Betsy
1966 6/4–6/10	Honduras, Southeast U.S.	51	Alma
1966 9/24–9/30	Caribbean, Mexico, Texas	293	Beulah. Major death toll was in the Caribbean and Mexico.
1969 8/17–8/18	Mississippi, Louisiana	258	Camille. Winds topped 200 m.p.h. Early warnings saved many lives, but some ignored warnings and perished. Twelve people, who refused to evacuate, and held a "hurricane party" instead, were among the victims.
1972 6/19–6/23	Florida, Virginia, Delaware, Pennsylvania	125	Agnes. Mortality rate low compared to damages—among the highest recorded for a hurricane.

It's a word born in the New World, as American a contribution to the English language as "potato" or "chile." *Yurakan* the Arawaks of Puerto Rico called it, and their fierce conquerors, the Carib Indians, feared nothing but *Yurakon*, the evil spirit who came from the sea. To the Mayas, the terrifying phenomenon was *Hunrakon*, the storm god, and to the Galibi Indians of the Guianas, it was a visitation from *Hyoracan*, the devil. The Spanish adapted it to their own language and called it *huracan*. And the English Colonists were soon writing home about terrible "hurry canes" and "harry canes," and finally, "hurricanes."

Hurricanes are spawned in the warm waters of the North Atlantic, between the coast of Africa and the Caribbean Sea: the closer to the African coast, the more dangerous they are to the United States. Hurricanes gain strength the longer they travel—mostly over water—if they survive.

The birth and survival of a hurricane depend on two conditions—heat and humidity—that is what the meteorologists describe as a low-pressure area. A high-pressure region—cool, dry air—repels a hurricane, and can mean certain death to it, unless the storm can find some warm, muggy situation to sustain it. When those conditions exist on land, not too far from the sea, they attract a hurricane like a magnet. Hurricanes, however, tend to weaken and die more quickly over land, but not without putting up a good fight and doing lots of damage. And, as we said, the longer they take to get to land the greater the damage.

Hurricanes from Africa, the Cape Verde Islands, and the farthest reaches of the West Indies usually strike the United States in autumn or at summer's end—late August, September, October. These are the storms that make September the cruelest month up and down our East Coast, from Florida to Maine and even into Canada. They have not often ventured into the Gulf of Mexico, but when they have, they've caused some of the worst natural disasters on record.

Mostly, however, it's been the Caribbean hurricane that's plagued the Gulf Coast. Born closer to home, they strike in June, July, or early August, and tend to be weaker and smaller than their more distant relatives.

A hurricane is a doughnut-shaped storm, a cyclone, with winds revolving around a calm center, or "eye." Those winds must revolve at a minimum of 74 miles per hour to qualify as a hurricane. Sometimes, they rotate at a speed up to 130 miles per hour, and have been known to top 200 miles an hour. But a 74-mile-per-hour wind is quite enough to cause mass misery and devastation, as both our Gulf and Atlantic coasts will attest.

And who should know better than those two areas of this country that are most vulnerable to hurricanes? Together with the Caribbean Islands, they make up our hurricane belt. The Pacific Coast has its own problems with nature, but hurricanes do not seem to be one of them. Apparently, the waters of the North Pacific are too chilly to give life and sustenance to a hurricane. (There are no hurricanes in the cold waters of the South Atlantic, either.)

There are other warm-water areas in the world with enough heat and humidity to generate hurricanes. In Australia, they call them "willy-willys." In the Bay of Bengal and the Arabian Sea, they are known as tropical "cyclones." In the warm waters of the Pacific, they are "typhoons." It was with the typhoon, in fact, that the practice began of calling storms by girls' names.

It happened during World War II, when the U.S. Navy and Air Force set up weather-tracking stations in the Pacific. The men, remembering their girls back home, began naming typhoons for them. "Marge" may have been the first. The U.S. Weather Bureau had been trying for years to find some simple way to differentiate one hurricane from another in a given year. Since there are generally several storms a season, identifying them by longitude and latitude can be pretty confusing. Identifying them by girls' names, in alphabetical order (the first storm of the year named with *A*, the second, *B*, and so on) was clear and simple.

Because the word "cyclone" has been used for both, some people believe that tornadoes and hurricanes are the same. A hurricane may spawn a tornado, but they are two different storms. A hurricane is always born at sea. A tornado needs no such soft birth or exacting conditions, and they have appeared in every state of the Union. Hurricane winds rarely reach 200 miles per hour. Winds of 350 to 450 miles per hour are more a tornado's speed. Hurricanes usually go forward at a slow but steady speed of 12 to 15 miles per hour. Tornadoes can

HURRICANES

117

rush forward at speeds over 60 miles an hour. A tornado can demolish in an instant what it may take hours for a hurricane to do, but it cuts a much smaller swath. Usually about 200 yards wide, it is a dwarf compared to the hurricane, which can cover a distance 50 to 1,000 miles wide, and the hurricane lives for weeks.

Hurricane of Independence, 1775

Date	Location	Fatalities	Remarks
9/2–9/9	North Carolina to Nova Scotia	4,170	The span between dates indicates time span between hurricane's destinations. This may be the worst hurricane ever to hit the Eastern Seaboard—if records are correct.

It happened in September, just as the opening frays of the American Revolution were beginning. From town and countryside, George Washington was collecting his raggle-taggle army, making militiamen of farmers. Back home, times would be tough without the full supply of manpower to help out. A blow to the delicate balance of the early domestic economies could mean disaster.

And then disaster struck on September 2. It hit first in eastern North Carolina. Said the *North Carolina Gazette:* "We had a violent hurricane . . . which has done a vast deal of damage here . . . 150 lives being lost at the Bar, and 13 in one neighborhood at Matamisket." Almost as important, in terms of the war effort, was the total loss of the corn crop and the great damage to other crops. The balance had been shaken. But the North Carolina Legislature, in what may have been this country's first emergency-relief act, allowed forty shillings extra to militamen for the purchase of food en route to their encampments. That meant less had to be taken from home.

The hurricane blasted its way north, hitting Virginia, Pennsylvania, and New England. Some places were hit hard, others spared from all but a bad gale. Still, nervous Colonists wondered if this weren't some deadly sign.

Then came the news from Nova Scotia, Canada. Four thousand sailors, mostly British, were reported drowned. The English had taken the bigger beating.

Last Island Hurricane, 1856

Date	Location	Fatalities	Remarks
8/11	Last Island, La. (also known as Isles Dernieres)	400	Island was destroyed, but nobody knew about it for days. Word trickled back, then newspapers in New Orleans began getting letters from survivors and visitors.

Reprinted from the *Daily Picayune,* August 17, 1856:

LAST ISLAND INUNDATED

Shocking Loss of Life

The rumor which prevailed yesterday on the destruction of Last Island in the late storm is probably too true. We have only some general reports of the greatness of the disaster, and a few vague particulars of the loss of individuals and families.

In the meantime, we subjoin such items as we have been able to gather. The following letters will show the excitement caused by the reception of the intelligence of the disaster at Brashear City, and the promptness with which steps were taken to send relief to the survivors.

Bayou Boeuf, August 14, 1856

Dear Pic.—You may have heard ere this reaches you of the dreadful catastrophe which happened on Last Island on Sunday the 10th inst. As one of the sufferers it becomes my duty to chronicle one of the most melancholy events which have ever occurred. On Saturday night, the 9th inst., a heavy northeast wind prevailed, which excited the fears of a storm in the minds of many; the wind increased gradually until about ten o'clock Sunday morning, when there existed no longer any doubt that we were threatened with imminent danger. From that time the wind blew a perfect hurricane; every house upon the island giving way, one after another, until nothing remained. At this moment everyone sought the most elevated point of the island, exerting themselves at the same time to avoid the fragments of buildings, which were scattered in every direction by the wind. Many persons were wounded; some mortally. The water at this time (about 2 o'clock P.M.) commenced rising so rapidly from the bay side that there could no longer be any doubt that the island would be submerged. The scene at this moment forbids description. Men, women, and children were seen running in every direction, in search of some means of salvation. The violence of the wind, together with the rain, which fell like hail, and the sand blinded their

eyes, prevented many from reaching the objects they had aimed at.

At about 4 o'clock, the Bay and Gulf currents met and the sea washed over the whole island. Those who were so fortunate as to find some object to cling to were seen floating in all directions. Many of them, however, were separated from the straw to which they clung for life, and launched into eternity; others were washed away by the rapid current and drowned before they could reach their point of destination. Many were drowned from being stunned by scattered fragments of the buildings, which had been blown asunder by the storm; many others were crushed by floating timbers and logs, which were removed from the beach, and met them on their journey. To attempt a description of this sad event would be useless. No words could depict the awful scene which occurred on the night between the 10th and 11th inst. It was not until the next morning, the 11th, that we could ascertain the extent of the disaster. Upon my return, after having drifted for about twenty hours, I found the steamer *Star*, which had arrived the day before, and was lying at anchor, a perfect wreck, nothing but her hull and boilers and a portion of her machinery remaining. Upon this wreck the lives of a large number were saved. Toward her each one directed his path as he was recovered from the deep, and was welcomed with tears by his fellow sufferers, who had been so fortunate as to escape. The scene was heartrending; the good fortune of many an individual in being saved was blighted by the news of the loss of a father, brother, sister, wife or some near relative.

As I stated before, not a single building withstood the storm. The loss of property is immense, amounting to at least $100,000; the principal sufferers being John Muggah & Co., Thomas Maskel, P. C. Bithel, Gov. Hebert, Thos. Mille, L. Desobry, Lynch, Nash, A. Comeau, and others. The loss of baggage belonging to visitors on the island at the time, which is complete, amounts to at least $5,000, besides about $10,000 in money on those who were drowned, which was nearly all recovered by a set of pirates who inhabit the island. The bodies of those who were recovered had been invariably robbed by these men. It was an awful scene to see the avidity of these heartless beings to pillage the dead. I hope that the hand of justice will take hold of them and dispose of them as they deserve.

Telegraphed to the New Orleans Picayune.
F. A. ABBOT, Reporter, 70 Wall street, New York.

CONGRESSIONAL.

(By the Southern Line.)

WASHINGTON, Aug. 12.—In the Senate, to-day, the Naval Appropriation bill was passed without any material amendment.

In the House, the Pacific Railroad bill was partially considered to-day, and will doubtless be passed to-morrow, with provisions for the construction of three roads. Forty-six private bills were also passed.

The National Intelligencer.

A statement that the National Intelligencer had decided to support Mr. Buchanan for the Presidency is declared to be erroneous.

Treaty with Venezuela.

The President sent to the Senate, to-day, for approval, a treaty of commerce and friendship, which has been effected with Venezuela.

Later from Texas.

ARRIVAL OF THE PERSEVERANCE.

The steamship Perseverance, Capt. Shepard, from Indianola and Galveston, arrived early this morning. A list of her passengers will be found in the Marine column.

THE LAST ISLAND CALAMITY.

FURTHER PARTICULARS.

The express train, with those of the survivors of the Last Island calamity rescued by the steamboat Major X. V. Aubrey, whose destination was this city, arrived at Algiers at an early hour this morning. By it we have further particulars respecting the awful occurrence.

Complete   Press

NG PLAIN DEALER.

R REGULAR AFTERNOON EDITIONS.

EIGHT PAGES---PRICE ONE CENT

Last Regular Edition

2,819

Is the number columns of advertising printed by The Plain Dealer in

EXCESS

of that printed by The Leader in the eight months of 1900 ending Sept. 1. This equals 402 full pages of The Leader.

VELAND, MONDAY EVENING, SEPTEMBER, 10, 1900.   NO 25

LOSS OF LIFE IS APPALLIN?

KNOCKED OFF HIS CAR.

Sprinkling Wagon Causes Serious Injury to Conductor Wedgewood.

O. N. Wedgewood, a conductor, was collecting fares from the passengers of a westbound Woodland avenue car about 6:30 o'clock Monday morning, and when near Putnam street a sprinkling cart brushed him from the running board of the trailer. He fell to the pavement and sustained a scalp wound and injuries to his back. J. W. Keebler's ambulance took him to the Huron Street hospital. He is married, forty-eight years old and lives at No. 32 Norton street.

COUNCIL WILL TAKE UP BRIBERY CHARGES

Board of Control Suggests That Councilmen Toland, Lapp and Green Investigate Fire Alarm Scandal.

Recommended Fire Alarm Contract be With Held Until Rumors of Boodling Are Cleared Up.

Two investigations will likely be authorized at the meeting of the city council this evening. One will be conducted by a committee consisting of Councilmen Toland, Lapp and Green, if the suggestion of the board of control is adopted, and the other will be made by the prosecuting attorney and grand jury, if the sense of an informal meeting of councilmen held Monday is embodied in a resolution and adopted.

At the meeting of the board of control the following resolution was adopted:

The within resolution is returned to the council. The board is still of the opinion that the Gamewell company is the lowest and best legal bidder and that if a contract is made on the bid submitted it should be with that company.

"Since the within has been referred to the board of control, presumably for some advice to the council concerning the same and there having come to the notice of the board through the publication in the newspapers that certain methods have been or are being resorted to, for the purpose of procuring contracts with the said Gamewell company or for defeating the same, and wherein this board is without power, to subpena and examine under oath witnesses of and concerning said charges, while the council or a committee thereof has such power, it is therefore recommended that said council appoint a committee of three, consisting of

read the resolution authorizing a contract for the fire alarm system with the Gamewell company. It had been referred back to the board by the council without recommendation, he said.

Director Hogsett said that inasmuch as the resolution had come back without recommendation he supposed the council wanted more light. He therefore presented the above report. It was read to the board and was adopted without debate.

Before the meeting of the board of control the matter was gone over in the private office of Mayor Farley, that official having returned from Georgian bay Sunday. The action stated was agreed upon.

Before the board of control meeting there was an informal gathering of councilmen in the committee room at the city clerk's office. President Steuer and Councilmen Lapp, Klingman, Flower and O'Donnell were present. The charges made by Councilman Toland were discussed, as were also the rumors of boodling in connection with the Gamewell contracts.

The councilmen finally agreed that a resolution should be introduced at the meeting Monday evening requesting Prosecutor Keeler to take up the charges made by Councilman Toland, if that gentleman had anything tangible to support his assertions that a corrupt ring existed in the council and that it was the most corrupt he had known in his councilmanic career of six years.

Contrary to expectations President Steuer did not call on the prosecutor Monday morning to renew his request for an in-

Most Destructive Hurricane Years Passed Over Texas Doing Terrible Damage.

Reported That in Galveston Alone Fifteen Hundred People Are Dead.

Property Loss Reaches $10,000,0 and Not a Building Escaped Injury.

DALLAS, Tex., Sept. 10.—Additional particulars of the storm which sw over Galveston Saturday night show that about 1,500 persons were drowned and $ 000,000 worth of property destroyed.

There is not a building in the city that was not damaged to some extent. the bath houses on the beach were destroyed and their attendants drowned. T Sealin hospital was destroyed and most of the patients drowned. The grain elevators were destroyed, one of them containing 1,000,000 bushels of wheat. The B high school and the Rosenberg school buildings were destroyed and many person who had taken refuge in them killed. Eight big steamships in port were all wrecked

All three railroad bridges and the county bridge across to the mainland at V ginia Point were swept away and the bridge tenders and their families drowned loss of life and property is simply appalling. The entire island was submerge water was eight feet deep on Tremont avenue, probably the highest point in the

WORK OF RESCUE BEGUN AT GALVESTON

Hurricane victims strewn on rubble was a common sight in Galveston. This picture appeared on the cover of *Collier's Weekly*, September 29, 1900.

Alvin, Texas, twenty miles from Galveston, laid waste by winds a waters of the great hurricane.

Galveston Horror, 1900

Date	Location	Fatalities	Remarks
9/8	Galveston Island and Texas Gulf Coast	6,000+	List of 6,000 was for city of Galveston only. More died in other towns on Galveston Island and the Texas mainland.

It still holds the record for being the worst natural catastrophe in the history of the United States. Only the longest-running epidemics or droughts have wreaked more havoc, but it took them years to do it. In twelve short hours, the Galveston hurricane devastated an island, destroyed a wealthy city, made homeless paupers of its residents, and killed more than 6,000 people. No one on the island was left untouched.

There'd been talk of a hurricane for days—from the time the Weather Bureau began tracking a newborn cyclone down near the West Indies. It looked to be heading for the States, for Key West, Florida. From there, it would probably veer northeast, up the Atlantic Coast, toward the Carolinas—at least that's what they thought on the Texas coast. That's how hurricanes usually behaved. They rarely headed west into the Gulf of Mexico, and certainly not as far up as Texas. Folks still talked about the hurricane of 1875, but as one old-timer later put it, "We lived through that one."

Only the Weather Bureau seemed nervous. By September 4, they realized the hurricane could head either way, northeast or northwest, and issued warnings both to the East Coast and throughout the Gulf area as far west as Galveston. By September 6, the news was definite. The hurricane was in the Gulf. Whether Galveston lay in its path or not, nobody knew for sure.

Dr. Isaac M. Cline, chief of the Weather Bureau at Galveston, was worried. Though shipping warnings did not say it was absolutely certain the hurricane would strike Galveston—and that prevented him from making an official hurricane warning—the signs were there. To the few anxious souls who called, he said the same thing. If they lived in a very sturdy house, well off the Gulf beach, they could stay put; otherwise, they were advised to make their way to the mainland if—and while—they could.

Just how bad the storm would be, even Dr. Cline didn't know. But he did understand the vulnerability of his little island.

Line drawing depicting the plight of Galveston from the Cleveland *Evening Plain Dealer*, September 12, 1900.

1. THE SPLENDID CITY OF GALVESTON IN THE WILD FURY OF THE HURRICANE. 2. WRECKS OF SHIPPING AND GRAIN ELEVATOR AT THE GALVESTON WHARF. 3. THE GALVESTON STRAND, A PRINCIPAL STREET, IN THE HEIGHT OF THE STORM. 4. GALVESTON CUT OFF FROM RAILROAD COMMUNICATION BY WIND AND WAVE.

GALVESTON AND THE TEXAS COAST SWEPT BY AN AWFUL HURRICANE.

"SCENES" BY F. CRESSON SCHELL, FROM PHOTOGRAPHS AND DESCRIPTIONS.—[SEE PAGE 107.]

Galveston Island is 27 miles long from east to west, and 5 miles wide, at its widest, from north to south. In some spots—most notably the east end where the city of Galveston is located—it's little more than a mile wide. It forms a barrier beach between the coast of Texas and the Gulf of Mexico, which can be a very rough sea at times. The highest point in the city is 20 feet above sea level, causing mainlanders to wonder throughout its history why it simply hadn't remained a deserted barrier beach.

But the very conditions that made Galveston vulnerable also made her great. The Gulf's access to the Atlantic made the city a perfect shipping port, serving otherwise landlocked parts of the South and Southwest. The island's beautiful beaches on the Gulf side also made it a perfect sea resort, serving the same area. Rich Texans built grand houses on the beaches, some in excess of a million dollars, and the tourist trade was brisk. With all they had invested in the place, it's small wonder that residents were reluctant to leave.

At noon, a new wind started blowing from the south, and the Gulf began to boil. For the first time, beach residents became frightened and started calling the Weather Bureau in earnest. All afternoon, Dr. Cline relayed the same message: "The worst is not over—yet."

By nightfall, the worst had arrived. The island was submerged in a wild sea. Winds estimated at 125 miles per hour splintered houses like matchboxes. "To go upon the streets was to court death," said one eyewitness.

The storm raged for hours. And then suddenly, at midnight, the wind started to die. A little after 1:00 A.M., the waters began to subside very quickly.

Dr. Cline himself had been swept to sea, but he and his daughter were washed back to the island by the tide, and by the time the waters withdrew he was reunited with his brother and his other children. He never saw his wife again. Interestingly, by the time he died, in 1955 at age 94, he had become one of the world's leading authorities on weather, the most famous in his field. But Dr. Cline, and all the other Galveston survivors, had yet to face the dawn.

"When the people who had escaped death went out at daylight to view the work of the tempest and floods, they saw the most horrible sights imaginable." That was the most conservative of the eyewitness reports. Rescue boats, coming

F. Cresson Schell painted these scenes of the destruction of Galveston and the Texas coast for *Frank Leslie's Illustrated*, September 22, 1900.

From the front pages of the Cleveland *Evening Plain Dealer*, September 12, 1900.

In the aftermath of the hurricane, looters were shot on sight. Blacks were blamed until white "ghouls" were also discovered. In the days that followed, reports of black heroism began appearing in the press, but it is recorded that 90 blacks were "executed" for "robbery."

over from the mainland, were horrified at the hundreds of bodies floating in the bay. Former State Senator Wortham, investigating the damage, reported, "Along the Gulf front, human bodies are floating around like cordwood."

But the worst sights were in the city itself. Said Wortham, "Great piles of human bodies, dead animals, rotting household furniture, and fragments of houses themselves are piled in confused heaps right on the main streets of the city." And beneath the debris, from six to twenty feet below, were more corpses. Sometimes the dead were the lucky ones. "In one pile of debris," reported a rescue worker, "we found a woman . . . who was injured and pinned down so she could not escape. A guard came along, and, after failing to rescue her, deliberately shot her to end her misery."

To add to the gruesome situation, the hurricane was followed by an intense heat spell, causing the bodies to swell and turn black and making them totally unidentifiable. Worse, the corpses, decomposing rapidly in the heat, threatened to finish the job the hurricane had begun. Left in the open, they would breed disease and create an epidemic that could totally depopulate the island.

The roof of Galveston's Catholic Orphans' Home went into the flood waters when the building gave way, and 75 lives were lost.

"A Cry from Southern Texas" was the title of this drawing from the Cleveland *Evening Plain Dealer*, September 12, 1900.

Clara Barton and her assistants of the Red Cross Society went to Galveston to help with relief work. According to reports she collapsed from overwork.

The dead needed to be disposed of quickly. But they couldn't be buried. The ground was saturated—the flood had even washed up those who had been laid to rest in the cemeteries — and the burial of 6,000 people could not be accomplished quickly, not even in trenches, which was tried.

While the city fathers were looking for a better plan, that element which seems to accompany every catastrophe reared its head in Galveston. The looters came out to rob the dead of their jewels and valuables. Swollen fingers that made it difficult to remove rings were cut off. One man was found with twenty-three adorned fingers in his pockets. Bejeweled ears weren't safe, either.

Meanwhile, the city fathers had come up with a desperate plan to rid the island of its dangerous dead. They would take them out in barges and bury them in the sea which had taken the lives of most of them.

Hundreds of corpses were taken out in the Gulf and dumped but they didn't stay there. All came washing back to the beaches with the tide.

By now, there was a deadly stench over the city and everyone knew what had to be done. They had wanted to avoid it, but last resorts were at hand. They had to burn their dead—and in as great heaps as they could.

Gathering great piles of debris and corpses together, a torch was set to each. Galveston became a city of funeral pyres.

For some the funeral pyres were too much to bear. They left Galveston, never to return.

But more stayed on. Most of Galveston's residents wanted to rebuild both their lives and their city. They wanted a huge sea wall—made of mortar and stone—that could hold back the Gulf at its wildest.

The city was rebuilt and they got their sea wall. Since then, Galveston has been visited by hurricanes, some of them very bad, but they've never had anything to compare with that incredible, terrifying night that cost so much. The sea wall has done its job.

Miami Hurricane, 1926

Date	Location	Fatalities	Remarks
9/18	Miami and Moore Haven, Fla.	243	Hurricane turned Miami from a boom town into a solid, well-built city, and the most hurricane-conscious place in the world.

> June, too soon.
> July, stand by.
> August, look out you must.
> September, remember.
> October, all over.
>
> *Hurricane Watch*

Old Miami hands are no strangers to hurricanes. Today houses are built to withstand the eternal enemy: corner posts set deep; long, low roofs or flat tops that won't catch the wind; poured concrete houses if the building is new. Even the tiniest houses sport substantial shutters that are not for decoration in this part of the world. And at summer's end, weather reports are listened to regularly.

But 1926 was different. The Weather Bureau detected nothing until it was almost too late. And to make matters worse, there were lots of newcomers in Miami that year. The Miami land boom had brought so many thousands of them that they outnumbered the natives.

Weathermen at Miami had not spotted the hurricane that made its way past the Cape Verde Islands on September 6. How they missed it remains a mystery, but the first they heard of it was on September 15, when it had already passed Puerto Rico. Startled, their only hope was that it wouldn't hit Miami.

September 16 was a day of watchfulness, even for old-timers, who kept their eyes peeled out of habit. But there were no familiar signs — no blood-red sunset. All the same, the Weather Bureau released the story of the hurricane to the papers, which ran it on the seventeenth, a day that dawned warm and clear and beautiful. Natives were perplexed. Where was the dark, yellow-green air you could cut with a knife? That's what preceded a hurricane. Newcomers left work early so they could get in some time on the beach.

The Weather Bureau watched and worried. By 10:00 P.M., they were sure the hurricane would hit. By 11:00, hurricane flags—red with black centers—were put up and every man

Above: A street scene after the Miami hurricane. The militia was called in to protect the city from looters. *Below*: Steel yacht once owned by Kaiser Wilhelm was built by Krupp to be "indestructible," but the captain and crew perished in Biscayne Bay.

The wind huffed and puffed and blew down many brick walls, making Miami residences look as flimsy as dolls' houses.

against doors and windows to keep out the wind. But they couldn't stop the water. People spent the night on floating beds, struggling to hold their heads and children above water.

Then suddenly, at 6:10 A.M., the wind died down completely. The sun came out, shining as if it was high noon. People looked at each other in amazement. Was it over?

It was not over, and native Floridians knew better than to leave their houses. But those who'd never experienced a hurricane rushed from their shelters in relief.

What they saw stunned them. The streets of Miami were obliterated by rubble. Huge boats had been lifted from the water, some landing in the city itself. Houses were gone, or swaying precariously. The city looked as though it had been bombed. And running through the streets was a crazy man— no doubt pushed over the edge by the storm—shouting for them to go indoors.

Richard W. Gray, weatherman, knew what all the natives knew. This was the eye of the hurricane—that perfect, calm center. The other half of the hurricane was coming, would be upon them at any moment.

At 6:47 A.M., just 35 minutes later, the calm was shattered. A wind blowing at 130 miles per hour began to smash everything the first half of the hurricane had missed.

The second half of the hurricane probably did more damage than the first. When it was over, more than 400 people were dead. Three hundred had died in Moore Haven alone. It was a miracle that only 114 people from Miami had perished. But the trial by wind and water had rapidly made old hands of Miami newcomers. No more shanties, no more tents, no more flimsy buildings. They joined citizens' committees to rebuild, helped revise the Miami building code, and became, like the Floridians before them, the most hurricane-conscious folk in America.

Miami will never again be so unprepared for a hurricane. They learned to plan and build against it. But there were other newcomers, to other parts of Florida, who would have to learn the same lesson the same hard way.

that could be rounded up was on the phone, relaying the news, asking everyone to call their neighbors.

The Weather Bureau was especially worried about the new community west of Miami—Moore Haven on Lake Okeechobee—and other outlying areas. Messages were sent, but many of the folk out that way had never even heard of a hurricane. And more people than not went to bed without a worry.

At 3:00 A.M., the people of Miami were roused by a roaring shriek. It was a wind blowing at 120 miles per hour and knocking out every line of communication and lighting system in its path.

People cowered in the dark as their shelters blew down around their ears.

Those with more substantial shelter moved heavy furniture

Photo essay of the ravaged Florida coast, reprinted
from *Mid-Week Pictorial*, September 29, 1928.

Lake Okeechobee, 1928

Date	Location	Fatalities	Remarks
9/16	Southern Florida, Puerto Rico	2,000	Worst damage was in Lake Okeechobee area.

Death and Destruction Ride on the Wings of the Hurricane That Sweeps Over Porto Rico and Lashes the Florida Coast

Mid-Week Pictorial, Week Ending September 29, 1928

A FLOODED SCHOOLHOUSE: THE BELL AND SOME OF THE CHILDREN'S SEATS
Can Be Seen, the Roof of the Schoolhouse at Canal Point, Lake Okeechobee, Fla., Having Been Torn Away by the Hurricane. It Was in This Lake That Hundreds Perished.
(Times Wide World Photo.)

DEVASTATION AT WEST PALM BEACH.
A Typical Scene Showing the Appalling Wreckage Left by the Great Tornado, Which Has Claimed About 800 Lives in Florida and Done Many Million Dollars' Worth of Damage.
(Times Wide World Photos.)

WRECKAGE IN ROCKFORD: THE ILLINOIS TOWN
Swept by a Tornado Which Resulted in at Least Fourteen Deaths.
(Times Wide World Photos.)

RUINS THAT ONCE WERE HOMES Along the Fair East Coast of Florida.
(Times Wide World Photos.)

A CITY BOMBARDED BY NATURE.
Battered and Devastated by the Pitiless Hurricane, This Street in West Palm Beach Typifies Many Other Scenes Along the East Coast of Florida.
(Times Wide World Photos.)

T HURRICANE OF RECENT YEARS IN THE WEST INDIES.
A STREET IN SAN JUAN, PORTO RICO,
l From the Appalling Havoc of Thirty-six Hours of Wind and
Rain Which Devastated the Whole Island.
(Fox News.)

WHAT THE TORNADO DID to One of the Main Streets of West Palm Beach.
(Times Wide World Photo.)

FALLEN LIKE A HOUSE OF CARDS: SOME OF THE HANDIWORK OF MAN
After the Great Tornado Had Swept Across It in San Juan Before Continuing Its Course Up the East Coast of Florida and Further North, Its Fury Gradually Dying Down.
(Fox News.)

ANOTHER VIEW OF A STREET in West Palm Beach, Fla., After the Worst Tropical Storm in the History of the State.
(Times Wide World Photos.)

HOUSES AT LA PERLA,
Near San Juan, Porto Rico.

127

On Florida's east coast, they understood about the new monster hurricane in 1928. It had left 600 dead in Guadeloupe, 300 dead in Puerto Rico. But westward, on Lake Okeechobee, with its newly hacked-out farmlands and boom towns, communications were primitive. Since weathermen didn't seem to think the storm would hit Florida, nobody went to tell the lake dwellers.

East coasters didn't care what the weathermen thought. Mindful of the hurricane of '26, they nailed themselves in against the storm, and they were right. On September 16, the hurricane struck West Palm Beach and headed westward for the big lake. It suddenly occurred to everyone that Okeechobeans knew nothing about the storm. Volunteers raced down in trucks and cars. People who heard about the hurricane—many didn't—took the sturdiest shelter they could find. Those who reached the few big hotels were lucky. One group of fifty got out on a raft in the middle of the huge lake and took their chances there.

At nightfall, the wind began to blow. The rain pelted. The lake overflowed and began to spread. Houses full of people blew over into the water. Those not crushed by flying timbers were drowned. Some tried to climb trees for safety and were bitten by deadly water moccasins fighting them for safe territory.

It was over by morning. Lake Okeechobee now covered an area the size of the whole state of Delaware. Beneath the now-placid waters were 2,000 dead. Only a few survived — those who'd sheltered in the big hotels and every one of those fifty people who'd taken their chances on the lake itself.

Submerged, roofless schoolhouse—bell in foreground—was among the few structures left standing at Lake Okeechobee. The roof was torn off by the wind.

Florida Keys, 1935

Date	Location	Fatalities	Remarks
9/2	Florida Keys	408	Among highest winds ever recorded for a hurricane—up to 250 m.p.h.

The hurricane of '35 was the most vicious ever seen by natives of the Florida Keys.

The small-centered hurricane heading toward them had circular winds of over 250 miles per hour. Nobody could be prepared for that.

Up in Miami they knew there were at least 400 men in the Keys who weren't prepared for any kind of hurricane at all. The Government had sent about 700 jobless veterans of World War I—misplaced persons of a sort—to live in a barracks out there. Of them, 300 had spent the day in Miami. But the others were back at the barracks, which was no protection against what was coming.

A rescue train made it down to the Keys, picking up veterans and natives, whoever wanted to come along. As it started making its way back, the train was swept from the tracks.

On September 2, counting veterans and natives, there had been some 800 people in the Keys. On September 3, 408 were dead.

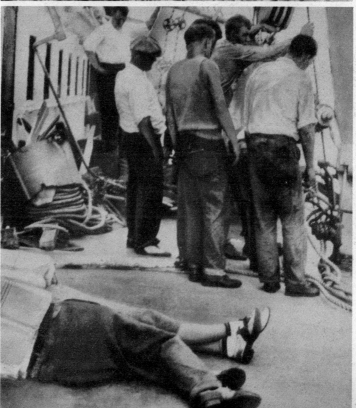

Far left: Aerial view of Lower Matecumbe Key showing the destruction in one section of a community that once included 300 houses as well as churches, schools, and docks. *Above*: This rescue train had been sent to the Florida Keys to pick up the 800 veterans the Government had housed there. The train was swept from the tracks and over 300 veterans died. *Below*: Aboard the hurricane-tossed liner, *Dixie*, off the Florida coast. Crew members repair damaged lifeboats while passengers sleep on deck awaiting rescue.

Hurricane of '38

Date	Location	Fatalities	Remarks
9/21	Long Island, New England, Montreal	600–700	Damage estimated from $50 million to $500 million. Problem was that New Englanders, who'd never seen a hurricane, had no insurance, and thus no claims were recorded.

9 Die, 39 Missing In L. I. Hurricane

N.Y., THURSDAY, SEPTEMBER 22, 1938

First Pictures From Stricken Area | Westhampton

City Wins Grant Of $12,000

THREE CENT

New England kids used to hear the story all the time. There was a man, living somewhere among them, who'd yearned for a barometer all his life. Not just any barometer, but the best made. Finally, in his middle years, he decided it was time to fulfill his life's dream and sent to New York City for the finest barometer money could buy.

It arrived on a hazy, humid day in September, much like the hazy, humid days that had dominated most of the summer and early fall. Carefully, he took the precious cargo from its wrappings, and took a long, loving look — then flew into a fury. The needle on the barometer was way down, pointing to the spot that clearly indicated hurricane weather.

Hurricane! Why, there hadn't been a hurricane in those parts in over a hundred years—never, some said.

Bitterly disappointed, he shook the thing, pounded it, some even say he kicked it. The needle stayed. Obviously, the damn thing was a fake.

His dream shattered, he rewrapped it, enclosing a note that told the store what he thought of them and their barometer. Then off he went to the local post office to mail the damn thing back.

When he returned home—there was no home. It had been totally destroyed. For most of New England, the hurricane of '38 had begun.

Surprise is the key word when you talk about the hurricane of '38. It arrived unannounced, unexpected, and some never knew what hit them until it was long gone.

Not that the Weather Bureau was totally unaware of the big hurricane that had come lurking past the Cape Verde Islands. It had given them quite a tug, in fact, when it looked to be heading straight for Miami. But it suddenly turned north about 300 miles short of the mainland. The Bureau heaved a sigh of relief, but kept watch as the storm meandered north, up past the Carolinas. From there, it seemed to take a sudden leap and disappear. Out to sea, believed the Weather Bureau, with waning interest.

The hurricane had taken a great leap, indeed, but not out to sea. According to Joe McCarthy in his book *Hurricane* (New York, 1969), it was hurrying toward just the right conditions to give new life to an old cyclone. A great mass of warm, humid

air enveloped the entire Northeast, from the New York area up past New England, perfect sustenance for a hurricane. And with its circular winds whirling at more than 100 miles per hour, it hurried forward at an unprecedented 60 miles per hour. Faster than a tornado, it raced toward the muggy feast. And there, sticking out in its path was Eastern Long Island, like a finger that vainly cautioned the winds to slow down.

Labor Day had come and gone, and so had a lot of people who'd made up the summer crowds on Eastern Long Island that year. Those who could had stayed. Long Island beaches are spectacular in autumn, wind and ocean putting on a clean, fine show.

Oceanfront property from Westhampton to Southampton is largely on a narrow strip of barrier beach, with the Atlantic Ocean on one side and Shinnecock Bay on the other. Homes are large and stately and very solid. So nobody was frightened when the wind began to blow. This vivid show was what they had paid for, and by two in the afternoon, neighbors were inviting each other over to watch the wild Atlantic surf through large picture windows.

But by three, the windows were blowing in, and by 3:30, big houses were being blasted apart by wind and waves. Those who panicked, and stayed, perished. Those who tried immediately to make their way to the mainland had such a harrowing experience that they wondered why they were bothering. The ultimate horror was a great wall of water — forty feet high — that came at them from the ocean, either crushing everything beneath or sweeping it all into the bay.

The storm struck Southampton first, but the story was the same all over Eastern Long Island. Inland areas were spared some of the ocean's destruction but it was a mess there, too. Most everything had been destroyed on the barrier beaches. Fire Island, separated from Long Island by Great South Bay, had been flattened and laid bare.

By 5:00 P.M., the hurricane was over — for Long Island at least. Cold, near-naked survivors made their way to the inland villages and stared in horror at the destruction. Some of them didn't know yet just what it was they'd been lucky enough to live through. Some thought it was a kind of weather freak, something only their little piece of the ocean had gone through.

Left: Water-soaked and wind-swept house in Hadlyme, Connecticut, which was tossed back from the roadway by the hurricane and then flooded by the Connecticut River. *Right*: In New London, Connecticut, ships were cast ashore near the derailed trains at the railroad station (upper right).

Finished in Long Island, the hurricane of '38 ripped its way through New England. It howled across Long Island Sound, smashing and flooding its way up to Hartford, Connecticut, almost in the middle of the state. But the real damage was done down east—in New London, open to the ocean; Norwich, on the Thames River, which is open to the sea; and in Stonington, also on the coast. The damage was so terrible that relatives from out of state, trying to reach trapped families, were sure all were dead.

The same sea waves that battered southeastern Connecticut wreaked havoc on Rhode Island's seashore. Napatree Point, Watch Hill, parts of Newport went the way of Long Island's sea resorts, with even more death and damage as a result. Wind and waves poured into Narragansett Bay, causing immense floods in Fall River—no stranger to catastrophe—and annihilation to nearby towns. But the worst sight, and maybe the strangest, was Providence, a major modern city turned into a tempestuous ocean all its own.

It was late afternoon, almost quitting time, when the 100-mile-per-hour wind and the rising water hit Providence. People were still at work in office buildings, and, if they were smart, they stayed there. Shoppers and pedestrians thronged the streets. Those lucky enough to be high watched in horror as the people on the streets struggled against the incredibly fierce wind and water to get to safety. People would get halfway across a street and then drop out of sight.

For hours people sat in the office buildings, in darkness or candlelight, watching the terrible drama below. When the wind died down a bit, they were treated to a peculiar sight.

The Mall, Providence, after flood waters began to recede.

Beneath the waters outside they could see lights eerily glowing and moving about, looking like great, luminous sea scavengers.

They were scavengers. The looters had arrived, in full underwater regalia and apparently very well organized, to begin stripping bare the submerged stores. There was no one to stop them. And as one Rhode Islander put it, "Well, at least none of our looters drowned."

The hurricane moved on to Massachusetts. A great sea wave, like the one seen on Long Island, poured into Buzzards Bay, nearly obliterating the little towns around its shores. Then, with the force of several atom bombs, it plowed a path of death and destruction through the middle of the state. It did the same in New Hampshire. In less densely settled Vermont, it destroyed two-thirds of the state's sugar maples.

By ten that night, the storm had reached Canada and was definitely waning. But not before it showed the people of Montreal a little tropical hell.

New England had been hit hardest by the hurricane. But by the time relief and the Red Cross arrived, they were digging out and making plans, regaling each other with tales of the hurricane. One minute it was a heartbreaking story of a neighbor's child who'd been wrenched from his father's arms and carried away. The next minute, the same person would tell you about the old-timer who, after the hurricane, had come up to one of the makeshift morgues. Looking at each of the unidentified bodies in turn, he remarked, "Nope, t'ain't me."

Everybody had a story, and one enterprising Yankee, thinking to recoup his losses, marched around Boston Common sporting a sign that read, "For a quarter I'll listen to your story of the hurricane."

Hurricane Agnes, 1972

Date	Location	Fatalities	Remarks
6/19–6/23	Florida, Virginia, Delaware, Pennsylvania	125	Mortality rate low compared to damages—among highest recorded for a hurricane.

"**G**et out. Get out now. If you have not evacuated Wilkes-Barre, get out now."

All day long, broadcasters in Pennsylvania's big Wyoming Valley urged residents of Wilkes-Barre and surrounding towns to leave the area, and the residents listened and left. The

results? In an area hit by the hurricane described as the "greatest natural disaster in the history of the United States," only six people were killed. And Wilkes-Barre is a large industrial city. People lost everything, were left homeless, and destitute. But many had survived because of an early-warning system that had worked. Other regions weren't so lucky, or so vigilant. Yet, in a way, the story of Wilkes-Barre is the story—and lesson—of Agnes.

The year began with talk of hurricanes. Early on, in January, Mrs. R. Bolton, former Vice President of the National Organization of Women, urged the United States to stop naming hurricanes after women. In fact, she wanted them to stop using the word "hurricanes" all together. Call them "himicanes" and name them after U.S. senators, she suggested.

Everybody laughed, except the Office of Emergency Preparedness in Washington. Mrs. Bolton hadn't solved any

Left: Shopping center in Kingston – Edwardsville area of Pennsylvania after the hurricane. Many local businessmen were ruined by Agnes. *Right*: You can't go home again after a hurricane like Agnes.

problems for them, but she had started folks thinking about hurricanes long before the season, which is just what the office director, G. A. Lincoln, considered important. A nine-state Preparedness Conference was organized and held in Miami, where Mr. Lincoln told 350 officials of the urgent need for a public-education program on hurricanes and their consequences.

The conference was held on May 9 and 10—and none too soon. On June 16, a big cyclonic storm was sighted off the Yucatan Peninsula, not yet a hurricane but strengthening.

On June 17, the storm had picked up force. It was now a hurricane heading for Florida. The Weather Bureau named her Agnes.

Everything about Agnes was early. Spawning tornadoes on the perimeter of her land-bound front, one man was killed and thirty-five injured in Florida on June 18—the day *before* Agnes arrived.

On June 19, people on the Florida peninsula were urged to evacuate. Agnes was heading straight for them, full-blown and tough, and would arrive that day. Smart Floridians were gone when she struck. She churned her way through the middle of the state—leaving twelve dead behind her—and headed inland to Virginia, Maryland, Pennsylvania, and New York, areas which were usually on the outer edges of the hurricane track. In some spots she weakened, her winds less than hurricane force. But by weakening, she released torrential rains as deadly as any wind. Bays and rivers, already swollen with spring rains, could not contain themselves and spilled over into river valleys with horrendous results. An immense infusion of fresh water destroyed most of the softshell clams in Chesapeake Bay and disrupted its ecology.

Worst hit were low-lying cities and towns situated along Pennsylvania's long, ambling Susquehanna River—Wilkes-Barre, Kingston, parts of Scranton. Harrisburg, the state capital, might just as well have been built in the middle of the Susquehanna River. The city was over its head in the swollen river's waters.

The cities and surrounding countryside were hit so hard that people were left almost entirely without material resources. It was a year or more before some of them would recover. Federal assistance, emergency-recovery funds, and tax abatements would be talked about and acted upon well into 1973. Comedian Bob Hope organized a telethon to raise funds

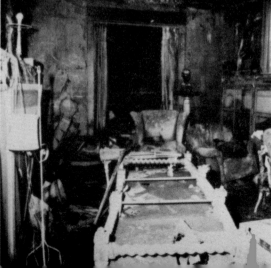

Above: Governor's mansion at Harrisburg, capital of Pennsylvania, surrounded by waters of the Susquehanna River. *Below*: Interior views of Riverside Drive homes in Wilkes-Barre, Pennsylvania.

Agnes' most bizarre trick was uprooting the dead from their resting places and transporting them 3 miles and farther. People found caskets and human remains in their backyards, and 550 bodies and caskets were reburied in a mass grave.

Wilkes-Barre wholesale district in flames—one of the dangers that accompanies all hurricanes.

for the victims of Agnes, with performers such as Zsa Zsa Gabor and David Janssen helping out.

Agnes, however, had left other wreckage in her wake—125 dead. However, far lesser storms have taken far more lives. Fair warning and the willingness of people to take heed — to value their lives above their goods and to believe the experts— probably saved more lives than any other circumstance connected with Agnes.

In almost every hurricane mentioned so far — with the exception of such surprise visitors as the hurricane of '38—the same could have been true. Perhaps it will be in the future.

The tornado is nature's most violent storm, usually small, but destructive, vicious, and spectacular. Nobody knows just how fast the whirling internal winds of the "twister" rotate. Every wind-measuring device laid in its path has been destroyed, but meteorologists estimate that it rotates at speeds of 200 to 450 miles per hour.

The tornado moves forward, backward, or sideways in unpredictable ways at speeds of 35 to 75 miles per hour, and sometimes rips along at 100. Fortunately, it is rarely more than 200 yards wide, usually travels a distance of only 5 to 20 miles, and lives a matter of mere minutes. But a town can be wiped out in a minute, and cities have been nearly demolished in less than five. Now and then a giant tornado is born, a mile wide and several hundred miles long, which can destroy in a couple of hours what an enormous hurricane might take days to destroy. Moreover, the conditions that create one tornado can give life to as many as a hundred at a time, and can cause the single twister to divide and multiply with terrific speeds. Such storms have covered more than a thousand miles.

The conditions needed to spawn a tornado can occur anywhere at any time. There is no state in the Union which has not had at least one tornado, no month of the year when a twister hasn't appeared somewhere. What happens is that a low-pressure area—a blanket of warm, humid air—is covered by a blanket of cold, dry air. The cold air keeps the warm air from rising. Similar conditions cause smog in some places, such as New York and California. However, sometimes the warm air finds a "hole" in the blanket of cold air and forces its way up as rapidly as possible. The faster it rises, the more turbulence it creates, until the tornado is born. Most of the time, it can actually be seen—a dark pendant cloud, wide at top, narrow at bottom, like a funnel. The dark cloud is the twister, and sometimes it hangs above the earth, sometimes it touches down. The damage is done where it touches down.

The center of the tornado is believed to be a hollow vacuum that sucks everything up into its vortex. The column of wind surrounding the vortex smashes every-

thing in its path. The tornado also does something to the air around it, besides filling it with incredible flying rubble. It creates an area of extreme low pressure. When it passes over a house in which all windows and doors are closed, the higher pressure inside the house causes the building to explode like a bomb. That happens to most houses during a tornado unless some smart person has opened the windows on the side of the house away from the storm.

Although tornadoes occur anywhere at any time, there is a region and a season for the biggest ones. The region is the South, primarily the Gulf states, and the Midwest. The season is spring, from its earliest stirrings in February to June. In February and March, the Gulf Coast starts to heat up and send out blankets of warm, humid air. But cold air is still moving down from the Rockies (both Canadian and American) and trapping the Gulf's hot sticky air beneath it. Thus Oklahoma and Illinois are the most dangerous places to be in spring. Not far behind are Arkansas, Alabama, and Texas. Georgia, Missouri, Tennessee, Mississippi, Indiana, Kentucky, Minnesota, Ohio, South Carolina, and Wisconsin are also beset by the deadly funnels, and everyone in Kansas sees a twister or two a year.

In this chapter we have listed only the big tornadoes that have taken the most lives. Yet every year, there are scores of tornadoes that take only one or two lives. In the past 50 years, we've had only 2 years in which less than 100 tornadoes raised their heads. In the same period, there was no year without at least 28 deaths, and usually, fatalities have been over 100. Of course, that makes no mention of damages to property.

Despite early-warning systems, tornadoes are unpredictable. Meteorologists may recognize the signs of a coming tornado, but there is no telling exactly where the funnel will strike. It may tear one town to pieces and leave a neighboring town unscathed. In tornado-torn regions, residents have built storm cellars in which to save life and limb, if not property. But it's necessary to be near the cellar when a tornado strikes, for it is the cat of the storm family and pounces suddenly and with fury.

Deadly funnel over Dallas, Texas, April 2, 1957.

TORNADOES

IMPORTANT AMERICAN TORNADOES

DATE	LOCATION	FATALITIES	REMARKS
1840 5/7	Natchez, Miss.	317	First of the really big tornadoes to be observed and accurately recorded.
1882 ?/?	Grinnell, Iowa	100	Town was a heap of firewood afterward. Every breeze caused fear for years to come.
1884 2/18	Southern U.S.	800	Six states contributed to death toll in the worst series of tornadoes in U.S. history.
1890 3/27	Louisville, Ky.	106	Tornado cut path 300 yards wide through city in minutes and traveled 75 miles beyond.
1896 5/27	St. Louis, Mo., East St. Louis, Ill.	306	Damage in St. Louis was 5 times that in East St. Louis, but deaths were about evenly divided.
1903 6/1	Gainesville, Ga.	98	Most of the town's large black population was away at a picnic that day, which helped to keep death toll down.
1913 3/23	Omaha, Nebr.	100	Omaha's Easter Sunday tornado left a trail of ruin ¼ mile wide, 5 miles long.
1916 6/5	Arkansas	100	Series of twisters.
1917 5/26	Mattoon and Charleston, Ill.	101	Single twister left trail 293 miles long, the longest *continuous* path on record. Tornadoes that have traveled farther have skipped over areas in broken paths.
1919 6/22	Fergus Falls, Minn.	59	Town demolished.
1920 3/28	South and Midwest	100	10 tornadoes broke out in Illinois, Indiana, Ohio, Michigan, Alabama, and Georgia.
1924 6/28	Sandusky and Lorain, Ohio	85	Started at Sandusky, hit Lorain 5 minutes later, tornado's trail was ¼ to ½ mile wide, 25 miles long.
1925 3/18	Missouri, Illinois, Indiana	689	Death and destruction were the work of one tornado, the worst single twister in U.S. history.
1926 11/25	Belleville to Portland, Ark.	53	An odd time for a big tornado in Arkansas, proving twisters of any size can strike any time, anywhere.
1927 4/12	Rock Springs, Tex.	74	Large part of town wiped out.
1927 5/9	Arkansas, Missouri	92	Hardest hit was Poplar Bluff, Mo., with 87 dead.
1927 9/29	St. Louis, Mo.	90	Tornado left path 300 yards wide, 5 miles long.
1932 3/21	Southern U.S.	362+	Five states stricken. Many of the missing were never accounted for.
1936 4/5–4/6	Tupelo, Miss., Gainesville, Ga.	455	Series of twisters raged through 6 Southern states. But Tupelo and Gainesville were hardest hit, with over 400 dead.
1938 9/29	Charleston, S.C.	75	Single twister.
1942 3/17	South and Midwest	111	Single twister.
1942 4/27	Rogers and Mayes Counties, Okla.	52	Oklahoma has had tornadoes every month of the year, day and night.
1944 6/23	Ohio, Pennsylvania, West Virginia, Maryland	150	Theory prevailed that tornadoes did not occur in hilly regions, until this one tore through the mountains of West Virginia and Pennsylvania.
1947 4/9	Texas, Oklahoma, Kansas	167	Tornado began in White Deer, Tex., and traveled 221 miles.
1949 1/3	Louisiana, Arkansas	58	New Year's tornado took everyone by surprise.
1952 3/21–3/22	Mississippi Valley	343	Series of 31 twisters tore through Arkansas, Tennessee, Missouri, Mississippi, Alabama, Kentucky, leaving 1,409 wounded, 3,591 homes destroyed.
1953 5/11	Waco, Tex.	114	Series of twisters struck city.
1953 6/8	Michigan, Ohio	142	Series of twisters rampaged through area.
1953 6/9	Massachusetts	92	Tornado struck Worcester vicinity; unusually large for area.
1955 5/25	Kansas, Missouri, Oklahoma, Texas	115	Series of tornadoes—80 dead in Udall, Kan., alone.
1965 4/11	Midwest	271	Indiana, Illinois, Michigan, and Wisconsin were all hit.
1966 3/3	Mississippi, Alabama	118	Series of tornadoes—58 dead in Jackson, Miss., alone.
1971 2/21	Mississippi	181	Delta region hit.
1974 4/3	South and Midwest	310+	Series of tornadoes hit 11 states, plus Windsor, Ontario, Canada.

Twisters, Twisters, Everywhere, 1884

Date	Location	Fatalities	Remarks
2/18	Southern U.S.	800	Six states contributed to death toll in the worst series of tornadoes in U.S. history.

It was more like an infernal visitation than a phenomenon of nature. Tornado gave birth to tornado. They split apart like giant demons in a nightmare, and they tore through six states, smashing town after town from the face of the earth. From Georgia, North Carolina, South Carolina, Alabama, Louisiana, and Tennessee came tales of instant destruction.

At Rockingham, North Carolina, the fury struck with such suddenness that no one had time to run. People were carried as much as 300 yards through the air, then smashed to the ground with killing force. The birds of the air, as well as all the chickens, were picked clean of feathers. The air was thick with flying fence rails and timbers, and some women were later found with heads pierced by fence rails. In a place where the tornado was 400 yards wide, "everything was swept off the face of the earth as by fire." It was all over in two or three minutes.

Oxmoore, Tennessee, was reduced to a woodpile. People were whirled through the air with their children clutched in their arms in a last effort to save them. A woman was found dead in a swamp, with a live infant on her bosom. "A most terrible tale," reported one newspaper, "comes from Jasper, in Pickens County, Georgia." A large number of children were in school when the teacher saw the "portending clouds." Understanding what the clouds portended, he dismissed his students, with orders to run for home immediately. On the way, the children spotted the funnel, and ran into an empty building, where they huddled together. The twister lifted the building and carried it away, while crashing timbers "killed and mangled the little ones." Jasper was bereft of almost all its youth.

The tornado that struck Columbus, Georgia, split and went off in two directions, east and north. Oxmoore, Tennessee, was one of the victims of the northern terror. The eastern tornado followed a course well known "ever since 1804." This "weather-beaten path" was from a half to three miles wide and went through three counties. The eastern tornado smashed its way along this route, then divided again and went on.

Macon, Georgia, on a "well-worn path" of its own, lost many people. Although its citizens were familiar with tornadoes and prepared for them, the twisters of 1884 struck with terrible force and suddenness.

All over South Carolina, plantations that had survived the

The devastation of Mt. Carmel, Illinois, 1877—not as bad as 1884, but typical of the destruction caused in small towns.

"The Great Tornado" of 1860 was the worst anyone had seen until 1884.

Twenty-two coffins in Camanche, Iowa, after "the Great Tornado" of 1860.

Date	Location	Fatalities	Remarks
5/27	St. Louis, Mo., East St. Louis, Ill.	306	Damage in St. Louis was 5 times that in East St. Louis, but deaths were about evenly divided.

The tornado that struck St. Louis in 1896 was like an uninvited, voracious monster who came to dinner —and six miles of St. Louis was dinner.

The day started badly. By noon, the sky was a filthy tell-tale gray, dark toward the earth, topped by lighter gray cumulus clouds. That must have given a tug to old-timers, who knew the signs well, but no one seemed inclined to utter the word *tornado*. A storm was coming, that much was conceded as the day grew darker. By late afternoon, store awnings were rolled up, windows were shuttered, and residents on the streets began seeking shelter in a casual way. On the Missouri River, steamers and ferries and small craft were made secure to their moorings and hatches were battened down. The crews and passengers remained aboard the vessels.

At first they got a storm. But what a storm! By 5:30, the wind was up to 80 miles per hour, enough to tear up telegraph poles, tear down chimneys, and rip off the brick facades so fashionable in the business district. If it hadn't been so early in the year, the residents might have sworn one of those Gulf hurricanes had finally made it all the way up to Missouri. In the river, waves surged as high as ocean surf, the rain came down in torrents, and great bolts of lightning rent the air, which was now cat's-eye green. The wind increased, up to 120 miles per hour, it was claimed. But it wasn't a tornado.

Although the violence of the storm was frightening, in less than half an hour it was over. The damages could be repaired; the injuries were not fatal. In relief, the people turned to each other—at least it had not been a tornado. Within ten minutes, their relief was shattered.

The people who lived at the western edge of the town near the railroad tracks heard it before they saw it. At 6:10 P.M., there was a roar like a thousand trains. People rushed to their windows. There it was, between the tracks of the Missouri-Pacific Railroad and the poorhouse. An old lady became the first fatality before the tornado even entered the city. One look and she died of fright.

The funnel began to move like a great elephant trunk, sucking up everything in its path. It moved east after knocking down the poorhouse. It picked up a horse, carried it a 100

Civil War were swept clean. At Bradley, every house was leveled to the ground. "The cyclone," reported one resident, "lasted only about a minute." Its path "passed within 100 yards of the track left by the cyclone of 1875."

Palmetto, Georgia, was struck by three tornadoes—at 2:00 P.M., 4:00 P.M., and 6:00 P.M. Most of the town was gone, and at the end of the day, survivors were pelted with hailstones the size of partridge eggs.

Out-of-town newspapers were slow to report the wide-spread destruction. "Telegraph wires are prostrated in almost every direction," reported the *New York Times*. "It is impossible to get trustworthy particulars." In short, they could scarcely believe their ears. But the reporters who made their way to the affected areas were willing to believe anything after they saw the destruction. "The loss of life and property have been incredible," one wrote. Clinton, Louisiana, was gone. Harris, Georgia, had suffered two cyclones, and was in almost as bad shape. Raleigh and Richmond, North Carolina, were devastated, Cave Spring, Georgia, had suffered a fearful loss of life. At Chester, North Carolina, two freight trains had been lifted from the tracks to the station platform. The townspeople considered leaving them there as a monument to the worst tornado they had ever seen. Reporters who had gone from state to state agreed it was the worst. No tornado or series of tornadoes had torn up as many thousands of miles of earth, obliterated as many towns, or killed as many people. To date, the twisters of 1884 still hold the record.

yards, and threw it down a well. It ripped up trees by the roots and sent them through the roofs of houses. The desirable residential section of Lafayette Park was stripped almost bare, and the twister played tricks with the houses that were left standing. Roofs were blown off huge homes, only to be replaced with little roofs lifted from small homes. At Compton Heights, great chunks torn from houses were refilled with airborne debris carried by the funnel. In a smart residential section where pianos were apparently the status symbols, 25 grand pianos were said to have flown through the air at one time, only to be dropped and turned into mahogany toothpicks.

Relentlessly, the funnel sped east to the business section. Down went the Exposition Building, the armory, the insane asylum, and the old city hospital. A rheumatic patient was lifted from his bed and set down—gently, he said—in the yard below. He hobbled to shelter.

In the old part of town, amid the crowded tenements, the twister did its cruelest work. There were no gentle settings-down here. Tenements were ripped to pieces. Some seemed to be taken apart brick by brick. Buildings that were occupied by 20 to 30 people became heaps in less than a second. At 6:20, the twister reached the Missouri River. It had finished with St. Louis.

Ruins of Martel and Tremont Hotels, St. Louis, where 40 people were killed on the spot. Clock in foreground stopped at 5:15 P.M.

Twister strikes Eads Bridge, St. Louis. Artist was an eyewitness of the scene.

THE ST. LOUIS TORNADO—DESTRUCTION IN ST. LOUIS.—[SEE PAGE 594.]

1. Anchor Hall, Jefferson and Park Avenues.   2. Church at Tenth and Soulard Streets.   3. On South Broadway.   4. Residence on Mississippi Avenue opposite Lafayette Park.   5. Mount Calvary Protestant Episcopal Church, Jefferson and Lafayette Avenues.   6. On South Broadway.   7. Ninth Street and Park Avenue—three persons were killed under these Trolley Cars.   8. Missouri Avenue west of Lafayette Park.

In ten short minutes, more than half of St. Louis was destroyed. A path of devastation, from a half to a mile wide and six miles long, showed where the funnel had been. The survivors could still see the frightful twister now, skipping across the river as it smashed sixteen steamships and other craft to bits. People rushed down to the shore to help the victims who had been thrown into the water. Luckily, the boats had all been moored near shore, and drowning fatalities were light.

The last the people of St. Louis saw of the twister, it was bearing down on their sister city of East St. Louis, across the river in Illinois. Dipping and bobbing, it tore out of sight.

The tornado had swept through St. Louis on a Wednesday. By Friday, nearby cities had sent in doctors, nurses, and whatever assistance they could. The city had begun to dig its way out of the rubble, and had recovered most of its dead — more than 150. St. Louis had also received news of its sister city across the river. The tornado had cut through East St. Louis in an erratic path some seven miles long, in less time than it had taken to get through St. Louis. It had behaved less dramatically and had caused about one-fifth the material damage, but it had claimed nearly the same number of lives before wandering out into the countryside to die. It was neither the most violent nor long-lived tornado on record, but for St. Louis and its sister city, it was too violent and too long-lived.

Left: Various scenes of the destruction in St. Louis. *Above:* Military patrols guard ruins against looters in St. Louis.

Monster Tornado, 1925

Date	Location	Fatalities	Remarks
3/18	Missouri, Illinois, Indiana	689	Death and destruction were the work of one tornado, the worst single twister in U.S. history.

At one o'clock on a Wednesday afternoon, Reynolds County, Missouri, was visited by a tornado that no one recognized as a tornado. Born close to the ground, with no pendant cloud or tell-tale funnel, it appeared to be a seething blackness — a fog of turbulent clouds and boiling winds that moved forward at 57 miles per hour. The black mass touched ground in one or two places, causing more terror than havoc, and moved east toward the Mississippi River.

The amorphous tornado dropped down before it reached the Mississippi River, killing 2 at Annapolis, 10 at Biehle, 1 at Altonburg. By the time it hit Cape Girardeau, killing 12, the air was filled with timbers and debris torn from towns it had already struck. The falling wreckage should have announced it was a tornado, but no warnings were sent ahead.

Traveling now at 59 miles per hour, the tornado moved into Illinois and descended on the city of Murphysboro. It demolished 60 per cent of the town—152 city blocks disappeared. Everything over 10 feet high was flattened, including the John Driver School with 200 students in session. Before the

Above: Schoolhouse wreckage in Murphysboro, where many children were killed. *Right:* Wiped-out section of West Frankfort.

people of Murphysboro could lift their heads, the tornado was in De Soto, where it tossed bodies a mile and a half out of town. The De Soto public school was destroyed with 125 students and teachers inside. Then the tornado hugged the ground all the way to West Frankfort, home of the Orient Mine, the largest coal mine in the United States. The mine was ruined, and much of the mining city with it, in less time than it takes to recite the pledge of allegiance.

By now, everyone knew it was a tornado, but still no warnings were sent to the towns in the path of the invading tornado. Perhaps there was no time or means to do so. The debris-filled black fog went on to Parrish, then drove through several small towns until it reached Mt. Carmel, Illinois, on the Indiana border. Without missing a beat, but increasing its forward speed to 68 miles per hour, it crossed over into Indiana and smashed through the cities of Griffin, Owensville, and Princeton. At last, 12 miles out of Princeton, 219 miles from where it began, the tornado died. It had taken only 3 hours and 18 minutes to get there, and had left a path of death and desolation that no single tornado has ever equaled in this country. In Murphysboro alone, 234 had been killed, many of them children. More than 100 perished in West Frankfort, 100 were dead in De Soto, 75 in Parrish and over 200 had died in less than half an hour in Indiana.

Eight tornadoes had been born on that fateful Wednesday, but it took only one to leave three states in shock for weeks.

Fires after the tornado added to Murphysboro's problems.

A Tale of Two Cities, 1936

Date	Location	Fatalities	Remarks
4/5– 4/6	Tupelo, Miss., Gainesville, Ga.	455	Series of twisters raged through 6 Southern states. But Tupelo and Gainesville were hardest hit, with over 400 dead.

SUNDAY NIGHT

It was a Sunday night, and Tupelo, Mississippi, was in a relaxed mood. In the fine residential section on the west side of the city, people lingered to enjoy the last of the day before the Monday rush began. In the streets, church-goers were strolling home from evening service. Others had come out to savor the spring evening. Among the strollers was Douglas Benoit, with his wife and three children. All at once, he heard a loud eerie noise. "It sounded like every whistle in Tupelo was blowing," he later said. He'd never heard a sound like it, but every instinct told him what it was. Seeing an open manhole in the street, he hurried his wife and children to it, pushed them down the hole, and jumped in after them—just in time. Overhead, the biggest tornado Tupelo had ever seen was ripping up the city.

It was 8:17 P.M. when Douglas Benoit heard that eerie sound. The twister, born a mile outside the western limits of the city, destroyed the suburb of Willis Heights on the way in. Local meteorologists stated that it was 400 yards wide, whirled at 300 to 400 miles per hour, and traveled forward at 5 to 6 miles a minute. In less than a second, it eradicated 15 blocks of Tupelo's best residential section. In the twinkling of an eye, the city's reservoir of drinking water was destroyed. Power lines were dead, and the city was in darkness. A large part of the business section was tossed into the middle of the main streets. With a last blow at outlying telephone wires, it scooted out of town—3 to 4 minutes after it had entered.

The city was in utter confusion. Some survivors didn't know what had hit them, and many were in deep shock. Great torrents of rain began to fall, which slowed down rescue operations considerably. Despite the downpour, which lasted all night, and the total darkness, the search for the injured and dead went on.

In the rich residential section, people looked in amazement at the total destruction. How had they survived? One woman seemed to know for sure why she was still alive. The wife of a wealthy publisher, her pride and joy was a very large refrigerator. As her walls came down around her, she grabbed

Gainesville, after tornado struck business district during morning rush hour.

Two-story house demolished in Tupelo.

Tupelo, Miss. 145

Funnel caught by amateur photographer.

her canary and took shelter in the refrigerator.

As the night wore on, the death toll climbed to 145. The number of injured was appalling — close to 1,500, and they were jammed into the city's one hospital. The final count of those killed on the spot by the twister was 216, but that did not include the victims outside of town, for the twister made its way 20 miles to Itawamba County before it died.

MONDAY MORNING

It was Monday morning, and Gainesville, Georgia, was caught up in the first-of-the-week rush. Nearly everyone in the city was on their way to work, mostly in the cotton mills in the main business area.

William Dozier, city clerk, was already at work. All at once, he thought he heard all the windows crashing in. He ran to look and was blown clear across the office. Outside, the biggest tornado Gainesville had ever seen was smashing its way across the city.

It was 8:45 A.M. when William Dozier heard the crashing windows. The twister, first spotted in the suburbs northwest of the city, struck Brennan College on its way in. Then, on the western outskirts of the city, there appeared not one but two tornadoes. They took up separate paths of destruction but came together again just west of Grove Street. Half a mile wide, the two-in-one tornado left a wake of rubble 14 blocks wide and 2½ miles long. It tossed cars in the air like toys and picked up running people, hurling them yards away. A large part of the business district was demolished. Giving a last whirl, it again split in two parts, which took separate paths out of town. It was 8:48 A.M. Just 3 minutes had passed.

No sooner had the twin tornadoes left town than fires began to break out in every quarter. Fire trucks were almost useless to do anything about them, for they could not be driven through the rubble that clogged the roads. In some areas, rescue workers had to race with fires in the search for survivors.

How many were lost in the fires is unknown, but the total number injured in every way was 934. Killed during the tornado were 185 persons. By week's end, the count had risen to 203. To handle the dead, the town's three biggest cotton mills had to be turned into temporary morgues.

Right: Remains of business district, Gainesvi

The Wright airplane flying at 75 feet one minute before the crash in which a passenger was killed and Orville Wright injured. *Below:* The wrecked airplane, showing broken propeller at left.

There are two ways things stay in the air. The first is the way birds do it: powered flight by a creature that is heavier than air—called "aviation," or heavier-than-air flight. The second is the way that things lighter than air stay up in the air for a long time. As early as the eleventh century, men were saying that if you could fill a large globe with some gaseous substance that was lighter than air, you could fly. This was called "aerostation," or lighter-than-air flight. But the substance capable of keeping a globe afloat in the air remained a mystery until 1782.

In that year, two French brothers, the Montgolfiers, noticed that smoke, or "vapors," rose from a fire. If you could inflate a big cloth globe with these vapors, maybe it would rise, too. It did, and stayed up for ten long minutes. Hot air, it seemed, was lighter than cool; but when the air cooled, the globe came down.

French physicist J. A. C. Charles about the same time filled a varnished silk globe with lighter-than-air hydrogen gas. It was a great success and rose 3,000 feet, but when it came down, 15 miles from Paris, frightened farmers tore it to pieces. This caused the French king to issue to his people a description of the make and purpose of balloons.

By the twentieth century, the Industrial Revolution and advances in science had given us power with the engine. The wind-driven balloon was joined by the power-driven dirigible.

People were still experimenting with heavier-than-air craft—the glider, it was called, with a streamlined body and stationary wings that rode on air currents. Without an engine, however, it could not fly from New York to Paris. In 1903, the Wright brothers successfully attached an engine, and the airplane was born. In World War I the plane really came into its own. Smaller than the dirigible, it was also much faster, just right for hit-and-run bombardment from the skies.

After the war, although the world went plane crazy, the dirigible still ruled the skies as a long-run passenger carrier. It was a dirigible, in fact, that started the first regularly scheduled flights between Europe and America. Still, there were problems. Most dirigibles were inflated with hydrogen, highly explosive, and fire was always a danger. There was also helium, a non-flammable, lighter-than-air gas, but many people were frightened by the thought of how many would be killed in one dirigible crash. At that time, a plane might carry 20 persons; a dirigible was likely to have 70 passengers aboard, which seemed too many lives to lose in one accident.

Ironically, after World War II and the "victory through air power," the size of planes grew steadily. In the 1950's, planes began to carry more than 50 passengers. Today we lose from 70 to over 100 persons in a single crash, but have never dreamed of abandoning the airplane. There is constant talk, moreover, of making planes big enough to transport as many as 500 people in a single flight. True, planes are safer than they used to be. There is greater quality control in building the vehicles, and our increasing knowledge of the skies gives us more control over actual flight. But life being what it is, the worst air disaster may still be in the future.

AIR CRASHES

149

IMPORTANT AMERICAN AIR DISASTERS

DATE	LOCATION	FATALITIES	REMARKS
1933 4/4	New Jersey coast	72	U.S. dirigible *Akron II* crashed. Biggest air disaster of its time.
1937 5/6	Lakehurst, N.J.	36	German dirigible *Hindenburg* caught fire and exploded. It was the end of the dirigible as a commercial craft.
1945 7/28	New York City	13	U.S. Army B-25 ripped into Empire State Building.
1947 6/13	Leesburgh, Va.	50	Pennsylvania Central DC-4 crashed into mountain.
1947 10/24	Brice Canyon, Utah	52	United DC-6 crashed into hillside.
1949 6/7	Puerto Rico	54	U.S. Strato Freight crashed in water.
1949 11/1	Washington, D.C.	55	Bolivian fighter plane collided with Eastern DC-4.
1950 6/24	Lake Michigan	58	Northwest Airlines DC-4 exploded over Lake Michigan.
1951 3/23	North Atlantic	53	U.S. Air Force plane wreckage found off Ireland.
1951 6/30	Rocky Mountain National Park	50	United DC-6 crashed.
1951 8/24	Decoto, Calif.	50	United DC-6B crashed.
1951 12/16	Elizabeth, N.J.	56	Nonscheduled flight plunged into river after take-off from Newark.
1952 4/11	San Juan, P.R.	52	Pan Am DC-4 crashed.
1952 11/23	Elmendorf Air Force Base, Alaska	52	U.S. Air Force plane crashed.
1952 12/20	Moses Lake, Wash.	87	U.S. Air Force C-124 crashed.
1953 6/18	Tokyo, Japan	129	C-124 crashed; biggest peacetime Air Force disaster.
1953 7/12	Wake Island	58	Nonscheduled plane plunged into Pacific.
1955 3/22	Honolulu, Hawaii	66	U.S. Navy plane hit cliff.
1955 8/11	Edelweiler, West Germany	66	Two U.S. Air Force planes collided.
1955 10/6	Laramie, Wyo.	66	United DC-4 crashed into mountains.
1956 6/20	Atlantic, south of New York City	74	Venezuelan Super Constellation went into ocean.
1956 6/30	Grand Canyon, Ariz.	127	TWA Super Constellation collided with United DC-7.
1957 8/11	Quebec, Canada	79	Maritime Central DC-4 charter plane crashed.
1959 2/3	New York City	65	American Airlines Electra plunged into East River.
1960 1/18	Richmond, Va.	50	Capitol Viscount crashed into swampy ravine.
1960 2/25	Rio de Janeiro, Brazil	61	U.S. Navy transport collided with Real DC-3.
1960 3/17	Tell City, Ind.	63	Northwest Airlines Electra exploded in flight.
1960 10/4	Boston, Mass.	62	Eastern Airlines Electra fell into harbor.
1960 12/16	Staten Island, N.Y.	135	United DC-8 and TWA Super Constellation collided over Staten Island. All lost in worst air disaster in U.S. history.
1961 2/15	Berg, Belgium	73	Sabena Boeing 707 crashed into lettuce field. Lost 18 members of U.S. Olympic Figure-skating Team.
1961 9/1	Chicago, Ill.	78	TWA Constellation crashed into field outside city.
1961 9/10	Shannon, Ireland	83	President Airlines DC-6 charter crashed.
1961 11/8	Richmond, Va.	77	Chartered Imperial Airlines Constellation crashed in woods.
1962 3/1	New York City	95	American Airlines Boeing 707 plunged into Jamaica Bay.
1963 6/3	Pacific, off Alaska	101	Northwest Airlines DC-7 charter crashed.
1963 12/8	Elkton, Md.	81	Pan Am Boeing 707 crashed in field.
1964 2/25	New Orleans, La.	58	Eastern Airlines DC-8 crashed into Lake Pontchartrain.

DATE	LOCATION	FATALITIES	REMARKS
1964 3/1	Lake Tahoe, Calif.	85	Nonscheduled carrier plane crashed.
1964 5/11	Clark Air Force Base, Philippines	75	U.S. military transport crashed.
1965 2/6	Atlantic, near Kennedy Airport, N.Y.	84	Eastern Airlnes DC-7B went into ocean.
1965 6/25	El Torro, Calif.	84	Military plane hit mountain.
1965 11/8	Cincinnati, Ohio	58	American Airlines Boeing 727 crashed into hillside.
1966 4/22	Ardmore, Okla.	84	Military-chartered Electra crashed.
1967 1/27	Cape Kennedy, Fla.	3	Apollo spacecraft burned on launching pad, killing three astronauts.
1967 7/19	Hendersonville, N.C.	82	Piedmont Boeing 727 collided with private Cessna 310.
1967 11/20	Cincinnati, Ohio	70	TWA Convair 880 crashed near airport.
1969 9/9	Shelbyville, Ind.	83	Allegheny DC-9 collided with student pilot's plane.
1970 11/14	Huntington, W.Va.	75	Southern Airways DC-9 crashed in mountains.
1971 9/4	Juneau, Alaska	111	Alaska Airlines Boeing 727 crashed into mountains.
1972 12/29	Miami, Fla.	100	Eastern Airlines Lockheed Tristar crashed on approach to Miami International Airport.
1973 7/31	Boston, Mass.	89	Delta Airlines jetliner crashed in heavy fog at Logan Airport.
1974 1/27	Pago Pago, American Samoa	96	Pan Am Boeing 707 crashed.
1974 9/11	Charlotte, N.C.	69	Eastern Airlines DC-9 crashed while landing.
1974 9/8	Ionian Sea, off Greece	80	U.S.-bound TWA airliner plunged into sea.
1975 6/24	Kennedy Airport, N.Y.	112	Boeing 727 crashed trying to land, apparently battling wind shear. Worst civilian single-craft crash in U.S. history.

Early attempts at aviation frequently came to grief.

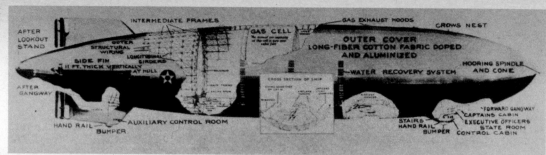

Diagram of the *Akron*.

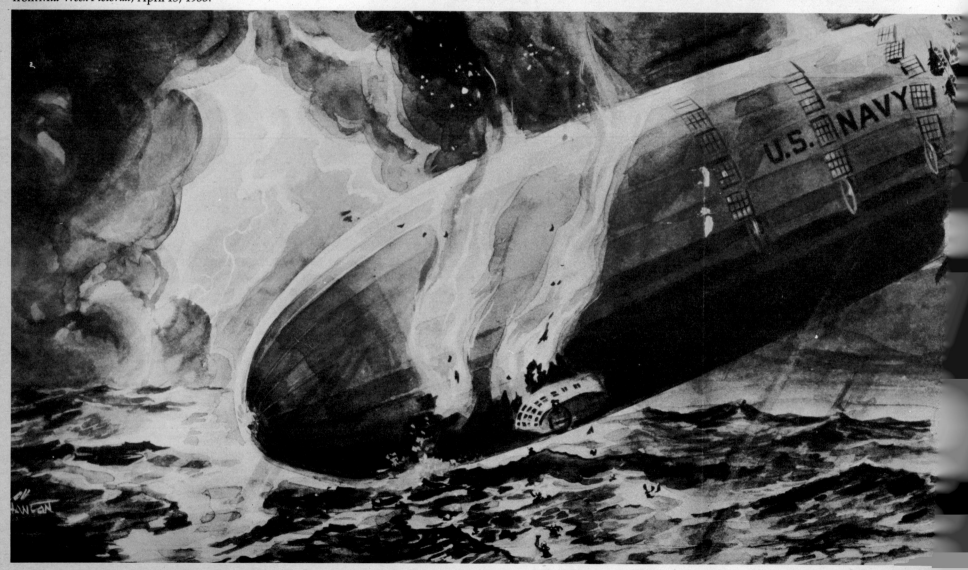

Artist's conception of the crash of the *Akron*, from *Mid-Week Pictorial*, April 15, 1933.

"Akron II," 1933

Date	Location	Fatalities	Remarks
4/4	New Jersey coast	72	U.S. dirigible *Akron II* crashed. Biggest air disaster of its time.

Reprinted from the *Booklyn Daily Eagle*, April 4, 1933:

A NEWS REPORT

U.S.S. *Akron*, largest airship in the world, crashed at sea at 12:30 A.M. today, about 25 miles off Barnegat, New Jersey, with 76 men on board.

Only five men have been found. Two of the five are dead. This makes the crash by far the greatest disaster in the whole of lighter-than-air flight — a history which has been spotted by major tragedies.

Coast Guard vessels, which sped to the rescue, reported that the *Akron* had been struck by lightning and caught fire. The Navy Department so reported to President Roosevelt.

Lieut.-Commander H. V. Wiley, executive officer of the *Akron* and one of the three known survivors, in a later wireless, made no mention of a lightning bolt hitting the craft or of its catching fire.

Officers of the Third Naval District in New York discounted the earlier reports.

The definitely established facts are that the *Akron* was caught in a violent electrical storm. With rudder control torn away, the ship descended to the water and was demolished by the impact.

Chairman Vinson of the House Naval Affairs Committee asserted that no more large airships would be constructed in the United States.

It was the worst American air disaster up to that time, and may remain the worst dirigible catastrophe on record. But was it some basic flaw in the concept of lighter-than-air flight that made the United States abandon almost all development in this area of aviation? Or was it the passenger-carrying capacity of the big ships, making any accident a major tragedy, that scared Americans off?

By 1933, the heavier-than-air craft, or airplane, was a common sight. They were faster than dirigibles, there were lots more of them, but on a one-to-one basis, they were just as dangerous. They crashed into fields, mountains, and oceans with alarming frequency. But they were smaller; as mentioned before, it was a rare plane that could carry more than 20 passengers at a time. And although 20 people killed in a plane crash was tragedy enough, 72 killed at once was intolerable.

The Germans thought otherwise. They hadn't had a dirigible disaster in ten years and they believed the floating behemoths were the coming thing in passenger transportation. And so Germany set out to build the biggest dirigible in the world.

The "Hindenburg," 1937

Date	Location	Fatalities	Remarks
5/6	Lakehurst, N.J.	36	German dirigible *Hindenburg* caught fire and exploded. It was the end of the dirigible as a commercial craft.

She was the queen of the skies. She could carry more passengers and crew than any airship before her. The biggest and most elegant dirigible ever designed, she had three decks, a ballroom, dining rooms, lounges, reading rooms, writing rooms, quarters for the crew, and 31 luxurious staterooms built to accommodate 72 passengers in high comfort. She was a flying luxury liner, and everybody wanted to travel on her. There was always a waiting list.

VOL. 10—NO. 240   Telephone: ATlantic 6100   MORNING, MAY 7, 1937.   ★ ★ ★ ★ ★   THREE CENTS

HINDENBURG CRASH KILLS 41 AFTER BLAST OVER LAKEHURST

Bursts Into Flames Landing At Lakehurst   MYSTERY EXPLOSION

She wasn't American, but the United States, specifically the mooring station at Lakehurst, New Jersey, was part of her regular run, and American citizens were among her regular customers. After the *Akron* disaster, the United States had officially given up the dirigible as a national interest. But this new airship was the realization of a dream that for years had been very important to America—to the whole world, in fact. She was the first regularly scheduled transoceanic flight to carry passengers, a landmark in commercial travel.

If she was important to the world, she was certainly important to the country that gave her life, Germany, and to the image of the people who ran that country, the Nazis. They loved being ahead of the whole world, and at one point it was even suggested that the airship be named the *Adolph Hitler*.

Hitler declined the honor. Air travel was still risky, and whatever went up often came down with a crash. If anything went wrong, the world might take it as an omen. And so she was named the *Hindenburg,* for the German statesman President Paul von Hindenburg, who, ironically, only four years before had done battle with the Nazis over their treatment of the Jews. But he was dead now, and did not care about omens.

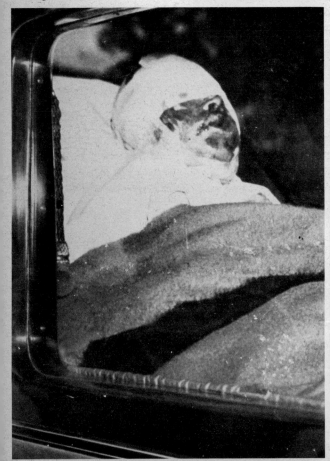

Rescue crew removing body of victim. *Below left:* Seriously burned survivor. *Below right:* Thirteen-year-old boy of *Hindenburg* who survived disaster.

Despite Hitler's fears, the *Hindenburg* appeared to be very safe — safer than an ocean liner, some swore. She made many scheduled flights between Germany and South America, and her regular trips between Frankfurt and Lakehurst, New Jersey, were without mishap.

During the late winter of 1936, she was taken out of commission and refitted so she could take on more passengers. There was talk of engine trouble her first time out, on a kind of propaganda flight around Germany. But everything was examined and adjusted. She was in perfect shape for her first transatlantic run of 1937.

She started out for Lakehurst on May 3, booked to capacity. The trip was smooth as silk with no hint that anything was wrong—right up to the moment she was due to arrive.

It was early in the morning, on December 6. At Lakehurst, a small crowd began to gather in the pouring rain. The *Hindenburg* was due in at 8:00 A.M., and friends, relatives, and reporters had arrived early to meet the passengers.

Everybody scanned the sky, hoping for a glimpse of her. Eight o'clock came without a sign of the *Hindenburg*.

Authorities at Lakehurst told everyone not to worry. Her captain, Max Pruss, had sent a radio message. He could see storm clouds brewing and was going to circle for a while until the winds and rain abated.

The crowd murmured approvingly. Small wonder the Germans hadn't had a dirigible accident in fourteen years. Small wonder the *Hindenburg* was queen of the skies.

By late afternoon, it was still raining and the crowd was becoming restless. Some of them had been there all day. Others had come and gone several times. The airship was more than nine hours late. She'd been in the air for over seventy hours. Where was she?

By early evening, it had stopped raining, and the Lakehurst authorities got word that Captain Pruss was bringing in the ship.

Then, suddenly, at 7:00 P.M., she was in view — huge and silver and glistening—a stately queen floating to her mooring.

Herbert Morrison reported, in what turned out to be one of the most famous broadcasts ever made, "The *Hindenburg* is floating down like a feather, ladies and gentlemen. The ropes have dropped and they have been taken hold of by a number of men in the field."

Inside the dirigible, the passengers could see the crowd waving and smiling. They waved back. There was a sudden soft thump — just the ship hitting the mooring station, the passengers thought. And then they saw everyone on the field running away from the ship!

Not everyone outside the ship saw it at first. But Herbert Morrison had. He was right in the middle of his smooth commentary, telling the folks at home that "the back motors of the ship are holding just enough to keep it . . . it's broken into flames! It's floating! This is terrible!"

The fire seemed to come out of the tail, and someone in the crowd yelled, "Run!" The crowd, seeing the tail aflame, ran. Then suddenly there was an explosion.

"This is one of the worst catastrophes in the world!" lamented Morrison, practically weeping into the microphone. "Oh, the humanity and all the passengers."

Passengers began leaping from the ship to the ground. One man, a professional acrobat, made the jump safely. "Aren't I lucky?" he later asked. Others weren't. Some jumped to their death as the *Hindenburg* rose high above her mooring. By the time she came back down, it was too late for the others.

Some of the crew who jumped clear began helping passengers, hurting themselves in the process. One crewman was so badly burned during his rescue maneuvers, he would later beg someone to shoot him because he couldn't stand the pain. Mercifully, he died.

The flames from the *Hindenburg* shot 500 feet up in the air, and within 32 seconds, she'd been incinerated.

"I told you, it's a mass of smoking wreckage," reported Morrison. "Honest, I can hardly breathe. Folks, I'm going to have to stop for a moment because I've lost my voice. This is the worst thing I've ever witnessed."

By the time it was over, 36 people were dead and at least a score were injured. Dead also was the fate of the dirigible as a practical passenger-carrying aircraft. The news, the publicity, and the terrible newsreel films caused panic to the public.

And other things were happening to make the production of the big dirigible impractical. The Germans needed small, fast, heavier-than-air fighter planes. They were getting ready to fight a war.

Coffins with 26 of the 35 victims, lined up on a pier in New York ready for mass funeral services. All the caskets are covered with Nazi flags except for one with an American flag. Caskets were shipped, after services, to Germany.

...MTON PRESS

SATURDAY EVENING, JULY 28, 1945.

★★★

City Edi[tion]
Complete Financ[ial]

PRICE FOUR

BOMBER STRIKES, FIRES EMPIRE STATE BUILDING

19 Known Dead, 3 Elevators Fall 80 Floor[s]

Attlee Selects Aides In New Labor Regime, Then Speeds to Big 3

Potsdam—(AP)—Prime Minister Clement R. Attlee and Ernest Bevin, his newly appointed foreign secretary, arrived at Potsdam tonight from Britain for an immediate resumption of the Big 3 Conference.

Mr. Bevin said shortly before his appointment that he thought "blunt Lancashire" better than "polished diplomatic phrases" in present international relations.

Mr. Attlee himself took the posts of minister of defense and first lord of the treasury, which were also held by Mr. Churchill.

Herbert Morrison, new lord president of the council and Mr. Attlee's principal understudy, was left in charge of the country.

Mr. Attlee and Mr. Bevin departed after the six senior members of the Attlee cabinet, named last night, took the oath from King George VI.

Mr. Morrison and Mr. Bevin, longtime trade union leader, are destined to play principal roles in the government that ousted Mr. Winston Churchill.

Mr. Morrison will devote most of his time to leading labor's 2 to 1 majority in Commons.

Mr. Attlee's selection of the six labor party stalwarts as the nucleus of his cabinet was hailed by the British labor press as constituting a "new deal" in British government.

Chief among the new cabinet members is blunt-talking Mr. Bevin, 64, bespectacled, 250-pound

trade union leader who succeeds Anthony Eden as Britain's foreign secretary.

Other cabinet selections were: Hugh Dalton, chancellor of the exchequer; Mr. Morrison, lord president of the Council and leader in the House of Commons; Arthur Greenwood, lord privy seal; Sir Stafford Cripps, president of the board of trade; Sir William Allen Jowitt, lord chancellor.

Revamped Big 3 Near Final Decision

Potsdam—(U.P)—The Big 3 were scheduled to resume their conferences today, with British Prime Minister Clement Attlee replacing the defeated Winston Churchill. Indications were that the meetings have reached the final decision

Congress Will Control Use of Troops--Truman

Washington—(AP)—President Truman made known today he will seek majority-vote approval of both the House and Senate for any military agreements reached under the United Nations Charter.

The alternative would be sion of a

Job Guarantee Is Ord[ered]

New York—A B-25 bomber crashed and exploded in the seventy-eighth floor of the Empire State Building today and the upper part of the tallest building in the world instantly became a blazing inferno for hundreds of office workers perched 1,000 feet above the street. The plane was lost in a fog when it struck. It broke into a giant, spectacular burst of flame. The explosion rocked midtown Manhattan. Two hours later police reported at least 19 known dead. Flames raged out of control in six floors of the building for 40 minutes. The plane struck the north side of the building, penetrated a wing of the floor, destroyed everything in its path and went out the south wing of the building. Part of it landed on the roof of the 12-story Waldorf Building on 33d Street. Six of the dead were reported to be soldiers, some of them presumably members of the plane's crew of five. Only the fact that it was Saturday morning, when many offices are closed, prevented a major catastrophe. The seventy-eighth floor was unoccupied. In the War Relief Service of the National Catholic Welfare Council on the seventy-ninth, several persons were killed.

Three elevators crashed from the eightieth floor. Glass and debris rained down.

Nine bodies were reported found on the 79th floor. Three bodies were taken from two of the fallen elevators. The third was empty.

By the United Press

An enormous crowd gathered in the street and the largest amount of fire fighting apparatus ever assembled in New York City was rushed out in four fire alarms. Glass and debris continued to shower down for almost an hour.

The 34th Street foyer of the building was converted into an emergency receiving Station. Bellevue Hospital sent all available doctors, nurses and disaster equipment.

Planes Cowling Is Stuck in Building

First reporters to fight their way up past the smoke clouded sixty-ninth floor found the cowling of the plane still stuck to the side of the building. The point where the plane struck was near a bank of 10 elevators. All floors from the 69th to the 79th were littered with debris. About 20 feet inside the window nearest where the plane struck lay one of the B-25's engines and half a propeller. A fragment of a propeller was imbedded in a wall.

Office windows were shattered 10 floors up.

Office windows were shattered 10 floors below the seventy-eighth story men, police, priests, doctors down the stairs

HOW GR[EAT]

Empire State Building, 1945

Date	Location	Fatalities	Remarks
7/28	New York City	13	U.S. Army B-25 ripped into Empire State Building.

Lieutenant Colonel William Franklin Smith, Jr., had certainly done his share of flying in the past few days. Two days earlier, he'd flown his B-25 from Sioux Falls, South Dakota, to Newark, New Jersey. The next day, he took off for Bedford, Massachusetts, with Staff Sergeant Christopher S. Domitrovich for company. The following morning, the two started back for Newark, with enlisted Navy man Albert Perna, who was hitching a ride aboard the U.S. Army bomber.

It was a little past 9:30 on a very foggy morning when they reached La Guardia Airport, where they planned to head west across Manhattan for Newark. They contacted La Guardia's control tower to check weather conditions.

The tower told Smith to put down as soon as possible. The fog was really bad, visibility close to zero. And the tower man added, "I can't even see the Empire State Building."

Minutes later, according to witnesses, Lieutenant Colonel Smith and company saw the Empire State Building—right in front of their plane! Smith tried desperately to climb, but never got past the seventy-ninth floor. With an explosion that rocked New York for two miles around, the plane crashed through the building between the seventy-eighth and seventy-ninth floors.

On Thirty-fourth Street, thousands of New Yorkers saw the upper reaches of the Empire State Building burst into flames. Stunned, they watched a huge company of fire-fighters battle uncontrollable flames for forty minutes. It was New York's most bizarre air disaster—nobody doubted that. It was one day short of being far worse.

Smith had taken his fatal flight on a Saturday, when most of the offices in the huge skyscraper were empty. The fog had kept tourists from taking the excursion to the observation tower, where little could be seen, anyway. (One die-hard group that had gone up was led to safety down flights of stairs by a cool-headed tour guide.) The seventy-eighth floor, hardest hit, was totally empty. But on the seventy-ninth floor, a group of women and girls were busy working for the Catholic Welfare Conference, and in other offices individual men had come in to clean up the week's tasks. Ten of them would not live to work another day.

Most of the victims were women from the Welfare Conference. One man, working in another office on the same floor, was found dead on a ledge seven stories below. The three men in the plane had died on impact. Thirteen dead.

Despite their astonishment, most New Yorkers could remember predicting this very catastrophe. The building was so high, the seaport city so frequently shrouded in fog, it was bound to happen.

After it did happen, something was done. Today, a huge beacon lights up the skies high above the building, penetrating fog and darkness, and few planes fly directly over mid-Manhattan.

Left: The B-25 Bomber that crashed into the Empire State Building left a huge hole, 18 feet wide by 27 feet high, in the 78th and 79th floors. *Right:* A section of the plane landed on Thirty-third Street.

Collision Over Staten Island, 1960

Date	Location	Fatalities	Remarks
12/16	Staten Island, N.Y.	135	United DC-8 and TWA Super Constellation collided over Staten Island. All lost in worst air disaster in U.S. history.

"I remember looking out of the plane window, at the snow below, covering the city. It looked like a picture out of a fairy book. It was a beautiful sight."

Eleven-year-old Stephen Baltz was aboard a United Airlines

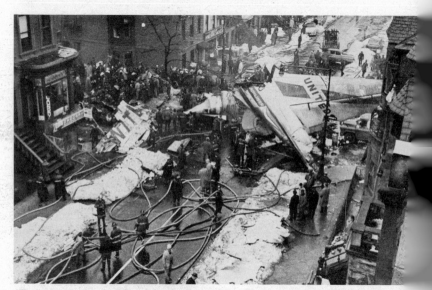

The United DC-8 lies in the middle of Seventh Avenue, Brooklyn, after the collision. The TWA plane crashed in Staten Island.

Tail section of the United DC-8 that crashed in Brooklyn after colliding mid-air with a TWA Super Constellation.

DC-8, headed for New York City's Kennedy Airport.* Along with seventy-six fellow passengers and a crew of seven, Stephen had come from Chicago to see the sights of New York during the Christmas season. To add to the enchantment that December 16, it had begun to snow long before Stephen's plane approached the city, and by the time his plane was over Staten Island, only minutes away from landing, the city was blanketed in white, its lights set off like jewels. It was Stephen's first—and last—sight of New York.

"Suddenly, there was an explosion. The plane started to fall and people started to scream. I held on to my seat and then the plane crashed. That's all I remember."

Argosy magazine, like some few other publishers in New York, had their printing done at a plant in Ohio. On December 16, the staff members were waiting impatiently for a shipment of proof to arrive. If they could read it and get it out fast, the magazine could go to press well before Christmas and they'd all have a little free time to finish their shopping and to celebrate. All day they waited, then suddenly they could no longer think about their proof. A news bulletin had come in. Two planes had collided in mid-air over Staten Island. One was a United Airlines DC-8, the other a TWA Super Constellation.

Later they learned that the TWA jet, headed for New York's La Guardia Airport, was coming from Ohio with their proof aboard. All they knew then was that the ill-fated TWA jet had fallen into New York Bay, which separates Staten Island from Brooklyn, and that all 43 of its crew and passengers had been lost.

The DC-8 jet had crashed into a Brooklyn street, killing 8 pedestrians and narrowly missing a school with 1,700 children in attendance. All passengers and crew aboard the DC-8 were dead, except for one — the little boy named Stephen. He'd been thrown from the plane, and was suffering from severe burns and injuries. His condition was critical.

The collision had taken place on a Friday. On Monday, *Argosy* magazine got its proof, with apologies. The printed material had been aboard the TWA jet from Ohio. It had been locked in a steel box and had survived the crash.

The staff stared at the proofs in amazement and horror. When they'd left work on Friday, the death toll had been 134. Over the weekend it had grown to 135. Little Stephen had fought hard but unsuccessfully for his life. A loss of 135 lives, and the proofs were in perfect condition. The staff could certainly get the magazine out on schedule and have time for shopping, but at the moment, it just didn't seem to matter.

*Kennedy Airport was then named New York International Airport and was familiarly called Idlewild, the place where it was located outside the city.

Berg, Belgium, 1961
U.S. Figure-skating Team Tragedy

Date	Location	Fatalities	Remarks
2/15	Berg, Belgium	73	Sabena Boeing 707 crashed into lettuce field. Lost 18 members of U.S. Olympic Figure-skating Team.

She lived in Berg, Belgium, just three miles out of Brussels. She had seen many planes before, but this one, flying so low, was different. She couldn't take her eyes from it.

"I could see people looking at me from inside the plane and gesturing," she told a reporter. "I held my hand up to them. Then the plane stopped — right in the air! It was as if it were hanging there on something. The whole plane was shaking, as if struggling to get moving again. But something was holding it back. Then, an amazing thing happened. The plane began to point to the sky. The whole nose began to rise upward. In a few seconds, the plane was pointed straight toward heaven. Then it fell like a stone—straight down. I could see the people inside waving at me. I waved back."

In less than a second, she was waving at nothing. The Sabena Airlines jet hit the ground and exploded into flames, spewing out its contents like so much kindling.

The 18 members of the U.S. figure-skating team boarding the ill-fated Belgian airliner.

Within minutes, help arrived, but it was too late. All 73 persons aboard the American-built Boeing 707 were charred, lifeless bodies. The plane had crashed into a lettuce field, trapping two farmers in the burning debris. One was killed. His was the only immediately identifiable body.

The take-off from New York had been a happy one. Aside from the usual contingent of tourists who were delighted to be on holiday, there was a young pregnant woman, on her way to join her G.I. husband in Europe, two men about to have long-overdue reunions with aging parents, and vacationing Belgians, glad to be going home (the plane was bound for Brussels).

But happiest and most spirited of the lot were eighteen young people. They were the American Figure-skating Team —champions every one—and America's hope for the upcoming 1964 Olympics. They were on their way to Prague, Czechoslovakia, for the world skating championships. There were Laurie and William Hickox, a brother-and-sister team; Ila and Ray Hadley, also brother and sister; and Patricia and Robert Dineen, husband and wife. There was an entire ice-skating family aboard. Mrs. Maribel Vinson Owen, who'd won the U.S. figure-skating title nine times, was accompanying her champion daughters to Prague. Daughter Maribel, 20, had just won a doubles title with her partner Dudley Richards, also on the plane. Laurence Owen, 16, was the North American figure-skating champion, and a sure candidate for top honors in the 1964 Olympics. Everybody said so, but no one could have known what would happen in a lettuce field in Belgium.

What went wrong with the Sabena jetliner was never determined. All that the Brussels authorities learned was that something had gone wrong before the plane approached the airport. During the last twenty minutes of the flight, the pilot had not made contact with the airport, extraordinary on even the most routine flights, and they could only guess that he couldn't make contact.

The first they saw of the plane, it came careening in over the airfield, low, but at full speed. Then banking crazily, it overshot the field entirely, winding up in Berg, three miles away.

The description given by the woman at Berg indicates that the pilot was trying desperately—by his fingernails practically — to climb and gain altitude. As for the passengers who gestured to her, were they waving or appealing for help? Were they told they were in an emergency situation?

Several of the bodies were found crouched between seats, the usual emergency position. Others were found embracing, as though to comfort each other against the common enemy.

Apollo Spacecraft, 1967

Date	Location	Fatalities	Remarks
1/27	Cape Kennedy, Fla.	3	Apollo spacecraft burned on launching pad, killing three astronauts.

It was the biggest irony in the history of the American space program. Men had been sent into orbited flight sixteen times and had returned without a broken fingernail. On January 27, 1967, no space flight had been planned. It was just a routine test session, with astronauts who'd been through the real thing.

Colonel Virgil "Gus" Grissom had made two space flights, the first American astronaut to do so. He was looking forward to his third launching, aboard the first manned Apollo flight, which was due to go off on February 27. That's what this test was all about — another in a series of simulated launchings aboard the Apollo.

Lieutenant Colonel Edward White had been the first American to walk in space. Tethered to his craft, he'd cavorted outside the ship, saying, "It's fun. I'm not coming in." Like Gus, he anticipated being one of the first astronauts to man the Apollo.

Lieutenant Roger Chaffee, the rookie of the group, had wanted to be an astronaut from the first time he'd ever heard the word. In a month he'd be going up with the big kids. Like Gus and Ed, he'd been through the simulated launchings before, and all were totally familiar with the Apollo. When they entered the capsule, at 1:00 P.M., it was as if they were going to their rooms, without fear or even excitement. They donned their inflatable suits and did their usual tasks until countdown time, when they strapped themselves to their couches.

At 6:30, countdown should have started. But something delayed it for a moment—and suddenly all hell broke loose. From inside the capsule came a cry: "Fire aboard spacecraft!"

Everyone ran for the hatch, to let the men out, but the heat drove them back. They watched, not daring to imagine what was happening inside.

Six minutes later, the hatch opened by itself. "The rest," as one news publication put it, "was silence." The Apollo space capsule was destroyed and the space program lost three of its most talented engineers and pilots — on the launching pad. They have yet to lose one in space.

Left to right: Virgil Grissom, Ed White, and Roger Chaffee

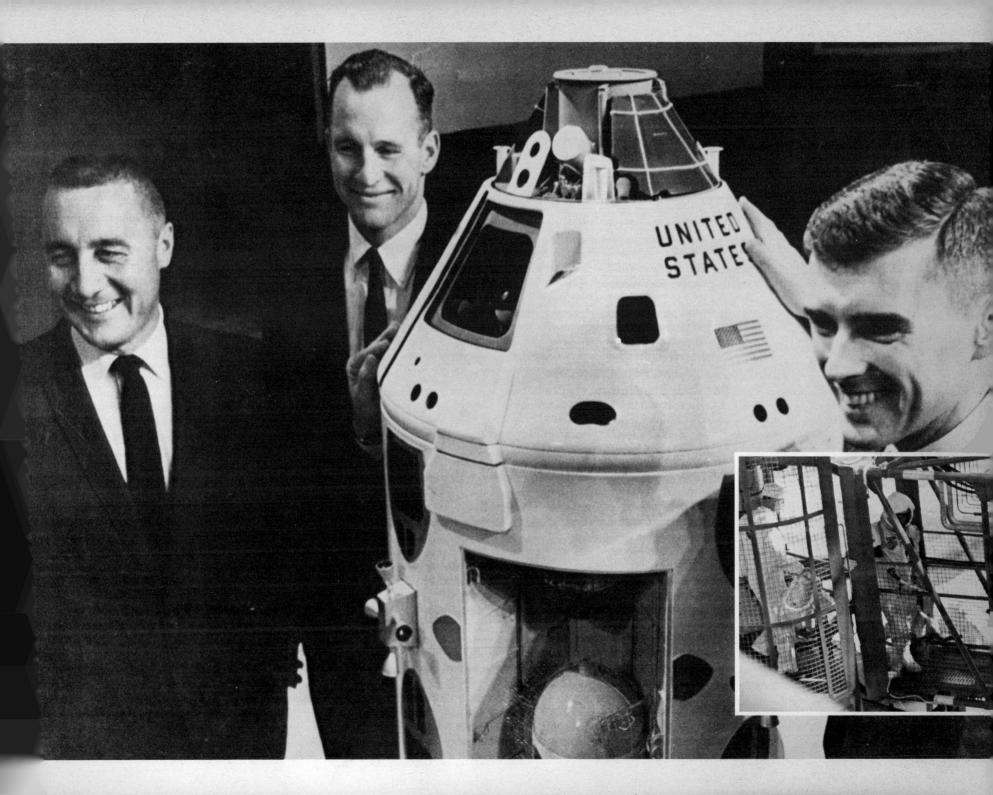

Jetliner Crash, Rockaway Boulevard, 1975

Date	Location	Fatalities	Remarks
6/24	Kennedy Airport, N.Y.	112	Boeing 727 crashed trying to land, apparently battling wind shear. Worst civilian single-craft crash in U.S. history.

It was almost four o'clock in the afternoon on a stormy day, Flight 66—an Eastern Airlines jetliner from New Orleans—was late. It was only minutes off-schedule, but air controllers at Kennedy Airport were having trouble with planes that were on time. A pilot with Flying Tigers who had just landed was telling them about hazardous "wind shear" conditions he had encountered on the runway.

Wind shear consists of two violent air currents moving in opposite directions, causing a localized turbulence that's hard to detect unless you're in it. It's strong and very dangerous to flying objects, sucking them down. Especially to a jet, which can't lose altitude too quickly without coming to grief, it's deadly.

The tower's instruments indicated nothing unusual with the wind pattern.

"I don't care what you're indicating," the pilot said. "I'm just telling you that there's such a wind shear on the final approach of that runway—you should change it to northwest."

Another plane, coming in right behind the Flying Tiger complained, too. But after that, two planes landed on the same runway with no trouble at all.

Before air controllers had time to think about it, the tardy Flight 66 appeared, requesting permission to land on the same approach. Right behind her was a National Airlines plane, waiting to use the approach. The tower told them both, "The only adverse reports we've had about the approach is a wind shear on short final and no braking reports. The approach end of the runway is wet."

Someone replied, "Okay," but the tower couldn't tell if it was Flight 66 or the National Airlines pilot. "Eastern 66, you read?" the tower asked.

There was no answer. Flight 66 had disappeared.

Rockaway Boulevard was just starting to fill up with early rush-hour traffic. One of the main arteries between New York City and Long Island, it would be jammed in another hour. Drivers were not especially surprised to see the big jetliner overhead. There was always a big jetliner overhead in that area.

Charred and blackened interior of the spacecraft seen through the hatch.

Then suddenly there was a flash of light—lightning, some thought—and the plane was gone.

"I saw the plane coming in," Neal Rairden, a mechanic at a gas station on Rockaway Boulevard, told reporters. "All of a sudden there was lightning. I looked up again, and the next thing I knew, the plane was gone and that was that."

Paul Moran, member of the Nassau County Police Department, had a similar experience. On his way home to Queens, he noticed the big plane approaching Kennedy Airport. Then out of the blue, it seemed to Paul, a lightning bolt appeared to strike the plane's tail. In seconds, the plane was gone from the sky, but this time the witness knew exactly what happened to it. It had crashed, almost in front of his car. He saw two figures hobbling away from the plane. "My God, are there any survivors?" he asked. They were too dazed to answer. And then the plane exploded into flames, massive pieces of it skidding across the highway like fireballs.

Police and firemen were on hand in minutes, but most of the passengers who'd been on Flight 66 were beyond help. Amidst the wreckage of the immense plane and rubble of the luggage lay 109 dead bodies, most of them burned and mutilated beyond recognition. But the sight of fourteen survivors kept the rescuers moving.

At the crash site, police, firemen, and volunteers sadly placed all human remains in plain pine boxes to be sent to the New York City Medical Examiner. Before they were through, the death toll would climb to 110. The body of a two-month-old infant, not listed on the plane's manifesto, had been found.

The charred and mutilated bodies were difficult—sometimes impossible—to identify. It took some people days to finally find a loved one. Some never did, and it was ultimately left to the medical examiner to make identification through dental charts, fingerprints and the like.

Before long, two survivors of the crash died in the hospital from their injuries, bringing the death toll to 112 and making the crash of Flight 66 the worst civilian single-plane disaster in the history of the United States.

And what were the findings of the investigation? Had the plane really been hit by lightning? Some of the witnesses allowed afterward that the illumination they thought was lightning might have been the plane itself exploding. A review of the taped conversation between tower and pilot, and the pilot's own remarks, seemed to indicate that the problem may have been wind shear. The pilot had heard the warning and thought he was prepared but then began losing altitude too quickly. In an apparent effort to pull the plane back up, he struck several approach lights, overshot the runway, and crashed. As were so many of his passengers, he was killed instantly.

Investigators probe engine remains at Rockaway Boulevard for clues to the cause of the crash.

Sheets cover bodies of victims, wreckage of jet is in background.

One look at the chart of mining disasters, and you know that mining must be the most dangerous occupation man has ever engaged in on a large scale. Every kind of deep mining has similar hazards—the collapse of tunnels under tons of earth, the sudden breakthrough of an underground spring that floods a mine, the fire that fills a ventilating system with suffocating smoke from which there is no escape. However, coal miners face the greatest danger of all in the alien underground environment.

Coal-mine explosions are the most frequent kind of mining disaster. Recently, of course, there have not been many coal-mine disasters, but that is because coal has not been much in demand since the late 1940's and early '50's, when oil became the principal fuel. Now the energy crisis may create a new need for coal, and thus cause an upsurge in mining catastrophes.

From the time coal was first taken from the earth, men understood the dangers of methane, or "marsh gas," as it was sometimes called. It was both poisonous and explosive. In the early days, miners took canaries into the mines with them. At the first sign of distress among the birds, who were very susceptible to the odorless gas, the miners ran for it. Since a lack of oxygen — and the presence of gas—makes lanterns dim, miners were soon wearing lamps on their hats, in order to detect the "bad air" in time.

Since then, many means have been devised to solve the problem of coal-mine explosions, such as various ventilation systems, but no entirely satisfactory solution has ever been found. The reason for this failure lies in the nature of coal mining. Following is an excerpt from *Harper's Weekly*, January, 1907, which explains what the problem was then. The problem is basically the same today.

"It is one of the tenets of the geologist that the lower we go for coal the more gas we strike. The use of electricity in mine haulage has been growing more and more general. Sparks from these electrical appliances quite frequently touch off the gas that is liberated in deep "shaft" mines.

"In a great many mines the roadways and shafts are exceedingly dry. In these the roadways often consist of coal which has not been taken out. Constant passing to and fro of the system of haulage; the constant passing to and fro of the army of mine employees; the action of the air currents upon the loose particles of coal carried in the cars—all work to charge the air with infinitesimally small particles of coal which are really lighter than air and are, consequently, carried in suspension. So long as the temperature of the air is normal there is absolutely no danger, but let something happen which will raise the temperature in a room, or ignite some of these fine particles of coal dust, and the explosive power of coal is demonstrated in an instant. The explosion seems to travel almost like a prolonged rumble of thunder. It may start from a given point and travel from chamber to chamber until practically the whole mine has been involved in a terrible catastrophe. The result is that the mine-workers are often burned by the explosion or are killed by the falling material dislodged by the shock. Instantaneous combustion of this kind uses up all the oxygen in a mine chamber, and the men are suffocated because the force of the shock has wrecked both the fan and the power-house and, consequently, has shut off the supply of fresh air. After one of these explosions comes the noxious product of the discharge, and then the death-dealing work of the explosion is completed. This, in fact, is what occurred at the Monongah Mine. Practically every known device has been used to keep down the dust, to keep the temperature lowered, and to avoid anything that would start an explosion of this kind; and yet, explosions do occur, and are likely to occur, with even greater frequency in the future.

"The principal ingredients of coal are fixed carbon and volatile matter, or gas. In some places the substance from which coal was made (originally decayed vegetation) had more gas than the coal could contain. In places it formed in reservoirs, hence the natural-gas belts. Where the quantity given off was not sufficient to establish one of these larger reservoirs, the gas collected in smaller spaces known as gas-pockets. The coal-miner quite frequently opens one of these pockets. If the air is not pure, it is quite easy to touch off this supply of gas and an explosion occurs. Even a smaller quantity of gas [is] sufficient to start a fire in conjunction with a large amount of coal dust.

"If the theory is at all correct, that the deeper we go the better grade of coal we find, it is equally true that the

MINING

EXPLOSION AT THE PUMPING-SHAFT.
HE DRUMMOND MINE HORROR.—[FROM SKETCHES BY THOMAS DORAN.]

IMPORTANT AMERICAN MINING CATASTROPHES

DATE	LOCATION	FATALITIES	REMARKS
1855 March	Coalfield, Va.	55	Coal-mine explosion.
1867 4/3	Winterpock, Va.	69	Coal mines exploded.
1869 9/6	Plymouth, Pa.	110	Avondale Mine caught fire.
1883 2/16	Braidwood, Ill.	69	Coal mine flooded, victims drowned.
1884 1/24	Crested Butte, Colo.	59	Coal-mine explosion.
1884 3/13	Pocahontas, Va.	112	Coal-mine explosion.
1891 1/27	Mount Pleasant, Pa.	109	Coal-mine explosion.
1892 1/7	Krebs, Okla.	100	Coal-mine explosion.
1895 3/20	Red Canyon, Wyo.	60	Coal-mine explosion.
1896 6/28	Pittston, Pa.	58	Coal-mine cave-in.
1900 5/1	Scofield, Utah	200	Coal-mine explosion.
1902 5/19	Coal Creek, Tenn.	184	Coal-mine explosion.
1902 7/10	Johnstown, Pa.	112	Coal-mine explosion in the same town as the Johnstown Flood.
1903 6/30	Hannah, Wyo.	169	Coal-mine explosion and fire.
1905 2/26	Virginia City, Ala.	112	Coal-mine explosion.
1907 1/29	Stuart, W. Va.	84	Coal-mine explosion.
1907 12/6	Monongah, W. Va.	361	Two coal mines exploded; worst mine disaster in U.S. history.
1907 12/19	Jacobs Creek, Pa.	239	Coal-mine explosion.
1908 3/28	Hanna, Wyo.	59	Coal-mine explosion.
1908 11/28	Marianna, Pa.	154	Coal-mine explosion.
1908 12/29	Switchback, W. Va.	50	Coal-mine explosion.
1909 1/12	Switchback, W. Va.	67	Coal-mine explosion.
1909 11/13	Cherry, Ill.	259	Coal-mine fire.
1910 5/5	Palos, Ala.	90	Coal-mine explosion.
1910 10/8	Starkville, Colo.	56	Coal-mine explosion.
1910 11/8	Delagua, Colo.	79	Coal-mine explosion and fire.
1911 4/7	Throop, Pa.	72	Coal-mine fire.
1911 4/8	Littleton, Ala.	128	Coal-mine explosion.
1911 12/9	Briceville, Tenn.	84	Coal-mine explosion.
1912 3/20	McCurtain, Okla.	73	Coal-mine explosion.
1912 3/26	Jed, W. Va.	83	Coal-mine explosion.
1913 4/23	Finleyville, Pa.	96	Coal-mine explosion.
1913 10/22	Dawson, N. Mex.	263	Coal-mine explosion.
1914 4/28	Eccles, W. Va.	183	Coal-mine explosion.
1914 10/27	Royalton, Ill.	52	Coal-mine explosion.
1915 3/2	Layland, W. Va.	112	Coal-mine explosion.
1917 4/27	Hastings, Colo.	121	Coal-mine explosion.
1917 8/4	Clay, Ky.	62	Coal-mine explosion.
1919 6/5	Wilkes-Barre, Pa.	92	Coal-mine explosion.
1922 11/6	Spangler, Pa.	77	Coal-mine explosion.
1922 11/22	Dolomite, Ala.	90	Coal-mine explosion.
1923 2/8	Dawson, N. Mex.	120	Coal-mine explosion.

DATE	LOCATION	FATALITIES	REMARKS
1923 8/14	Kemmerer, Wyo.	99	Coal-mine explosion.
1924 3/8	Castle Gate, Utah	171	Coal-mine explosion.
1924 4/28	Benwood, W. Va.	119	Coal-mine explosion.
1925 2/20	Sullivan, Ind.	52	Coal-mine explosion.
1925 12/10	Acemar, Ala.	53	Coal-mine explosion.
1926 1/13	Wilburton, Okla.	91	Coal-mine explosion.
1927 4/30	Everettville, W. Va.	97	Coal-mine explosion.
1928 5/19	Mather, Pa.	195	Coal-mine explosion.
1929 12/17	McAlester, Okla.	61	Coal-mine explosion.
1930 11/5	Millfield, Ohio	82	Coal-mine explosion.
1932 12/23	Moweaqua, Ill.	54	Coal-mine explosion.
1940 1/10	Bartley, W. Va.	91	Coal-mine explosion.
1940 3/16	St. Clairsville, Ohio	72	Coal-mine explosion.
1940 7/15	Portage, Pa.	63	Coal-mine explosion.
1942 5/12	Osage, W. Va.	56	Coal-mine explosion.
1943 2/27	Red Lodge, Mont.	74	Coal-mine explosion.
1947 3/25	Centralia, Ill.	111	Coal-mine explosion.
1951 12/21	West Frankfort, Ill.	119	Biggest shaft mine in the world exploded and caught fire.
1968 11/20	Mannington, W. Va.	78	Coal-mine explosion and fire.
1972 5/2	Kellogg, Idaho	91	Sunshine Silver Mine, one of the biggest in the world, caught fire.

deeper we go for coal the more gas we are bound to encounter. By the same process of reasoning it is very easy to determine that the deeper we go for coal the more danger there is going to be of gas and other explosives, and consequently, the more dangerous becomes the mining of coal.

"Another point established is this: the deeper we go for coal the more difficult it is to force fresh air down into the shafts. It is for this reason that mine disasters are going to increase in number and in severity in future, rather than diminish, unless some new means be found for overcoming these natural difficulties.

"There are three ways which have been adopted by some coal-mine operators. The first of these is a careful selection of the explosives used in the mines. Incidentally, in the use of explosives is found one of the most patent causes of mine disasters. The miner very often will overload the hole bored in the coal. When the powder is ignited the force of the explosion is much greater than the amount of work to be done requires, and the powder, which must exert itself somewhere, rushes out into the miner's chamber in a long flash of fire. This is called a "blow-out" or a "windy shot." If there is any gas in the room, or if there is any collection of coal dust, this blow-out, or windy shot, naturally ignites the gas or coal dust and an explosion can very easily occur. This in fact, is supposed to have been the exact cause of the mine disaster which occurred at Monongah, West Virginia.

[The second way is to hire professionals to set and ignite the explosives. This met with resistance among the miners, who regarded it as the creation of a privileged class.]

"A third preventive of mine explosions is to keep the air perfectly pure. It is realized that even the accumulation of dust is preventable, to a certain extent, by the free circulation of air. It is known, of course, that a liberal infusion of fresh air will so dilute gas as to remove, almost completely, the danger of an explosion.

"An auxiliary preventive is to keep down the dust in the mines. The mine operators in Wales have gone much further, in this respect, than the people of the United States, as they not only sprinkle the floors and the driveways of dusty mines, but also the sides of the shaft or slope as well as the coal in the cars."

169

THE AVONDALE COLLIERY DISASTER—BRINGING OUT THE DEAD.—Sketched by Theo. R. Davis.

Avondale Mine Disaster, 1869

Date	Location	Fatalities	Remarks
9/6	Plymouth, Pa.	110	Avondale Mine caught fire.

The Avondale Mine Disaster

Good Christians all, both great and small, I pray ye lend an ear,
And listen with attention while the truth I will declare;
When you hear this lamentation it will cause ye to weep and wail,
About the suffocation in the mines of Avondale.

On the sixth day of September, eighteen hundred and sixty-nine,
Those miners all then got a call to go work in the mine;
But little did they think that death would gloom the vale
Before they would return again from the mines of Avondale.

—G. G. KORSON, *Minstrels of the Mine Patch*

Reprinted from *Harper's Weekly*, September 25, 1869:

The scene of the terrible disaster was at the Avondale Colliery at Plymouth, about twenty miles south of Scranton, Pennsylvania. It is situated in the Wyoming Valley, on the steepest and most commanding side of the Shawnee Hills. This colliery was reported to be the best and largest in the valley. When in full working order it produced 700 tons of coal per day. For three months previous to the first of September it was idle, owing to the miners' strike. It was leased by the Lackawanna and Western Railroad Company, who also lease many other mines in the valley; and by this ingenious plan of leasing in place of opening mines themselves, they avoid the charge of being held responsible for the manner of their construction.

There is no doubt that the Avondale mine was one of the best and worst in the valley. The masonry-work, running down the sides of the shaft some twenty feet, was as strong as stone and cement could make it. The engine-house was firmly built, the machinery of the finest kind used in the colliery business, the breaker that covered the engine-house, and through which the broken coal was dispatched through a long shoot to the railroad track below, was built in the most substantial manner, and altogether the works to the casual observer seemed to leave no room for improvement. The shaft was sunk to a depth of 237 feet, with a space, 26 feet by 12, divided in the center by a wooden partition, on one side of which the pure air descended to the mine, and on the other the impure vapors ascended to the top and were dissipated abroad. After going in a sheer descent to the bottom of this shaft the explorer of the mine found on either hand two long galleries or avenues, one branching east 1,200 feet, and the other west 800 feet. Moving straight onward at right angles to the shaft, and at a distance from it of 220 feet, the furnace for creating a draught of air through the galleries and chambers of

the mine might be found blazing away in dangerous proximity to the wood-work lining of the passage-way reserved for the admission of the fresh air currents.

On the morning of September 6 a fire broke out, originating, as it appears, from this furnace. A spark ignited the dry scantling adjacent; the flames leaped forward to the bottom of the shaft, caught the wooden partition above-mentioned, climbed to the top, and involved the coal-breaker and the surrounding buildings in the conflagration. Whatever fresh air there was in the mine went to feed the fierce flame, while the sulphurous gases, having no longer an outlet, were forced back into the chambers and galleries of the colliery. As the buildings at the top of the shaft were consumed their ruins fell down and obstructed the only means of entrance to or of egress from the mine.

But what had become of the miners? Their families were congregated about the opening in great numbers; and the miners from all parts of the region rapidly arrived to rescue their comrades, if possible.

Left: Miners descending the shaft. *Right:* The heap of bodies found behind an extemporized barricade.

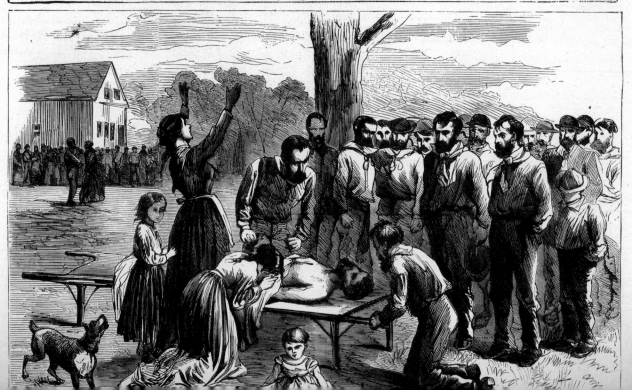

Above: Bringing out the exhausted miners. *Above right:* Ruins of the coal breaker. *Right:* Friends and family claim their dead.

About 6:00 P.M. a dog and lamp were sent down to test the air. The dog was found to be alive when drawn up, and the lamp had not been extinguished. Soon afterward a man went down, and after seven minutes returned and reported no difficulty in breathing, but said there were obstructions halfway down the shaft which he could not pass. The obstructions were removed so as to reach the bottom of the shaft by 7:15 P.M. The two men who had engaged in this work also penetrated a gangway about 60 or 70 yards, finding three dead mules, and reaching a barricade which the miners, retreating for safety, had extemporized to shut out the noxious gases.

The next two men who descended—Thomas W. Williams and David Jones—were suffocated to death. Except to recover the bodies of these brave men no further attempts were made to descend the mine until fresh air was forced down into the mine by means of a fan driven by a small engine. These preparations were not completed until 9:00 A.M. on the 7th. In the meantime a body of forty-six experienced miners was organized as a volunteer force to descend the shaft and make explorations. Several parties descended between 10:00 A.M. and 1:30 P.M., but they returned so completely exhausted that it was not considered safe to make any farther descent until the gangway was cleared of gas. Still four or five descents were made before midnight, but without effect.

Before 3:00 A.M. on the 8th two of the dead were found in the stable of the mine. At half past 6:00 A.M. a large number of miners were found dead on the east side of the plane. The next party which descended reported that they went up the plane, just beyond which a barrier was met, consisting of a car packed around with coal "culm" and clothing. This was cleared away, and a little further on a similar barrier was found. One man was found dead outside of the barricade. Upon the removal of this second barrier a pile of dead miners was discovered. These were found in all conceivable attitudes. Fathers had died embracing their children, and comrades locked in one another's arms. Evan Hughes, the Superintendent was found sitting down with his head resting upon his knees. The work of exhumation continued all day, and by 9:30 P.M. 72 bodies had been brought up. As the bodies were brought to the top of the shaft their faces were cleansed, and they were thus prepared for the recognition of their friends. By noon on the 9th, 108 bodies had been exhumed, after which none were found.

It is impossible to censure too severely the culpable carelessness of a mining company who, rather than provide, at the expense of a few thousand dollars, a second shaft for the safety of their workmen, preferred to risk this terrible loss of life. We are glad that measures have been promptly taken to provide relief for the families which have been made destitute by this sudden calamity.

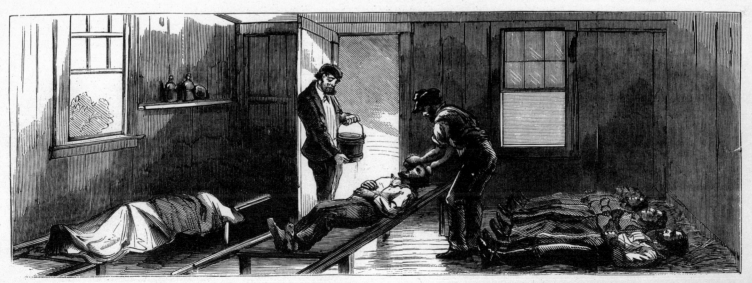

THE AVONDALE COLLIERY DISASTER—CLEANSING THE FACES OF THE MINERS PREPARATORY TO THEIR SEPULTURE.

Monongah Mine Explosion, 1907

Date	Location	Fatalities	Remarks
12/6	Monongah, W. Va.	361	Two mines exploded; worst mine disaster in U.S. history.

All the local people knew about the hollow hills of Monongah, West Virginia. The Consolidated Coal Company of Boston had honeycombed the hills with mine shafts and tunnels until it seemed the town might one day fall in. Even so, the 6,000 people who lived there were all connected with mining. Every family had at least one man who worked below ground.

The *New York Times* commented at the time that mining had once been the stronghold of Americans, but the "foreigners" had become the majority. The Monongah mines, however, had more Americans than any other mine in the country. But all the men were equal when it came to the danger of the mines. In 1907 alone, more than 800 men died in coal mines, most within one month. Nearly half of them died in the Monongah mines, in one day.

Early on Friday, December 6, 380 men entered the No. 6 and No. 8 mines of Consolidated. The two mines were connected underground, but one had its entrance on one side of the South Fork River, the other on the opposite side. Everything seemed to go as usual until 10:00 A.M. when an enormous explosion rocked Monongah. Everyone knew at once what it was.

The townspeople ran for the mines, and there they saw that the props holding up the entrance to No. 6 had been blown clear across the river. The entrance to the other mine was likewise a shambles, and both were blocked by tons of earth, rock, and coal. It would take rescuers a long time to dig down to the men trapped inside.

In the hills, however, there were several openings to No. 8. Such fervid hope was born in the hundreds of hysterical kinsmen who rushed to these holes that they could almost see the trapped men pouring out of the openings. But all that poured out of the entryways was volumes of the "black damp," the poisonous methane gas that had probably started the coal-dust explosion. At every opening, withering vegetation showed that the gas was there. No man could make his way through those fumes.

A huge rescue force gathered and was set to work at every point of entry and exit. Almost at once, six bodies and five injured men were pulled to the surface. The injured men could remember little of what had happened, and merely spoke of crowds of struggling, frantic men below them. It was guessed that they were not very deep in the mine when it exploded.

In Mine No. 6, rescuers discovered two things. One was a group of living miners whom they could not reach at the moment. The other was that the explosion had knocked out the ventilating system, and no one could stay long in the mine, which was now filled with bad air. The rescue workers broke up into teams, and went in short relays into the sickening air below. Each time, the groups tried to penetrate a little deeper, and each time, they returned without a survivor.

The efforts of the rescuers were heroic, but mostly in vain. Only 19 miners survived, most of whom had escaped immediately after the explosion. The bodies in the mine—361 of them—were torn and mangled and blackened. The majority of them had apparently died in the explosion or the fire that instantly followed. As for the group of living men sighted earlier, it was never discovered what happened to them or if they had ever really been seen.

Experts later concluded that one of the mine shafts had been filled with methane gas, which a miner, in setting off an excavation blast, had ignited. The gas not only had exploded but had ignited the highly flammable coal dust that is characteristic of West Virginia mines. Newspapers called the disaster the greatest in the history of bituminous-coal mining. It was the greatest mining catastrophe in the history of the United States.

Funeral Wreaths for Christmas, West Frankfort, Illinois, 1951

Date	Location	Fatalities	Remarks
12/21	West Frankfort, Ill.	111	Biggest shaft mine in the world exploded and caught fire.

Charlene Nicholson, 24, was home with her two young children that Friday night before Christmas. Her husband, Kenneth, 26, was on the night shift at the Chicago, Wilmington and Franklin Orient Mine, the biggest coal pit in the world.

This was the last night shift before Christmas. Next morning, the men would be free for the holidays. Many of them had brought their good clothes along to the mine, for they intended to start Christmas shopping with their families as soon as the shift was over.

At 8:30 P.M., the Orient Mine was torn apart by a blast so

terrific that "it knocked cars weighing several tons off of tracks and brought down overhead timbers!" It killed more than a hundred men.

The moment Charlene heard about the explosion, she called her mother. Not only was her husband at the mine, but an uncle as well. She wanted her mother to watch the children, so she could go there.

By the time she arrived, a fire was raging in the mine. Families were lined along Highway 37, and they just stood there in the chilling 19-degree weather. Charlene inched her way as near to the mouth of the mine as she could. She watched and waited.

Rescue workers were rushed to the mine from all parts of southern Illinois. Most of the volunteers were miners themselves, and some even had kinsmen in the mine.

At 10:30 P.M., the first body was brought up, and the West Frankfort High School gymnasium became a morgue. Begrimed rescue workers, wearing gas masks against the deadly methane that had caused the explosion, worked on through the night. They soon abandoned hope that they could reach most of the missing men in time. But not Charlene Nicholson.

Charlene waited at the mouth of the mine for six hours, never taking her eyes from the entrance, never becoming discouraged. Life in a coal-mining family had apparently taught her patience and faith. Both were rewarded. After six hours, she saw a grimy, tattered, but familiar figure. It was Ken. He had been working in a section away from the explosion. He had come out almost immediately, but had joined the rescue workers to search for other men. Charlene's joy was dimmed only by the fact that she would never see her uncle alive again.

Above and left: Hasty funeral arrangements are made while survivors mourn the death of the Sunshine miners.

By Saturday, the gymnasium was filled with bodies. All through the town, families began taking down Christmas wreaths and putting up funeral wreaths. The public Christmas wreaths in the town were also replaced with funeral wreaths. The Christmas programs planned in churches for that Sunday morning were canceled, and mourning services were held instead. The town was draped in black, the streets empty, in memory of the 111 men who died.

Sunshine Silver Mine, 1972

Date	Location	Fatalities	Remarks
5/2	Kellogg, Idaho	91	Sunshine Silver Mine, one of the biggest in the world, caught fire.

In the mountains of Idaho—in the northern panhandle between Washington and Montana—is a place called Silver Valley. It sounds like something out of a fairy tale, and perhaps it is for the people who profit from this richest silver-mining region in the country. For the men who work it, however, especially the men who were working the Sunshine Silver Mine in 1972, it is another story.

Discovered in 1884, the oldest part of the Sunshine Silver Mine goes down nearly 4,000 feet in the earth, about as far from sunshine as you can get. In 1972, temperatures in the mine sometimes soared above 100 degrees, and the men often could not work more than 30 minutes at a stretch without getting heat cramps that forced them to surface. The old timbers that kept the oldest tunnels from caving in were no doubt as dry as tinder and just as flammable, and high heat and dry tinder can lead to spontaneous combustion. At least that was the opinion of the Federal inspectors who, for several reasons, labeled the mine "unsafe."

There had not been a fire—or, apparently, a fire drill—in the mine since 1946. But after all, this wasn't a coal mine, with the constant dangers of methane gas and coal dust. The owners had provided some of the latest safety equipment, such as respirators, or "self-rescuers," which fit over the face and maintained artificial respiration. But no one knew how to use them.

By eleven o'clock Tuesday morning, the day shift was deep in the Sunshine Silver Mine when someone smelled smoke. It began to pour in through the fresh-air ventilators. No one saw the fire, but anyone who works in a mine knows the horror of smoke deep down in an airless space. No man can breathe smoke for many minutes and live.

There was a mad scramble for the main elevator shaft. The

Two miners were rescued after being trapped for one long week in the Sunshine Mine. The men were brought up from the 4,800-foot level by a rescue cage.

men closest to it were able to reach the top and fresh air. All at once, there was no elevator. Something had happened to the hoist in the fire below, and down there with it were nearly a hundred trapped men.

The news traveled fast to the people of Kellogg, a silver-mining community of 7,000. The mine was six miles away, and by the time they got there, barricades had been set up. Hundreds of miners from the area were let through to help with rescue operations, but the women could only watch the smoke billowing from the smokestack. "It just doesn't seem real, does it?" one wife said. "You read about it in other places, but it never happens here."

The rescue teams could not go down into the mine until the hoist had been repaired. Air was pumped into the ventilators, but each rush of air going in seemed to cause a rush of smoke through the smokestack. It was obvious that the fresh air was feeding the flames below.

All the same, they could not stop pumping. Spokesmen for the mining company mentioned that the mine had miles of twisting tunnels, many with fresh-air spaces. The men might make their way to them. Moreover, there were escape routes to the Polaris and Silver Summit mines a mile and a half east of the Sunshine. The men might reach them.

All day and into the night, smoke billowed from the stack. Rescuers in teams of five, wearing oxygen masks, went down into the mine. They searched for bodies and sealed off empty shafts from fire, smoke, and the fresh air that was only feeding the flames. There was no word that anyone had found their way through the escape routes to the Polaris and Silver Summit mines.

By week's end, 91 men had been found, all dead. How the fire started was a matter of conjecture. Some insisted that the fire had originated in the oldest part of the mine when heat had caused the ancient timbers to ignite spontaneously. Others held that there was evidence of faulty wiring below and that the fire had started electrically.

Whatever the cause, said the Sunshine Silver Mining Company, the fault was not theirs. The mine had been inspected by non-Federal officials days before and had been declared safe. The Federal inspectors insisted that their men had not come to the same conclusion.

The miners and the Federal Government were bitter. This was something that could not be allowed to happen again. For those families in Kellogg who had lost their men, the fight had gone out of them, at least for the time being.

Smoke from the underground fire in the Sunshine Mine.

Diagram of the position of the trapped men. (UPI.)

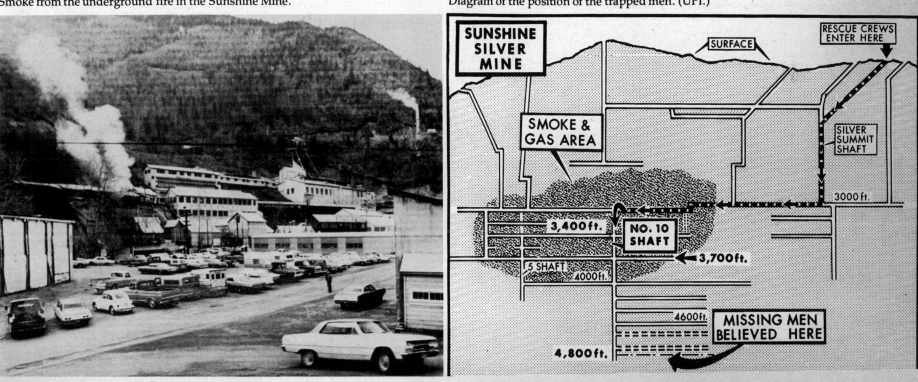

IMPORTANT AMERICAN EPIDEMICS

DATE	LOCATION	FATALITIES	REMARKS
1607 June–October	Jamestown, Va.	50	Apparent typhus epidemic killed nearly half of first English colony in America.
1618–23	Massachusetts	30,000	Unidentified pestilence wiped out entire tribe of Indians.
1699 August–November	Charleston, S.C., Philadelphia, Pa.	400	Yellow fever, already known in West Indies, struck continental colonies for first time.
1721–22	Boston, Mass.	899	Small pox epidemic affected 6,000 out of 12,000 population.
1793 July–October	Philadelphia, Pa.	5,000	Yellow fever raged through the city, nearly making it a ghost town until first fall frost stopped the disease.
1832 June–December	Nationwide	30,000(?)	Cholera swept the nation, killing at least 5,000 in New York, and 5,000 in New Orleans, which was hardest hit. Many thousands more perished across the nation, for which there is no accurate count. Our estimate is conservative.
1853–55	New Orleans, La.	5,000+	For three summers running, yellow fever struck the ''capital'' of the ''land of fevers,'' as the Middle South was called.
1878 July–October	South	14,000	Yellow fever struck entire lower Mississippi River Valley. Memphis, Tenn., was hardest hit.
1916	Nationwide	7,129	27,363 cases of polio reported.
1918 March–November	Nationwide	500,000	Spanish flu pandemic killed 21,640,000 people throughout the world. Almost every populated area on earth was affected.
1946 June–September	Nationwide	1,845	25,698 cases of polio reported.
1948 June–September	Nationwide	1,895	27,726 cases of polio reported.
1949 June–September	Nationwide	2,720	42,033 cases of polio reported.
1953 June–September	Nationwide	3,300	57,628 cases of polio reported.
1975–76	Nationwide	Current epidemic, count not yet complete.	Swine fever, a strain of the Spanish flu of 1918, is with us at this writing.

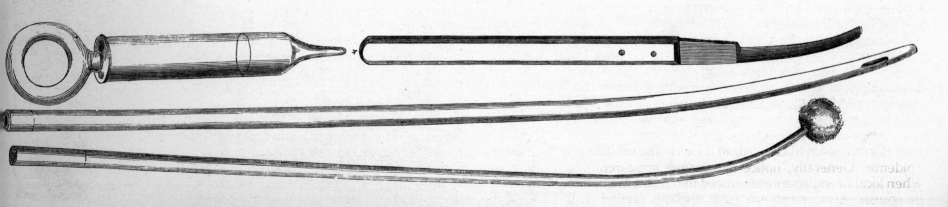

In the 1850's, Dr. Horace Green invented controversial instruments to remove parts of infected lungs.
When one of his famous patients died, Dr. Green was brought to trial.

An epidemic is the rapid spreading of a disease that affects many people in a short time. The disease is usually spread by contact between living creatures, human or otherwise, but the spreader need not be infected with the disease. The mosquito, for example, is a carrier, not a sufferer, of yellow fever. Epidemics have always been a tragic form of population control. In the annals of catastrophe, they are the worst mass murderers of all time, and have caused more deaths than crime or war.

Epidemics were well known to the settlers who first came to North America. The overcrowded, often filthy cities of Europe regularly had plagues, and the colonists brought epidemic diseases along with them to their new home. Which infectious diseases were native to the New World isn't known for sure. Captain John Smith, before assuming leadership of the colony at Jamestown, reported an epidemic among a tribe of Indians. He could not diagnose the disease. The Pilgrims who landed in Massachusetts in 1620 found that an epidemic was wiping out an entire tribe of Indians. They thought it was small pox. It soon became apparent—by the Indians' total lack of immunity to small pox—that they had never been exposed to it before meeting Europeans.

The colonists on the more populous East Coast could mark the beginning of an epidemic by the arrival of a ship with a sick person aboard, or even by news of the outbreak of an epidemic in Europe. Typhus, typhoid fever, small pox, and cholera came with the earliest settlers—typhus apparently with the Jamestown colonists, small pox with the Puritans around 1630. There were also reports of diptheria and scarlet fever. The colonists did not seem to know what these child-killers were, so perhaps they were born in the New World. There were also reports of killing polio and whooping cough, but they did not fill up the pages of the Catalogue of the Dead the way typhus, cholera, and small pox did. Actually, the Catalogue of the Dead was not an accurate record of fatalities. No town liked to admit it was in the midst of an epidemic. Generally, notice of a plague appeared only when local newspapers announced that it had finally run its course. Also, many epidemic diseases carried with them a stigma of shame. Cholera, for example, was thought to be a visitation from God upon lazy paupers and ethnically inferior peoples. If a family could help it, they kept their members from being listed as victims of such diseases. However, the severity of an epidemic could be estimated by the number of "fast days," "days of humiliation," and "days of prayers" called by local government and church. An epidemic was felt to be a punishment from God for wicked ways. Pious people offered to sacrifice themselves to appease the Almighty.

Medical men at last noticed that those who survived a case of small pox were immune to the next onslaught. It was reasoned that by giving a mild case of the disease to a person, he might become immune to a real attack. The result of their reasoning was variolization—deliberately injecting people with small pox. Not everyone favored it. Not only did it seem to be thwarting God's will, it sometimes killed you. But variolization seemed to reduce the death rate of small pox.

Meanwhile, in 1699, a new disease had been born in the colonies—yellow fever. Europeans called it the "American plague." Americans, observing that it arrived with ships from the West Indies, called it the "Barbadoes distemper." Because the fever and vomiting were usually accompanied by liver disorder and jaundiced yellow skin, it eventually became known as yellow fever. It appeared as far north as New York, but really thrived in the hot, humid lowlands of the South, especially in the lower Mississippi River Valley. Yellow fever was a late-comer, but along with the other infectious diseases, it remained a scourge almost until the twentieth century.

By 1800, vaccination had begun to be practiced. Vaccination induced cowpox—just one small pock—which with very little aftereffect made a person immune to small pox. By 1900, except for occasional outbreaks, the pox was under almost complete control. Modern sanitation, food sterilization, and water purification had virtually eliminated cholera. Fever-abating drugs, along with a variety of injections and vaccinations, had turned the "children's diseases"—whooping cough, measles, and mumps—into milder illnesses, not so deadly as they once were. Some of them, however, would continue to be fairly lethal until the 1930's and '40's. In 1900, Walter Reed discovered that by destroying the strain of mosquito named *Aëdes aegypti*, the world would be rid of yellow fever.

EPIDEMICS

Some diseases hung on, like polio, which seemed to become even worse in the twentieth century. Less competition from other diseases may have made it more virulent. Although it has never taken the number of lives other diseases have, its devastating effect of crippling deformity made it a major enemy. In 1956, after some vicious epidemics, Salk vaccine, administered by injection, was made available to the public. With periodic booster shots, it could make polio extinct. Several years later, Sabin vaccine, which could be taken orally, was introduced and seems to have eliminated polio.

Then there was—and is—the ubiquitous influenza. Every year, it seems, we have suffered a flu epidemic of some degree, and always a different strain: Asiatic flu, Spanish flu, Chinese flu, and so on. It comes in like the sniffles and goes out like pneumonia. We've never been able to eradicate it. Each year, it kills thousands, mostly among the very young and the very old. Certain serums or vaccines ("flu shots") seem to slow down some strains, but not to stop them. Even as this is being written, we are in the midst of a flu epidemic—"swine fever"—a strain of the deadly Spanish flu that killed so many in 1918.

Aside from influenza, science and constant vigilance seem to have wiped out the most fatal communicable diseases in this country, but indeed, the operative word still is "Vigilance!"

Burning down of Quarantine Hospital on Staten Island, New York, 1858. Quarantine hospitals were established to keep epidemics from spreading, but panic-stricken citizens frequently attacked the diseased who were housed in their area.

Jamestown, Virginia, 1607

Date	Location	Fatalities	Remarks
June–October	Jamestown, Va.	50	Apparent typhus epidemic killed nearly half of first English colony in America.

There were 105 colonists who were ready to set sail in three ships to establish an English colony in the New World. Captain John Smith was one of them. They had no illusions about the hardships they would face in this strange place. The previous English effort to plant a colony, at Roanoke, had ended in mysterious disaster (see the chapter "Disappearances").

The company's minister, the Reverend Robert Hunt, was feverish, weak, and very sick from the moment he boarded ship. The small band wanted to put him ashore before sailing, and so did the shipowners. Unlike most shipowners of the time, they kept their vessels scrupulously clean by airing them every day and swabbing them down with vinegar to "abolish the vehement funk." They knew about epidemics, and it occurred to them that they might be carrying the beginnings of one along with them. Since the reverend lived no more than twenty miles from the port of departure, it was no great effort for him to find his way home.

The Reverend Mr. Hunt, however, did not want to go home. His will later revealed that he suspected his wife of faithlessness. Whether his suspicions were true or not, the ships set sail with the reverend aboard.

After five or six weeks, the reverend's illness disappeared. He was a hard worker and a spiritual comfort, so everyone seemed happy he had not been left behind. The ships stopped first in the West Indies, where the men rested from the rigorous journey and consumed fresh food, which had been lacking at sea. Then they set sail northward, in the same direction as the ill-fated colonists of Roanoke Island before them. They landed north of Roanoke, and chose for their site a low-lying peninsula in a river they called the James River, after their king. They had been warned by earlier visitors not to choose a low site, because fever and pestilence seemed to breed in such spots. But the surrounding waters offered them some protection from unfriendly Spanish settlers and Indians, and they took the chance.

For ten days after their ships left them, everything seemed fine, except for an Indian skirmish or two. It was a hot June, and the waters of the river were brackish, but there were plenty of fish and fresh vegetation. On the eleventh day, a colonist came down with a strange malady. He was feverish and his joints swelled; there was weakness and finally a near paralysis. Soon, his fellow colonists showed the same symptoms.

Within a few months, everyone at Jamestown, including Captain Smith, was infected with the same disease. Only the Reverend Mr. Hunt seemed immune. And while they all tended the common stockpot — from which they all ate — it was probably the reverend who did most of the tending, since he wasn't sick. Likewise, when they were well enough to do it, they all took turns drying the sturgeon they caught, pounded into meal, and made into bread. Thus the food was much handled, by the sick as well as the sound, and probably a great deal by the reverend.

Nobody knew what they were suffering. According to Dr. Gordon Jones of Fredericksburg, Virginia, writing in *The Virginia Magazine of History*, the symptoms sound like beriberi, but as Dr. Jones points out, that disease is the result of a diet deficiency (lack of vitamin B$_1$). If the colonists of Jamestown had suffered such a deficiency on their long journey over, they had more than likely made up for it in the West Indies and in Jamestown. Their diet was varied and fresh, if not plentiful, and there seems to be no reason for beriberi.

Dr. Jones goes on to point out certain similarities between beriberi and typhus. Typhus is caused by a microorganism called rickettsia that is usually carried by body lice, which bite and infect their host. It attacks the nervous system, so temporary paralysis might result. (Dr. Jones also feels there is some connection between typhus and beriberi.)

There was uniformity in the length of time each person

A 1619 version of the arrival at Jamestown.

suffered the illness, which points to an infectious disease rather than diet deficiency. The symptoms disappeared after five or six weeks, the duration of the Reverend Robert Hunt's illness. The reverend may have been suffering from typhus. Lice on his body (they were hard to get rid of in those days) could easily have survived the trip and flourished in the hot lowland of Jamestown.

By November, the epidemic was over. It had left 50 dead in its wake. By later standards that may not seem bad, but the English portion of America had lost half its population — and had suffered its first epidemic.

Yellow Fever, 1878

Date	Location	Fatalities	Remarks
July–October	South	14,000	Yellow fever struck entire lower Mississippi River Valley. Memphis, Tenn., was hardest hit.

The ladies of Memphis always looked the other way when Annie Cook came strolling down the street. The gentlemen greeted Annie warmly, unless their wives were there. Then they looked the other way, too. She was never a guest at the best houses, although some of the men swore she owned the best house in Memphis. It was the Mansion House, on Gayoso Street, sumptuous, baroque, and filled with the fanciest ladies-for-hire in the South. Annie was not society's golden girl, but before the summer of '78 was over, she became the Saint of Memphis and her house a dwelling of mercy.

From late spring, Memphis had gone through periods of panic. First had come tales that the dreaded yellow fever was sweeping the West Indies. Ships from the Indies often put in at New Orleans, and from there, the fever could make its way up the Mississippi River to Memphis. It had done so before.

By July, newspapers reported an epidemic in New Orleans. The population was leaving the city, and those who were infected carried the disease with them. In early August, the word was that the fever had reached Grenada, Mississippi, not all that far from Memphis. The people of Memphis packed their bags, ready to desert their city at the first sign of black vomit, yellow skin, and raging fever.

Then one sultry August night, a Mrs. Bionda, who, with her husband, ran a food establishment on the banks of the Mississippi, was heard to complain about some mosquito bite she'd gotten. No one thought much about it, for it was not yet known that a mosquito carried the disease. The Biondas' riverside eatery (it was nothing so fancy as a restaurant) was like much of Memphis in those days — not very clean. Like other proprietors of public places, the Biondas dumped their garbage in the streets or shallows of the river. Naturally, flies and mosquitoes bred there.

On August 13, Mrs. Bionda died. The diagnosis was yellow fever.

Yellow fever epidemic in Memphis. *Left to right:* The survivor; woman and child found at home days after death; armed guards maintain barricades around city limits; mass burials of the dead. From *L'Illustration*, October 5, 1878.

In the records, Mrs. Bionda is the first reported case in the yellow fever epidemic of 1878 in Memphis. On the same day, 22 more cases were reported. During the next three weeks, 25,000 people, more than half the population of Memphis, fled the town, carrying the deadly virus with them and spreading it throughout Kentucky, Mississippi, and other parts of the South not yet stricken.

Left at home were 20,000 people — 6,000 whites with no means to leave, and 14,000 blacks in the same predicament. Among them were some who chose not to leave—the priests and ministers who refused to leave their flocks, doctors and nurses who would not desert their patients, and loyal citizens like Annie Cook, who decided to stay and help. Annie released her girls, but she stayed put and opened her Mansion House to the sick. Along with the clergymen, doctors, nurses, and volunteers from other parts of the country, she helped nurse the yellow-jack victims herself. For once, no one turned their backs on Annie. Of the 20,000 left in town, 17,000 were stricken, and Annie's loyalty was badly needed.

Through all the hot days of August and September, Memphis was like hell. The businesses were all shut down, and hardly anyone ventured into the streets. There were the carts that picked up the dead, endlessly loading them to be dumped at the nearest cemetery. There were mass funerals daily in common trenches, and even relatives were afraid to attend the services and be exposed to the fever. Sometimes, the only people in the streets were the dead, lying for days where they'd fallen, putrefying in the heat, so terrified were most citizens to approach the infected corpses.

Not all were afraid. Not the looters, for example, or those whom panic had sent on a perpetual drunk. Bolstered by alcohol, they were as frightening as the yellow jack. There weren't many, just enough to carouse at odd times in the streets or to dress corpses in strange carnival costumes and otherwise to create bizarre and terrifying scenes.

September drifted into hot and humid October, and still the death knell rang. Some people, who had been away from the city when the epidemic struck, refused to return even to collect their nearest kin who were dead or dying. Weird tales made their way out of the city: of a pregnant woman who had died and had a healthy child born afterward; of a deaf-mute twelve-year-old who had recovered from the fever able to hear and speak; of the Irishman, presumed dead in his shrouds, who rose in the middle of his funeral service demanding to know what was going on.

Finally, in mid-October, there was a killing frost, and with the heat went the yellow fever.

The fever was gone, but it had stolen 5,000 lives from the city.

Of the dead, 4,000 were white, 75 per cent of the 6,000 whites who had stayed in Memphis; the other 1,000 were black, less than 10 per cent of the 14,000 blacks who had stayed behind. All over the South, statistics seemed to say the same thing—blacks had greater immunity to this disease than whites. The statistics meant one thing: yellow fever had its origins in Africa.

Two dozen priests and 54 doctors had stayed to tend the sick. And many volunteers, among them, Annie Cook. A local newspaper wrote: "Annie Cook, the woman who after a long life of shame, ventured all she had of life and property for the sick, died September 11 of yellow fever which she contracted while nursing her patients. If there was virtue in the faith of the woman who but touched the hem of the Divine Redeemer, surely the sins of this woman must be forgiven her."

Memphis was hardest hit by the epidemic, followed by New Orleans, but all over the lower Mississippi Valley the fever had taken its toll. Tiny towns,with populations of little more than 2,000, were cut in half. Some were nearly wiped out.

Spanish Flu, 1918

Date	Location	Fatalities	Remarks
March–November	Nationwide	500,000	Spanish flu pandemic killed 21,640,000 people throughout the world. Almost every populated area on earth was affected.

It is the worst epidemic and the worst disaster in our history. It may well be the worst disaster in the history of the modern world. In a few short months, we lost ten times as many Americans as were killed in World War I. It happened, in fact, during the last year of that war and was so vicious that people suspected it was an act of war. There was even a theory that a German submarine had landed on one of our shores and deposited a vial of virulent germs, thus starting the great influenza epidemic of 1918. But the Germans were hit as hard as anybody by the disease, and besides, surfacing a submarine in the middle of Kansas, where the epidemic started in the United States, seems to be out of the question, even for the most determined German.

It started right in the middle of Kansas, at Camp Funston, an Army camp situated at Fort Riley. It began on March 5 with an outbreak of what seemed to be a very mild strain of influenza. It spread through the camp, and then through many Army camps, but there was little attendant pneumonia and subsequent death. The epidemic seemed to be confined to Army camps and Navy bases, and when the troops went overseas, they seemed to take the influenza with them.

The trip across the Atlantic did something to this flu. When it hit Europe, it was no longer a mild strain. The French called it *la grippe*, and it struck severely among the French, German, and British soldiers in the field. Then Scotland began reporting 10 and 15 deaths a day. Italy was hit, and alarming reports were soon heard from Greece, Macedonia, and Egypt.

As it spread, it grew in strength, and by May, it hit Spain so hard that it became known forever as the Spanish Flu. While it ravaged Europe, it also made its way to Asia, to inflict incredible death in China and India. Traveling across the Pacific, it touched down at Hawaii and came back home by way of Alaska and our West Coast. Whole Eskimo communities were wiped out. At the same time, it came back across the Atlantic to attack our East Coast. With horrible consequences, it spread itself out across the country.

The Spanish flu killed people at an extraordinary rate, and doctors were completely stymied. They merely knew that it was influenza—and a few even wondered if that was the truth. Much advice was given, some of it a little crazy. Most of it seemed to ration human contact in the same way goods were being rationed because of the war. People were warned not to shake hands. One New York doctor cautioned against kissing except through a handkerchief or face mask. Some cities held that face masks should be part of one's daily outfit, and the magazine *Popular Science Monthly* came up with a way to wear a mask and smoke at the same time. They suggested placing two cornplasters on the mask—one inside and one outside—and cutting a hole through the middle. The hole was to be just big enough for a cigarette, and of course, you had to fashion a cork of some sort to plug up the hole when you weren't smoking.

Theaters, sports arenas, and other public gathering places were closed, but nothing seemed to help. There were not enough doctors or nurses or hospitals for the suffering. Nor were there enough undertakers, gravediggers, or cemeteries for the dead. No one knew what to do, and if there had not been a war in Europe, there might have been utter national panic.

On November 11, the war was over, and very strangely—almost miraculously—so was the Spanish flu. The coincidence was eerie, but what is stranger and more wonderful is that the Spanish flu has never returned. We've had many flu epidemics since then, but none to compare with the epidemic of 1918.

Polio, 1949

Date	Location	Fatalities	Remarks
June–September	Nationwide	2,720	42,033 cases of polio reported.

Anyone who was a child in 1949 will never forget that summer. That was the summer many public swimming pools were closed down, and there were daily reports on water pollution at all the local beaches. Not that your mother would let you go to the beach, anyway, or to the movies or anyplace else crowds gathered. She was afraid you might catch something. If you got the slightest sore throat, she called the doctor.

That was also the summer the boy across the street got polio, the first kid you ever knew personally who did. You were forbidden to visit him because nobody knew how long the contagion period would last. But you went anyway. You stood outside the house, in back, and your friend showed you his withered arm through the upstairs window. He was lucky, he told you. His doctor said his muscles could be restored with exercise, but he had seen kids in the hospital whose bones were affected, and they'd be crippled for life. He'd seen others who'd gotten something called bulbar polio, and who would spend their lives in iron lungs. And you'd both heard about kids you knew who'd died from polio. You realized that if you finished the summer in the same shape you'd started it, you'd be a lucky kid.

Now that infantile paralysis is mostly a memory, it's hard to imagine what it was like in the forties. There had been bad epidemics before, but in this decade, polio flourished like an evil weed. Each summer began with an onslaught of fear that was all too often fulfilled by autumn time. By August, hospitals were crowded beyond reasonable capacity, and doctors didn't just make housecalls—they flew around the country to understaffed stricken communities, like constant commuters. In a panic over sanitation, planes dusted everything with DDT, and caused ecological problems that are still unresolved.

The summer of '49 outdid them all. It was the worst polio epidemic since 1916, a year that holds the record as the worst killer, if not crippler, in our experience with this scourge. For a while, it looked as though 1949 would be worse, and in some ways it was. There were far more cases reported, and if the fatalities did not mount up as high, it was bad enough. But in the polio epidemic of 1916, there was little courage and human dignity. Few communities responded to pleas for help from their neighbors. People fled their own towns and cities, and could find no place to stay elsewhere. If a town were stricken, surrounding towns put up KEEP OUT signs, and enforced the message with armed guards who were not afraid to use their weapons if they felt they had to. People were frightened, and perhaps you couldn't blame them.

People were frightened in 1949, too, but there was little of the panic and cruelty that had characterized early epidemics. Doctors and specialists from nonstricken areas responded to calls from stricken areas. Communities shared equipment and so did hospitals, and volunteers by the thousands took classes to learn how to use the methods and equipment that might restore the wasted muscles of polio victims.

Perhaps people in the forties could afford to be more generous than in previous decades. In 1916, for example, bulbar pneumonia meant almost certain death. Then, during World War II, the Air Force developed some high-altitude breathing equipment, and it became the basis for respirators that could keep bulbar victims alive. If doctors could keep such victims breathing for five days, they could save their lives. The fact that they would have to go through life encumbered by an iron lung did not seem like much of a problem when so many lives were at stake. By 1949, Sister Kenny and other experimenters had come up with hot packs, and special baths and therapy that seemed to restore the withered muscles of some victims.

But equipment was expensive and in short supply, and so were the personnel to operate it. Nonstricken communities responded immediately. Some had bought their own iron lungs, hot packs, and respirators during this decade, and they offered to send them on to communities who had greater need of them. Not even fear that polio might suddenly strike could move them to hoard the equipment that others needed. The airlines and railroads made special trips to transfer the heavy equipment and to transport volunteers to where they were needed in a hurry.

The National Polio Foundation—founded by the most famous victim of polio, Franklin Delano Roosevelt—had created an equipment pool during the earlier years of the decade, and they did it again, in 1949, making sure the equipment served as many people as possible.

It was a concerted effort and must certainly have helped to lessen the number of fatalities. In 1916, 27,363 cases had been reported; 7,129 had died. In 1949, 42,033 cases were reported; 2,700 died.

All the same, it was a heartbreaking summer. More than half the victims were children under ten years old. Nearly 25 per cent were between 10 and 20. The rest were adults of various ages. Only once more would infantile paralysis give us a worse summer than this — in 1953. Three years later, Salk vaccine was released to the public, and polio was on its way to becoming a disease of the past. This seems finally to have been accomplished with the introduction of the Sabin vaccine.

Linda Brown was the 1949 poster girl. Photo courtesy of the National Foundation, March of Dimes.

IMPORTANT AMERICAN DISAPPEARANCES

DATE	LOCATION	FATALITIES(?)	REMARKS
1587–90	Roanoke Island, N.C.	127	Settlers of Roanoke Colony were last seen in 1587. Had colony succeeded, it would have been first British settlement in America.
1854 March	North Atlantic, between England and U.S.	450	Immigrant ship *City of Glasgow* disappeared without a trace.
1872 June	Mississippi River, near Vicksburg, Miss.	55	Riverboat *Iron Mountain* vanished.
1872 November	North Atlantic, between U.S. and Europe	10	All aboard ship *Mary Celeste* disappeared. Ship was found intact, but no sign of crew. Despite relatively few lost, it is one of the most famous and bizarre disappearances.
1918 3/4	Off Barbados, West Indies	280	U.S. *Cyclops* vanished. Despite fact that World War I was in progress, there was never any evidence that the enemy had taken her.
1930 September–November	Anjikuni, Canada	30	Inhabitants of Eskimo village disappeared. All possessions, including food in cooking pots and all means of transportation, were left behind.
1956 10/10	Atlantic, north of Azores	59	U.S. Air Force plane vanished.
1957 3/21	Pacific	67	U.S. Air Force transport plane disappeared.
1962 3/16	Pacific, between Guam and Manila	107	Flying Tiger Super Constellation, chartered by Army, vanished.

From time to time, people or objects (both large and small) have vanished from the face of the earth with no apparent cause. To explain these disappearances, theories have been invented that range from ordinary earthly events to fantastic interplanetary occurrences.

Much has been written about time and space "warps" (holes in the sky or the sea), as well as about a "veil" that separates our own time continuum from another, through which people and objects may fall or be carried to some other time and space. Sometimes the space is said to occupy the same territory as our own, though invisible to our eyes. Thus people who disappear for unknown reasons are said to exist in another dimension, a fourth or even a fifth dimension that is undetected by our senses, which perceive only three dimensions. Some people believe that warps provide entrance to a totally different time and space, that alien (nonearth) beings, exerting enormous force, pull earthlings through holes to a space ship which whisks them away to a distant planet. Others think all permanently missing human beings are simply picked up on earth by UFO's and carried off.

A little less fantastic are the theories about the "trouble spots" of the world, where planes and ships disappear with alarming regularity. A large number of books have been written in the past decade about the Bermuda Triangle, which lies in an area of the North Atlantic Ocean where it is claimed that strange regional gravitational "pulls" have drawn ships and planes down—and even up—out of sight. Much has also been made of atmospheric conditions peculiar to the area—unusual amounts of clear-air turbulence and wind shear, those strong local wind currents that are not accompanied by clouds and are therefore invisible. Using a good deal of St. Elmo's fire and eerie fogs for dramatic effect, some theorists of the Bermuda Triangle have compounded the peculiar weather conditions and the warp theories into a hypothesis of their own.

Of course, there are many writers who maintain that only perfectly comprehensible accidents and disasters have happened to people and objects that disappear without a trace. It all seems mysterious only because no witnesses are left to tell what caused the disappearance.

We hope these writers are right, but in this chapter we have chosen disappearances that occurred without a clue as to why or how. We have stayed away from disappearances that could be readily explained, such as the ships that vanished in the 1800's, when there were no well-traveled shipping lanes between the New World and the Old. We've also steered clear of cases reported in the Bermuda Triangle, in favor of cases with fewer natural explanations. We've likewise avoided disappearances during wartime, for obvious reasons, unless those reasons did not seem to fit the circumstances.

In the days when communities around the world had little contact with each other, a disappearance was accepted as an act of God. It was usually too difficult to search for clues to what had happened. But in these days of instant communication and immediate search parties, things and people are still disappearing, and strange to say, we still don't always know the reasons.

The Lost Colony, Roanoke Island, 1587–90

Date	Location	Fatalities	Remarks
1587–90	Roanoke Island, N.C.	127	Settlers of Roanoke Colony were last seen in 1587. Had colony succeeded, it would have been first British settlement in America.

John White was uneasy. He had been named governor of a recently discovered territory in the New World, a place then called Virginia by the English in honor of their Virgin Queen, Elizabeth I. Governor White was charged with establishing a colony there, at Roanoke Island. Among those he had brought with him to settle on the island were his wife, his pregnant daughter Eleanor, and Eleanor's husband, Ananias Dare. What troubled Governor White was that he had to return to England, leaving his family behind.

Roanoke Island, near the mouth of a large sound and protected from the sea by a reef, had been discovered in 1584 during an expedition financed by Sir Walter Raleigh. The explorers thought the island a sylvan paradise, and they had been discovered, in turn, by a tribe of friendly Indians. The Indians lived nearby on an island that lay closer to the sea— Croatan Island. They took the explorers there in canoes and introduced them to their king, Wingina.

The explorers came home with tales of a primitive paradise, and a year later Raleigh financed an effort to establish the first British colony in the New World on Roanoke Island.

From the start, trouble appeared. There were tribes of Indians who were not friendly and who began to kill the settlers. The gentle King Wingina (the English translated his title as "king," not "chief") was apparently as frightened of these savages as the English were, and could offer no protection. Moreover, the settlers were unable to stand the primitive conditions of life during the winter months. They paddled by canoe to the outlying islands where sea-going vessels were likely to pass, and there, they got a ride home with Sir Francis Drake.

Raleigh financed a second try, and this time the colonists stayed. When a British ship stopped by, they found that the hundred or so settlers were all dead except for 15 men. Leaving 15 men behind to guard the settlement (it is not known if they were the same 15 men), the ship departed with a promise to return as soon as possible. When it did, the 15 were gone. One skeleton and various signs of violence gave clues to what had happened. They'd been attacked by Indians and carried off, or they'd managed to escape and were now lost or living among friendly Indians in the wilderness.

That was the history of Roanoke Island when Governor White arrived. Besides the ship's crew, he had brought 125 people with him from England. A baby had been born on the boat. Before he left, a baby would be born in the New World.

On August 18, 1587, Eleanor Dare gave birth to a daughter. She named the little girl for the territory in which the child had been born. Virginia Dare was the first English child to be born in the New World.

White was both delighted and fearful. His granddaughter, he felt, would become a legend to all Englishmen who came here, and he was sure many would. But he did not want to leave the child with so little protection. White and a party went over to Croatan Island to beg for King Wingina's help. Wingina was alarmed. The hostile savages were on his island at this very moment, and he warned White not to let anyone wander far from the Croatan Indian settlement. One of White's party did go fishing up the coast, and was killed. White kept up his efforts to gain Wingina's promise of protection. At length, King Wingina gave his word. He and his braves would look in on the settlers from time to time, and if there was trouble, the settlers were to come to him at once.

Wingina's promise apparently reassured White, for he now made ready to leave. He and the settlers devised ways of leaving messages for each other in case anything happened. If they had to leave the settlement they would carve a short message on a tree, or in some wood. If they were in trouble when they left, they would leave the sign of the cross, with or without a message. White promised to return within the year, and so he departed.

Governor White was unable to keep his promise. War broke out between England and Spain, and passenger vessels to the New World were unavailable until 1590.

Thus, three years after he'd set sail for England, White started back for Roanoke Island. He arrived on August 18, his granddaughter's third birthday.

As they approached the island, both White and the sailors expected the settlers to come out to greet them. The sailors called and sang, but no answer came. They landed, but there were no people. The entire population of the colony had disappeared. There were no signs of violence, no signs of destruction. Some of the houses had been taken down, but very neatly, as though by people who had decided to take their leave leisurely and without fear.

There was a message. Carved into the bark of a tree was the word CROATAN. The letters CRO were carved in another. But there was no sign of the cross over either message, no sign of the cross anywhere. Apparently, the settlers had been in no

This English painting from the early seventeenth century depicts the American Indian. The inscription reads: "The manner of their attire and painting themselves when they go to their general huntings or at their solemn feasts."

danger when they left. John White could only believe they had gone to join the Croatan Indians.

White was sure all were safe. The big ship could not land near the little island, so White would have to be taken there by canoe, but there were none. Nor could the captain of the ship spare the time or personnel to get White over there. There had already been too much delay in searching the settlement. He had to take his ship back to England. White decided to go with him, but to return as soon as possible on another ship. Meanwhile, he asked the captain to pass as close as possible to Croatan Island, in case there was anything to see. There was nothing to see, but that didn't dampen White's spirits. He was sure everyone was there somewhere. Actually, Croatan Island was so small that anyone on it should have been able to see the ship. If his people were there, wouldn't they hail an English ship?

White sailed home to England, and began to make plans to return to Roanoke to search for his lost colony. He never made it. Within a year, he was dead.

Seventeen years after the "Lost Colony" at Roanoke was understood to be lost, the first successful British settlement was established at Jamestown, and the surrounding territory, though quite a bit north of Roanoke, was designated as Virginia. Twenty years later, a huge area including Roanoke Island was named Carolina. In 1712, Carolina was split in two, and Roanoke Island became part of North Carolina.

Through all the name changes, interest in the disappearance of the Roanoke Island colonists never waned. In the 1700's, a tribe of Indians was found in Robinson County, North Carolina, 100 miles inland from Roanoke. They were light-skinned, some were blue-eyed, and they spoke Elizabethan English. They also bore family names that greatly resembled the family names of the settlers at Roanoke.

The Roanoke colonists may have married with friendly Indians, such as the Croatans, or perhaps it was later colonists. Many English family names were common and widespread, and many early settlers, especially in the Carolinas, left colonial society to live in the wilderness, sometimes among Indians, and often with Indian wives even if they chose to live in no society at all. The Elizabethan-speaking Indians might be the solution to the Roanoke riddle, but not necessarily.

In 1937, another theory materialized. Rocks with strange carvings were found strewn over 500 miles of territory, from North Carolina to Georgia. All carried messages in Elizabethan English, and all were signed by Eleanor Dare. The question was whether they were real or fake.

Experts at first claimed that they were old and that the language was genuinely Elizabethan, such as shewe for show,

The dangers of North Carolina's seacoast are symbolized by the ship wrecks in this illustration of the 1585 voyage to Roanoke.

or anye for any. However, the words were always spelled the same way. Elizabethans, said the experts, never spelled any word—including their names—the same way all the time. Uniformity in spelling is a relatively modern invention. Others claimed the messages were anagrams. If you read them up and down, for example, instead of across, you got a different message. One clearly read, "Fake." The consensus was that the rocks—which told of the sojourn in Georgia of Eleanor and the settlers, and of the widowed Mrs. Dare's marriage to an Indian chief—were not genuine.

Another theory was that the settlers had taken boats out to sea in an unsuccessful effort to return to England. If this was so, why was CROATAN carved instead of HOME?

The mystery of the Lost Colony remains a mystery.

The "Iron Mountain" Vanishes, 1872

Date	Location	Fatalities	Remarks
March	Mississippi River, near Vicksburg, Miss.	55	Riverboat Iron Mountain vanished.

It happened in broad daylight, but no one could ever be found who saw it happen. In fact, no one was ever found who knew how it had happened.

One June day, in Vicksburg, Mississippi, the steamer Iron Mountain was loaded for her usual run. She was to go up the Mississippi River to the Ohio, on to Louisville, Kentucky, where she'd drop off cotton and molasses, then up to Cincinnati, and on to Pittsburgh. She had made the run a dozen times with no problem. A full 180 feet long and 35 feet wide, she was no tiny ship. Towing her barges of cotton behind her, she was impressive.

With the last of her 55 passengers and crew aboard, the steamboat left the pier headed north and soon went round a bend in the river, which put her out of sight of Vicksburg. She was never seen again.

No one knew anything was wrong for about two hours, when the riverboat *Iroquois Chief* nearly ran down a string of runaway barges. The *Chief* maneuvered to a safe position and, once in control, chased down the barges. She knew they came from the *Iron Mountain*. Had the barges broken loose? If they had, the *Iron Mountain* would be coming down river in pursuit of them. But the *Iron Mountain* never showed up, and the captain and crew of the *Iroquois Chief* noticed that the ropes that had held the barges to the *Mountain* had been deliberately cut. River steamers cut loose barges only if they're in trouble. Had the *Iron Mountain* caught fire? Had her boilers exploded? The *Chief* began to search.

Other ships were notified and joined in the search, but to no avail. For hours they scoured the river. Whatever it was, it had happened in the Mississippi, because of the location of the loose barges. But search as they might, they could not find the *Iron Mountain*. Nor could they find anyone who'd seen her after she'd turned the bend outside Vicksburg. That part of the Mississippi was well traveled and populated. If she'd caught fire or exploded, someone would have seen it, and there would have been some debris. Aside from the barges, nothing was found of the *Iron Mountain*. Down in Vicksburg, they still tell the story of the ship that disappeared round a bend and . . . well, disappeared.

A Village Is Missing, 1930

Date	Location	Fatalities	Remarks
September–November	Anjikuni, Canada	30	Inhabitants of Eskimo village disappeared. All possessions, including food in cooking pots and all means of transportation, were left behind.

Anjikuni was a tiny Eskimo village north of the Canadian tundra, almost inaccessible after the snows started to fall early in autumn. The people of Anjikuni were warm and sociable, and over the years, they had made many friends among the trappers and hunters who ventured into the area. Although it was tough getting there after October, sometimes a friend would go out of his way to visit the Eskimos.

That's why trapper Joe Labelle was there that November. His work had taken him north, and then he'd decided to continue on so he could see his friends. He was sure they'd be delighted by the surprise visit, and he expected a warm and noisy welcome. All that greeted him in Anjikuni was a strange and deadly silence.

The silence was the first thing Joe noticed. The Anjikunis were an active people, and there should have been sounds of chatting and work. There were no barking dogs. No Eskimo village is without sled dogs, and the dogs always bark when an unfamiliar person enters the village.

Joe went to one of the huts and found a pot filled with food hanging over what had once been a fire. No one was in the hut. He went to another hut and saw that someone had been mending clothes. There was a bone needle stuck through some fur, as if the mender had left for only a moment. He went from hut to hut, and in each there were signs of normal activity that had obviously been interrupted as if temporarily. But not a living soul was to be found.

Had the people gone somewhere in a hurry? Their kayaks were still on the beach of Lake Anjikuni. Then Joe remembered something and ran back to look inside the huts. Near the doorway of each stood the Eskimo's most prized possession—his rifle. Joe knew the men would never go anywhere without their rifles, at least not without a struggle, but there was no sign of violence. Joe was a little frightened and called the Canadian Royal Mounted Police.

The Mounties soon arrived, and together with Joe, they went over the village with a fine-tooth comb. They found the dogs about 100 yards from the village, tied to tree stumps—and dead from starvation. Now the Mounties were alarmed. The Eskimos would not have left their dogs behind. They could not have left the place voluntarily. Yet there was no sign of foul play. Only one thing seemed peculiar. There had been a grave near the village, an Eskimo grave marked with a pile of rocks as memorial. The pile of rocks had been taken down and neatly stacked. Whatever had been beneath was gone.

The Mounties estimated that whatever had made the Eskimos move on had happened two months previously, and no one had been there since. It seemed the Anjikunis had been going about their ordinary activities when something had occurred that made them very carefully put down what they were doing as though they meant to resume work again in a minute. Had they been called outside by something? Nobody knew.

For months, the Mounties kept up a thorough and widespread search. There was no sign of a trail leading from the village, no hint to the direction they might have taken. The investigation spread to many towns, where it was hoped that members of the Anjikuni community might be found. But no native of Anjikuni was ever seen again, not in this world.

From Guam to . . . ? 1962

Date	Location	Fatalities	Remarks
3/16	Pacific, between Guam and Manila	107	Flying Tiger Super Constellation, chartered by Army, vanished.

The Flying Tiger was due to land in Manila at 3:16 A.M. It was coming from Guam, 1,600 miles of ocean away, with no islands along the route. Besides the crew, the plane carried 97 American soldiers.

It was the year we had begun to wonder if the United States was secretly engaged in war. The Government and military said no, we were just "advising" an army in Vietnam who was at war. All the same, the U.S. Army had chartered this Flying Tiger Super Constellation to pick up 97 soldiers and transport them, ultimately, to Saigon "to join the growing force of U.S. military men assisting in the battle against communist guerrilla forces," a spokesman for the Army said. Their first stop on the many-legged journey was Hawaii; the second, Guam.

At Manila, 3:16 came and went without a sign of the Flying Tiger. But planes were frequently a little late. It was close to 4:00 A.M. before personnel at the Manila air base began to worry. They contacted the air base at Guam, and were told that the Flying Tiger had reported to them about an hour after takeoff. It was flying at an altitude of 18,000 feet, all was well, and it had enough fuel to stay airborne until 8:22 A.M. There had been no word since. At 4:30, rescue planes began revving up their engines. At 5:00 A.M., the Flying Tiger was officially declared missing.

As soon as the word went out, all military facilities in the area joined the search. They knew the plane's flight pattern and covered every inch of the area from Guam to Manila as thoroughly as possible. Six air-sea rescue planes went out from Clark Air Force Base. The Seventh Fleet sent out nine search planes. The Coast Guard searched with ships and planes. A destroyer escort was sent out from Guam. Special rescue planes were sent out from Manila. They found nothing. They started again, going over the same ground, widening the search.

By now, the newspapers had hold of the story. One Army spokesman said the military's position was that the plane had crashed and been lost at sea. Another told newspapers it was the Army's "hope that the plane might have crashed in such a manner that there were survivors." Their hope might have been based on the reputation of the plane's captain, Gregory P. Thomas.

Captain Thomas had become somewhat of a hero in 1957 when he'd made a daring crash-landing on the mudflats of Jamaica Bay, in Queens, New York. He'd just taken off when his engines had begun to lose power. To avert a crash in thickly populated Queens, he'd swerved sharply and managed to belly-land in the bay's shallows. No one was hurt.

The search went on for weeks, but no oil slick, not even the tiniest speck of debris, was ever sighted. Activity was heaviest around the Pacific Ocean's Mariana Trench, the deepest water in the world. The Flying Tiger's last report put it slightly east of the trench, but if it went down in the Mariana, there would have been an oil slick, rubbish of some sort. Furthermore, the Flying Tiger had been using a well-traveled air lane. Someone should have seen something, if there was a crash.

The New York Times noted at the time that if the plane were found (with no survivors), it would be our worst air crash to date in the Pacific. The plane was never found at all, and is one of our biggest mysteries in the Pacific.